AAT

ASSESSMENT KIT

Intermediate Unit 5

Financial Records and Accounts

In this May 2002 edition

- Kit updated in the light of the asssessor's review of the previous edition of the kit

- Many additional Practice Activities

- New Simulation

- The June and December 2001 Central Assessments are included to attempt as 'mocks' under 'exam conditions'.

FOR ASSESSMENT IN DECEMBER 2002 AND JUNE 2003

BPP Publishing
May 2002

First edition 1999
Fourth edition May 2002

ISBN 0 7517 6424 8 (Previous edition 07517 6404 3)

British Library Cataloguing-in-Publication Data
A catalogue record for this book
is available from the British Library

Published by

BPP Publishing Limited
Aldine House, Aldine Place
London W12 8AW

www.bpp.com

Printed in Great Britain by W M Print
45-47 Frederick Street
Walsall, West Midlands
WS2 9NE

We are grateful to the Lead Body for Accounting for permission to reproduce extracts from the Standards of Competence for Accounting and to the AAT for permission to reproduce two of their simulations.

CONTENTS

Page

	Activities	Answers
Practice activities	3	309

> Practice activities are activities directly related to the actual content of the BPP Interactive Text. They are graded pre-assessment and assessment.

	Activities	Answers
Practice devolved assessments	117	391

> Practice devolved assessments consist of a number of tasks covering certain areas of the Standards of Competence but are not full assessments.

	Activities	Answers
Trial run devolved assessment	167	417

> Trial run devolved assessments are of similar scope to full simulations.

	Activities	Answers
AAT sample simulation	211	443

Contents

	Activities	Answers

Practice central assessments 245 459

> Practice central assessments are past central assessments set by the AAT.

Trial run central assessment: December 2001 291 487

> Trial run central assessments are full central assessments providing practice for the AAT's actual central assessment.

Lecturers' resource pack activities 495 -

> Lecturers' resource pack activities are practice activities and assessments for lecturers to set in class or for homework. The answers are given in the BPP Lecturers' Resource Pack.

ORDER FORM

REVIEW FORM & FREE PRIZE DRAW

Activities Answers Done

PRACTICE ACTIVITIES

Chapters 1-4 Accounting principles

Chapter 5 Capital acquisition and disposal

Chapters 6-11 Final acounts

Chapter 10 Incomplete records

Chapter 11 Clubs accounting and manufacturing accounts

Chapter 12 Extended trial balance

Activity Checklist/Index

Activities   *Done*

HOW TO USE THIS ASSESSMENT KIT

Aims of this Assessment Kit

> To provide the knowledge and practice to help you succeed in assessments for Intermediate Unit 5 *Financial Records and Accounts*.

To succeed in the assessments you need a thorough understanding in all areas covered by the standards of competence.

> To tie in with the other components of the BPP Effective Study Package to ensure you have the best possible chance of success.

Interactive Text

This covers all you need to know for assessment for Unit 5. Icons clearly mark key areas of the text. Numerous activities throughout the text help you practise what you have just learnt.

Assessment Kit

When you have understood and practised the material in the Interactive Text, you will have the knowledge and experience to tackle this Assessment Kit for Unit 5. This aims to get you through the assessment, whether in the form of a simulation or workplace assessment. It contains the AAT's Sample Simulation for Unit 5 plus other simulations. It also contains past Central Assessments including the June and December 2001 Assessments.

Passcards

These short memorable notes are focused on key topics for Unit 5, designed to remind you of what the Interactive Text has taught you.

Recommended approach to this Assessment Kit

(a) To achieve competence in all units you need to be able to do **everything** specified by the standards. Study the Interactive Text very carefully and do not skip any of it.

(b) Learning is an **active** process. Do **all** the activities as you work through the Interactive Text so you can be sure you really understand what you have read.

(c) After you have covered the material in the Interactive Text, work through this **Assessment Kit.**

(d) Try the **Practice Activities**. These are linked into each chapter of the Interactive Text, and are designed to reinforce your learning and consolidate the practice that you have had doing the activities in the Interactive Text. Depending on their difficulty, they are graded as Pre-assessment or Assessment.

(e) Then attempt the **Practice Devolved/Central Assessments**. These are designed to test your competence in certain key areas of the Standards of Competence and will give you practice at completing a number of tasks based upon the same data.

(f) Next do the **Trial Run Devolved/Central Assessments**. They are designed to cover the areas you might see when you do a full devolved assessment.

(g) Then try the AAT's **Sample Simulation** which gives you the clearest idea of what a full assessment will be like.

(h) Finally, try the December 2001 assessments under 'exam conditions'.

How to use this Assessment Kit

Remember this is a **practical** course.

(a) Try to relate the material to your experience in the workplace or any other work experience you may have had.

(b) Try to make as many links as you can to your study of the other units at this level.

A **helpful tip**: photocopy the pages containing the blank proformas, especially the trial balance, this makes it easier to work on the assessments as you flick from page to page.

Lecturers' Resource Pack activities

At the back of this Kit we have included a number of chapter-linked activities without answers. We have also included two practice devolved assessments and a trial run devolved assessment without answers. The answers for this section are in the BPP Lecturers' Resource Pack for this Unit.

Stop press

The AAT is planning to change the terminology used for assessments in the following ways:

(a) Central assessments to be called exam based testing
(b) Devolved assessments to be called skills based testing

As the plans had not been finalised at the time of going to press, the 2002 editions of BPP titles will continue to refer to central and devolved assessments.

UNIT 5 STANDARDS OF COMPETENCE

The structure of the Standards for Unit 5

The Unit commences with a statement of the knowledge and understanding which underpin competence in the Unit's elements.

The Unit of Competence is then divided into elements of competence describing activities which the individual should be able to perform.

Each element includes:

- A set of **performance criteria** which define what constitutes competent performance

- A **range statement** which defines the situations, contexts, methods etc in which competence should be displayed

- **Evidence requirements**, which state that competence must be demonstrated consistently, over an appropriate time scale with evidence of performance being provided from the appropriate sources

- **Sources of evidence**, being suggestions of ways in which you can find evidence to demonstrate that competence.

The elements of competence for Unit 5: Financial Records and Accounts are set out below. Knowledge and understanding required for the Unit as a whole are listed first, followed by the performance criteria and range statements for each element. Performance criteria are cross-referenced below to chapters in the Unit 5 Financial Records and Accounts Interactive Text.

Unit 5: Maintaining financial records and preparing accounts

What is the unit about?

This unit is concerned with the collecting and recording of information for the purpose of preparing accounts and maintaining effective records. It involves identifying the types of information that are required, recording it, making any appropriate calculations or adjustments and maintaining the appropriate records.

The unit requires you to have responsibility for collecting all the relevant information for preparing accounts and presenting it to your supervisor in the form of a trial balance or an extended trial balance. Also required are communication responsibilities relating to handling queries, making suggestions for improvements and maintaining confidentiality.

Knowledge and understanding

The business environment

- Types and characteristics of different assets and key issues relating to the acquisition and disposal of capital assets (Element 5.1)

- Relevant legislation and regulations (Elements 5.1, 5.2, 5.3 & 5.4)

- Main requirements of relevant SSAPs (Elements 5.1, 5.2, 5.3 & 5.4)

- Methods of recording information for the organisational accounts of: sole traders; partnerships; manufacturing accounts; club accounts (Element 5.2)

- Understanding the structure of the organisational accounts of: sole traders; partnerships; manufacturing accounts; club accounts (Element 5.2)

- The need to present accounts in the correct form (Element 5.3)

- The importance of maintaining the confidentiality of business transactions (Elements 5.1, 5.2, 5.3 & 5.4)

Accounting techniques

- Methods of depreciation: straight line; reducing balance (Element 5.1)

- Accounting treatment of capital items sold, scrapped or otherwise retired from service (Element 5.1)

- Use of plant registers and similar subsidiary records (Element 5.1)

- Use of transfer journal (Elements 5.1, 5.2, 5.3 & 5.4)

- Methods of funding: part exchange deals (Element 5.1)

- Accounting treatment of accruals and prepayments (Elements 5.2, 5.3 & 5.4)

- Methods of analysing income and expenditure (Element 5.2)

- Methods of restructuring accounts from incomplete evidence (Element 5.3)

- Identification and correction of different types of error (Elements 5.3 & 5.4)

- Making and adjusting provisions (Elements 5.3 & 5.4)

Accounting principles and theory

- Basic accounting concepts and principles - matching of income and expenditure within an accounting period, historic cost, accruals, consistency, prudence, materiality (Elements 5.1, 5.2, 5.3 & 5.4)

- Principles of double entry accounting (Elements 5.1, 5.2, 5.3 & 5.4)

- Distinction between capital and revenue expenditure, what constitutes capital expenditure (Element 5.1)

- Function and form of accounts for income and expenditure (Element 5.2)

- Function and form of a trial balance, profit and loss account and balance sheet for sole traders, partnerships, manufacturing accounts and club accounts (Elements 5.3 & 5.4)

- Basic principles of stock valuation: cost or NRV; what is included in cost (Elements 5.3 & 5.4)

- Objectives of making provisions for depreciation and other purposes (Elements 5.3 & 5.4)

- Function and form of final accounts (Element 5.4)

The organisation

- Understanding of the ways the accounting systems of an organisation are affected by its organisational structure, its administrative systems and procedures and the nature of its business transactions (Elements 5.1, 5.2, 5.3 & 5.4)

Element 5.1 Maintain records relating to capital acquisition and disposal

Performance criteria		Chapters in the Text
1	Relevant details relating to capital expenditure are correctly entered in the appropriate records	5
2	The organisation's records agree with the physical presence of capital items	5
3	All acquisition and disposal costs and revenues are correctly identified and recorded in the appropriate records	5
4	Depreciation charges and other necessary entries and adjustments are correctly calculated and recorded in the appropriate records	5
5	The records clearly show the prior authority for capital expenditure and disposal and indicate the approved method of funding and disposal	5
6	Profit and loss on disposal is correctly calculated and recorded in the appropriate records	5
7	The organisation's policies and procedures relating to the maintenance of capital records are adhered to	5
8	Lack of agreement between physical items and records are identified and either resolved or referred to the appropriate person	5
9	When possible, suggestions for improvements in the way the organisation maintains its capital records are made to the appropriate person	5

Range statement

1	Methods of calculating depreciation: straight line; reducing balance	5
2	Records: asset register; ledger	5

Evidence requirements

- Competence must be demonstrated consistently, over an appropriate timescale with evidence of performance being provided of records being maintained.

Sources of evidence

(These are examples of sources of evidence, but candidates and assessors may be able to identify other, appropriate sources.)

- *Observed performance*, eg maintaining records of capital acquisition and disposal; calculating adjustments; calculating profit and loss on disposal; resolving discrepancies, unusual features or queries; making suggestions for improvements in the maintenance of capital records and accounts.

- *Work produced by the candidate*, eg a fixed asset register; a completed fixed asset reconciliation; a ledger; journals; invoices; minutes from meetings; cash books; disposals account or equivalent; correspondence relating to capital acquisition or disposal; authorisation for expenditure.

- *Authenticated testimonies from relevant witnesses*

- *Personal accounts of competence,* eg report of performance.

- *Other sources of evidence to prove competence of knowledge and understanding where it is not apparent from performance*, eg reports and working papers; performance in independent assessment; performance in simulation; responses to verbal questioning.

Element 5.2 Record income and expenditure

Performance criteria	Chapters in the Text
1 All income and expenditure is correctly identified and recorded in the appropriate records	2
2 Relevant accrued and prepaid income and expenditure is correctly identified and adjustments are made	8
3 The organisation's policies, regulations, procedures and timescales in relation to recording income and expenditure are observed	2
4 Incomplete data is identified and either resolved or referred to the appropriate person	10
Range statement	
1 Records: day book; journal; ledger	1, 2, 7

Evidence requirements

- Competence must be demonstrated consistently, over an appropriate timescale with evidence of performance being provided from involvement with account records.

Sources of evidence

(These are examples of sources of evidence, but candidates and assessors may be able to identify other, appropriate sources.)

- *Observed performance*, eg recording income and expenditure; checking accounts; making adjustments; resolving incomplete data.

- *Work produced by the candidate,* eg nominal ledger listing; accruals and prepayments listings; petty cash book; journals for accruals and prepayments (reversibles) (recurring); invoices; minutes from meetings concerning incomplete data; cash books; disposals account or equivalent; correspondence relating to income and expenditure.

- *Authenticated testimonies from relevant witnesses.*

- *Personal accounts of competence,* eg report of performance.

- *Other sources of evidence to prove competence of knowledge and understanding where it is not apparent from performance,* eg reports and working papers; performance in independent assessment; performance in simulation; responses to verbal questioning.

Element 5.3 Collect and collate information for the preparation of final accounts

Performance criteria		Chapters in the Text
1	Relevant accounts and reconciliations are correctly prepared to allow the preparation of final accounts	7
2	All relevant information is correctly identified and recorded	6
3	Investigations into business transactions are conducted with tact and courtesy	6
4	The organisation's policies, regulations, procedures and timescales relating to preparing final accounts are observed	6
5	Discrepancies and unusual features are identified and either resolved or referred to the appropriate person	10
6	The trial balance is accurately prepared and, where necessary, a suspense account is opened and reconciled	2, 7

Range statement

1	Sources of information: ledger; bank reconciliation; creditors' reconciliation; debtors' reconciliation	6, 7
2	Discrepancies and unusual features: insufficient data has been provided; inconsistencies within the data	10

Evidence requirements

● Competence must be demonstrated consistently with evidence of performance being provided of collecting and collating information for sets of final accounts from different types of organisation.

Sources of evidence

(These are examples of sources of evidence, but candidates and assessors may be able to identify other, appropriate sources.)

● *Observed performance,* eg preparing accounts and reconciliations; investigating client's business transactions; preparing the trial balance; opening and reconciling a suspense account; resolving discrepancies or unusual features.

● *Work produced by the candidate,* eg control accounts/adjusted control accounts; bank reconciliations; trial balance; audit trail; suspense account; minutes from meetings; general ledger printout; copy of the extended trial balance; nominal ledger listing; correspondence relating to income and expenditure.

● *Authenticated testimonies from relevant witnesses.*

● *Personal accounts of competence,* eg report of performance.

● *Other sources of evidence to prove competence of knowledge and understanding where it is not apparent from performance,* eg reports and working papers; performance in independent assessment; performance in simulation; responses to verbal questioning.

Element 5.4 Prepare the extended trial balance

Performance criteria	Chapters in the Text
1 Totals from the general ledger or other records are correctly entered on the extended trial balance	12
2 Material errors disclosed by the trial balance are identified, traced and referred to the appropriate authority	12
3 Adjustments not dealt with in the ledger accounts are correctly entered on the extended trial balance	12
4 An agreed valuation of closing stock is correctly entered on the extended trial balance	9, 12
5 The organisation's policies, regulations, procedures and timescales in relation to preparing extended trial balances are observed	12
6 Discrepancies, unusual features or queries are identified and either resolved or referred to the appropriate person	12
7 The extended trial balance is accurately extended and totalled	12

Range statement

1 Adjustments relating to: accruals; prepayments	12

Evidence requirements

- Competence must be demonstrated consistently, over an appropriate timescale with evidence of performance being provided from preparing an extended trial balance across the range.

Sources of evidence

(These are examples of sources of evidence, but candidates and assessors may be able to identify other, appropriate sources.)

- *Observed performance,* eg entering totals and adjustments on the extended trial balance; tracing and correcting material errors; resolving discrepancies, unusual features or queries; extending and totalling the trial balance.

- *Work produced by the candidate,* eg extended trial balance; ledger accounts; transfer journal.

- *Authenticated testimonies from relevant witnesses.*

- *Personal accounts of competence,* eg report of performance.

- *Other sources of evidence to prove competence of knowledge and understanding where it is not apparent from performance,* eg reports and working papers; performance in independent assessment; performance in simulation; responses to verbal questioning.

ASSESSMENT STRATEGY

This unit is assessed by both **central assessment (exam based testing)** and by **devolved assessment (skills based testing.)**

Central Assessment

A central assessment is a means of collecting evidence that you have the **essential knowledge and understanding** which underpins competence. It is also a means of collecting evidence across the **range of contexts** for the standards, and of your ability to **transfer skills**, knowledge and understanding to different situations. Thus, although central assessments contain practical tests linked to the performance criteria, they also focus on the underpinning knowledge and understanding. You should in addition expect each central assessment to contain tasks taken from across a broad range of the standards.

Section 1

This section will include one or more accounting exercises from the following:

- **Trial balance**

  Example task: preparation of a trial balance from a list of balances given.

- **Extended trial balance**

  Example tasks: completion of the adjustments columns from information given. Extension of relevant figures into profit and loss and balance sheet columns.

  Note: Exercises involving the extended trial balance will not necessarily include all of the columns. Tasks could, for example, be based entirely around the initial balances and the adjustments columns. In this case, the remaining columns would not be required for the assessment.

- **Identification and correction of errors**

  Example tasks: candidates given a number of transactions and entries made. Errors and correcting journal entries to be identified.

- **Suspense accounts**

  Example tasks: suspense account required to balance a trial balance. Correcting entries to be identified to eliminate the suspense account balance.

- **Bank reconciliation statements**

  Example tasks: preparation of a statement to reconcile the opening balances and preparation of a further statement to reconcile the closing balances of a cash book and a bank statement.

- **Control accounts**

  Example tasks: preparation of a debtors control account from information given and reconciliation with the total of the sales ledger balances.

  There will also be a number of short answer questions from across the range of the Standards for the unit.

Section 2

This section will comprise of one or more practical exercises concerned with the processing, restructuring and production of information for different types of organisations. Candidates will be expected to be able to produce:

- Manufacturing accounts from data given;

- Information from data given and / or incomplete records for sole traders, partnerships and clubs.

  There will also be a number of short answer questions from across the range of the standards for the unit.

EXAMPLES. The processing, restructuring and production of information includes:

- calculation of opening and / or closing capital (accumulated fund for clubs);

- restructuring the cash and / or bank account;

- preparation of total debtors account and total creditors account to calculate, for example, sales and purchases;

- production of simple statements showing the calculation of gross profit and / or net profit and listing assets, liabilities and capital (or equivalent for clubs). These statements to summarise figures or to ascertain missing items of information;

- use of mark up and margin (the use of other accounting ratios is outside the scope of this unit);

- production of other statements and / or restructured ledger accounts. For example, to calculate expenses paid, expenses profit and loss figures, accruals and prepayments, profit or loss on the sale of an asset, provisions and subscriptions for the period.

Central Assessment Technique

Passing central assessments at this level is half about having the knowledge, and half about doing yourself full justice on the day. You must have the right **technique**.

The day of the central assessment

1   Set at least one **alarm** (or get an alarm call) for a morning central assessment

2   Have **something to eat** but beware of eating too much; you may feel sleepy if your system is digesting a large meal

3   Allow plenty of **time to get to where you are sitting the central assessment**; have your route worked out in advance and listen to news bulletins to check for potential travel problems

4   **Don't forget** pens, pencils, rulers, erasers

5   Put **new batteries** into your calculator and take a spare set (or a spare calculator)

6   **Avoid discussion** about the central assessment with other candidates outside the venue

---

Technique in the central assessment

---

1 *Read the instructions (the 'rubric') on the front of the paper carefully*

Check that the format of the paper hasn't changed. It is surprising how often assessors' reports remark on the number of students who attempt too few questions. Make sure that you are planning to answer the **right number of questions**.

2 *Select questions carefully*

Read through the paper once - don't forget that you are given 15 minutes' reading time - then quickly jot down key points against each question in a second read through. Select those questions where you could latch on to 'what the question is about' - but remember to check carefully that you have got the right end of the stick before putting pen to paper. Use your 15 minutes' reading time wisely.

3 *Plan your attack carefully*

Consider the **order** in which you are going to tackle questions. It is a good idea to start with your best question to boost your morale.

4 *Check the time allocation for each section of the paper*

Time allocations are given for each section of the paper. When the time for a section is up, you must go on to the next section. Going even one minute over the time allowed brings you a lot closer to failure.

5 *Read the question carefully and plan your answer*

Read through the question again very carefully when you come to answer it. Plan your answer to ensure that you **keep to the point**.

6 *Produce relevant answers*

Particularly with written answers, make sure you **answer the question set**, and not the question you would have preferred to have been set.

7 *Get the easy bits right*

Include the obvious if it answers the question, and don't try to produce the perfect answer.

Don't get bogged down in small parts of questions. If you find a part of a question difficult, get on with the rest of the question. If you are having problems with something, the chances are that everyone else is too.

8 *Produce an answer in the correct format*

The assessor will state **in the requirements** the format in which the question should be answered, for example in a report or memorandum.

9 *Follow the assessor's instructions*

You will annoy the assessor if you ignore him or her. The **assessor will state** whether he or she wishes you to 'discuss', 'comment', 'evaluate' or 'recommend'.

10 *Lay out your numerical computations and use workings correctly*

Make sure the layout fits the **type of question** and is in a style the assessor likes.

Show all your **workings** clearly and explain what they mean. Cross reference them to your answer. This will help the assessor to follow your method (this is of particular importance where there may be several possible answers).

11 *Present a tidy paper*

You are a professional, and it should show in the **presentation of your work**. Students are penalised for poor presentation and so you should make sure that you write legibly, label diagrams clearly and lay out your work neatly. Markers of scripts each have hundreds of papers to mark; a badly written scrawl is unlikely to receive the same attention as a neat and well laid out paper.

12 *Stay until the end of the central assessment*

Use any spare time **checking and rechecking** your script.

13 *Don't worry if you feel you have performed badly in the central assessment*

It is more than likely that the other candidates will have found the assessment difficult too. Don't forget that there is a competitive element in these assessments. As soon as you get up to leave the venue, **forget** that central assessment and think about the next - or, if it is the last one, celebrate!

14 *Don't discuss a central assessment with other candidates*

This is particularly the case if you **still have other central assessments to sit**. Even if you have finished, you should put it out of your mind until the day of the results. Forget about assessments and relax!

Devolved Assessment

Devolved assessment is a means of collecting evidence of your ability to carry out **practical activities** and to **operate effectively in the conditions of the workplace** to the standards required. Evidence may be collected at your place of work or at an Approved Assessment Centre by means of simulations of workplace activity, or by a combination of these methods.

If the Approved Assessment Centre is a **workplace**, you may be observed carrying out accounting activities as part of your normal work routine. You should collect documentary evidence of the work you have done, or contributed to, in an **accounting portfolio**. Evidence collected in a portfolio can be assessed in addition to observed performance or where it is not possible to assess by observation.

Where the Approved Assessment Centre is a **college or training organisation**, devolved assessment will be by means of a combination of the following.

- Documentary evidence of activities carried out at the workplace, collected by you in an **accounting portfolio.**

- Realistic **simulations** of workplace activities. These simulations may take the form of case studies and in-tray exercises and involve the use of primary documents and reference sources.

- **Projects and assignments** designed to assess the Standards of Competence.

If you are unable to provide workplace evidence you will be able to complete the assessment requirements by the alternative methods listed above.

Possible assessment methods

Where possible, evidence should be collected in the workplace, but this may not be a practical prospect for you. Equally, where workplace evidence can be gathered it may not cover all elements. The AAT regards performance evidence from simulations, case studies, projects and assignments as an acceptable substitute for performance at work, provided that they are based on the Standards and, as far as possible, on workplace practice.

There are a number of methods of assessing accounting competence. The list below is not exhaustive, nor is it prescriptive. Some methods have limited applicability, but others are capable of being expanded to provide challenging tests of competence.

Assessment method	Suitable for assessing
Performance of an accounting task either in the workplace or by simulation: eg preparing and processing documents, posting entries, making adjustments, balancing, calculating, analysing information etc by manual or computerised processes	**Basic task competence.** Adding supplementary oral questioning may help to draw out underpinning knowledge and understanding and highlight your ability to deal with contingencies and unexpected occurrences
General case studies. These are broader than simulations. They include more background information about the system and business environment	Ability to **analyse a system** and suggest ways of modifying it. It could take the form of a written report, with or without the addition of oral or written questions
Accounting problems/cases: eg a list of balances that require adjustments and the preparation of final accounts	Understanding of the **general principles of accounting** as applied to a particular case or topic
Preparation of flowcharts/diagrams. To illustrate an actual (or simulated) accounting procedure	**Understanding of the logic** behind a procedure, of controls, and of relationships between departments and procedures. Questions on the flow chart or diagram can provide evidence of underpinning knowledge and understanding
Interpretation of accounting information from an actual or simulated situation. The assessment could include non-financial information and written or oral questioning	**Interpretative competence**
Preparation of written reports on an actual or simulated situation	**Written communication skills**
Analysis of critical incidents, problems encountered, achievements	Your ability to handle **contingencies**
Listing of likely errors eg preparing a list of the main types of errors likely to occur in an actual or simulated procedure	Appreciation of the range of **contingencies** likely to be encountered. Oral or written questioning would be a useful supplement to the list
Outlining the organisation's policies, guidelines and regulations	Performance criteria relating to these aspects of competence. It also provides evidence of competence in **researching information**
Objective tests and short-answer	**Specific knowledge**

Assessment method questions	Suitable for assessing
In-tray exercises	Your **task-management ability** as well as technical competence
Supervisors' reports	**General job competence**, personal effectiveness, reliability, accuracy, and time management. Reports need to be related specifically to the Standards of Competence
Analysis of work logbooks/diaries	**Personal effectiveness**, time management etc. It may usefully be supplemented with oral questioning
Formal written answers to questions	Knowledge and understanding of the **general accounting environment** and its impact on particular units of competence
Oral questioning	**Knowledge and understanding** across the range of competence including organisational procedures, methods of dealing with unusual cases, contingencies and so on. It is often used in conjunction with other methods

BUILDING YOUR PORTFOLIO

What is a portfolio?

A portfolio is a collection of work that demonstrates what the owner can do. In AAT language the portfolio demonstrates **competence**.

A painter will have a collection of his paintings to exhibit in a gallery, an advertising executive will have a range of advertisements and ideas that she has produced to show to a prospective client. Both the collection of paintings and the advertisements form the portfolio of that artist or advertising executive.

Your portfolio will be unique to you just as the portfolio of the artist will be unique because no one will paint the same range of pictures in the same way. It is a very personal collection of your work and should be treated as a **confidential** record.

What evidence should a portfolio include?

No two portfolios will be the same but by following some simple guidelines you can decide which of the following suggestions will be appropriate in your case.

(a) **Your current CV**

This should be at the front. It will give your personal details as well as brief descriptions of posts you have held with the most recent one shown first.

(b) **References and testimonials**

References from previous employers may be included especially those of which you are particularly proud.

(c) **Your current job description**

You should emphasise financial **responsibilities and duties**.

(d) **Your student record sheets**

These should be supplied by AAT when you begin your studies, and your training provider should also have some if necessary.

(e) **Evidence from your current workplace**

This could take many forms including **letters, memos, reports** you have written, **copies of accounts** or **reconciliations** you have prepared, **discrepancies** you have investigated etc. Remember to obtain permission to include the evidence from your line manager because some records may be sensitive. Discuss the performance criteria that are listed in your Student Record Sheets with your training provider and employer, and think of other evidence that could be appropriate to you.

(f) **Evidence from your social activities**

For example you may be the treasurer of a club in which case examples of your cash and banking records could be appropriate.

(g) **Evidence from your studies**

Few students are able to satisfy all the requirements of competence by workplace evidence alone. They therefore rely on simulations to provide the remaining evidence to complete a unit. If you are not working or not working in a relevant post, then you may need to rely more heavily on simulations as a source of evidence.

(h) **Additional work**

Your training provider may give you work that specifically targets one or a group of performance criteria in order to complete a unit. It could take the form of questions, presentations or demonstrations. Each training provider will approach this in a different way.

(i) **Evidence from a previous workplace**

This evidence may be difficult to obtain and should be used with caution because it must satisfy the 'rules' of evidence, that is it must be current. Only rely on this as evidence if you have changed jobs recently.

(j) **Prior achievements**

For example you may have already completed the health and safety unit during a previous course of study, and therefore there is no need to repeat this work. Advise your training provider who will check to ensure that it is the same unit and record it as complete if appropriate.

How should it be presented?

As you assemble the evidence remember to **make a note** of it on your Student Record Sheet in the space provided and **cross reference** it. In this way it is easy to check to see if your evidence is **appropriate**. Remember one piece of evidence may satisfy a number of performance criteria so remember to check this thoroughly and discuss it with your training provider if in doubt.

To keep all your evidence together a ring binder or lever arch file is a good means of storage.

When should evidence be assembled?

You should begin to assemble evidence **as soon as you have registered as a student**. **Don't leave it all** until the last few weeks of your studies, because you may miss vital deadlines and your resulting certificate sent by the AAT may not include all the units you have completed. Give yourself and your training provider time to examine your portfolio and report your results to AAT at regular intervals. In this way the task of assembling the portfolio will be spread out over a longer period of time and will be presented in a more professional manner.

What are the key criteria that the portfolio must fulfil?

As you assemble your evidence bear in mind that it must be:

- **Valid**. It must relate to the Standards.

- **Authentic**. It must be your own work.

- **Current**. It must refer to your current or most recent job.

- **Sufficient**. It must meet all the performance criteria by the time you have completed your portfolio.

What are the most important elements in a portfolio that covers Unit 5?

You should remember that the unit is about **financial records** and **accounts**.

Finally

Remember that the portfolio is **your property** and **your responsibility**. Not only could it be presented to the external verifier before your award can be confirmed; it could be used when you are seeking **promotion** or applying for a more senior and better paid post elsewhere. How your portfolio is presented can say as much about you as the evidence inside.

Practice activities

2

1-4 *Accounting principles*

1   PICTURE THIS CASH BOOK   **Pre-assessment**

Picture This is a small firm operating a picture framing workshop. Its business is the framing of items submitted by business clients, mostly retail shops, all of whom are offered credit but many of whom pay by cash or debit/credit card. Its sole proprietor is Harry Gold.

All cash and cheques paid and received are recorded in an analysed cash book. All sales are charged to VAT at the standard rate of 17.5%. When performing bank reconciliations in previous months you have found that a number of items of income and expenditure have appeared on the bank statement for which you can find no information, and have had to seek clarification from Harry Gold by means of a formal memo.

Task 1

Refer to the paying in slip and the BACS list below.

Write up the receipts and payments sides of the cash book for these items and extract totals. Note that no discount was allowed against any of the receipts from debtors.

			Please detail cheques and cash overleaf		
DATE		**NOTES**			
31/10/X6	**bank giro credit**		£50	50	00
Cashier's stamp	Border Bank plc		£20	40	00
	1 High Street, Jedburgh NE7 7FG		£10	60	00
	ACCOUNT		£5	40	00
	Picture This		£2	10	00
	PAID IN BY		£1	5	00
	Harry Gold		50p	0	00
			Silver	0	00
NUMBER OF CHEQUES			Bronze	0	00
5		**TOTAL CASH**		205	00
		Cheques +		6,088	66
	SORT CODE NUMBER ACCOUNT NUMBER	**£**		6,293	66
	01-73-33 78269830				

BPP
PUBLISHING

Border Bank plc

1 High Street, Jedburgh NE7 7FG

Sort code 01-73-33

BACS Payment Listing

Payment ref: BACS

Name of customer: Picture This
Park Street
Jedburgh NE 5 7SD

Account number: 78269830

Date: 26 October 20X6

Authority is hereby given to Border Bank plc to make the following payments by BACS transfer from the account designated above

Payee	Sort code	Account number	Amount £
Sarah Johnson	72-09-25	87920348	1,239.87
Robert Callaghan	72-87-09	37849220	1,027.67
Yussef Mohammed	65-26-54	87349209	1,110.70
Total			3,378.24

Please make these payments as soon as possible and debit our account with the total shown above

Authorised signature   Date

Harry Gold   *26/10/X6*

CASH BOOK: RECEIPTS

Date	Details	Cash	Discount allowed	Sales Ledger Control	Cash sales	VAT	Capital	Interest
		£	£	£	£	£	£	£
20X6								
5 October	Cash/cheques	7,309.83	245.02	6,959.41	305.00	45.42		
9 October	BACS receipt	1,293.94		1,293.94				
12 October	Cash/cheques	2,738.64	67.00	1,212.86	1,298.54	227.24		
17 October	Cash/cheques	800.00		800.00				
24 October	Cash/cheques	5,309.30	278.27	3,663.72	1,400.50	245.08		
		205 00			174 47	30 53		
		6088 66		6088 66				
		5000·00					5000·00	
		459 35						459 35
		23745·37	590 29	20018·59	3178·51	548 27		

29204 72   5000 00   459.35

Practice activities

CASH BOOK: PAYMENTS

Date	Details	Cheque No	Cash	Discount received	Purchase Ledger Control	Other
20X6			£	£	£	£
1 October	Jedburgh County Council	DD	1,092.87			1,092.87
1 October	Society of Picture Framers	DD	250.00			250.00
2 October	Timbmet Wood Ltd	1397	3,298.93	45.00	3,298.93	
3 October	Glass Products Ltd	1398	5,209.36		5,209.36	
7 October	Lamination Ltd	1399	1,376.84	24.50	1,376.84	
10 October	The Contract Cleaning Co	1400	563.37		563.37	
11 October	Just a Minute Courier Company	1401	357.00		357.00	
12 October	Lynn's Caterers	1402	175.00		175.00	
15 October	Thor Stationery	1403	736.83	13.00	736.83	
16 October	Kinetic Electricity Ltd	DD	200.00			200.00
20 October	High Stick Adhesives	1404	245.09		245.09	
21 October	Big Gas Company Ltd	BACS	150.00			150.00
22 October	Quality Paper Company	1405	1,983.09		1,983.09	
24 October	Glass Ceramics Ltd	1406	3,736.94	51.00	3,736.94	
27 October	Chrome Sheeting Ltd	1407	398.65		398.65	
26 Oct	Picture The	BACS	3378.24		3378.24	
	Analysis:					
	Direct labour					
	Administration					
	Drawings					
			2297221			

Task 2

Refer to the bank statement for the month of October 20X6.

Perform a bank reconciliation as at 31 October 20X6 using the format below.

Bank reconciliation at 30 October 20X6

	£	£
Balance per bank statement at 31/10/X6		5010 53
Add: outstanding lodgement		
Less: unpresented cheques:		
Balance per cash book at 31/10/X6		
Cash book balance at 1/10/X6		(2,190.87)
Receipts		
Payments		
Cash book balance at 31/10/X6		
Adjustments to cash book:		
Amended cash book balance at 31/10/X3		

BPP PUBLISHING

Border Bank plc

1 High Street, Jedburgh NE7 7FG

STATEMENT

Account Name: Picture This

Statement no: 24

Account No: 78269830   **Sort code:**   01-73-33

Date	Details	Payments	Receipts	Balance	
20X6		£	£	£	
1 Oct	Balance brought forward			457.01	OD
2 Oct	DD – Jedburgh County Council	1,092.87		1,549.88	OD
2 Oct	DD – Society of Picture Framers	250.00		1,799.88	OD
6 Oct	CC		7,309.83	5,509.95	
8 Oct	Cheque issued 1395	523.99		4,985.96	
9 Oct	Cheque issued 1398	5,209.36		223.40	OD
9 Oct	BACS receipt		1,293.94	1,070.54	
9 Oct	Cheque issued 1396	1,209.87		139.33	OD
10 Oct	Cheque issued 1399	1,376.84		1,516.17	OD
13 Oct	Cheque issued 1400	563.37		2,079.54	OD
13 Oct	CC		2,738.64	659.10	
15 Oct	Cheque issued 1402	175.00		484.10	
16 Oct	DD – Kinetic Electricity	200.00		284.10	
18 Oct	CC		800.00	1,084.10	
20 Oct	Cheque issued 1403	736.83		347.27	
21 Oct	BACS payment – Big Gas Co	150.00		197.27	
24 Oct	Cheque issued 1404	245.09		47.82	OD
25 Oct	CC		5,309.30	5,261.48	
25 Oct	ATM withdrawal	100.00		5,161.48	
25 Oct	Debit card payment to Siren.com	248.97		4,912.51	
27 Oct	Cheque issued 1405	1,983.09		2,929.42	
27 Oct	BACS receipt from Harry Gold Personal Account		5,000.00	7,929.42	
27 Oct	Interest paid		459.35	8,388.77	
28 Oct	BACS payment – salaries	3,378.24		5,010.53	

Key   DD: Direct Debit   BACS: Bankers automated clearing services
       O/D: Overdrawn   ATM – automated teller machine cash withdrawal

Task 3

Update the 'cash' columns in the receipts and payments side of the cash book and calculate a balance that agrees with your reconciliation. Do not analyse the receipts or payments.

Task 4

Draft a memo to Harry Gold seeking clarification of any receipts or payments as necessary.

Task 5

Assuming Harry's response indicates that the queried payments are personal expenditure by him, and that queried receipts other than interest are payments of capital by him, analyse the receipts and payments that you have entered in, and further analyse the 'other' column on the payments side of the cash book.

2 TOUCHSTONE CASH BOOK   Assessment

Touchstone Cycles Ltd is a small chain of cycle shops. Its business is to sell cycles, cycling equipment and repairs to the general public and certain business clients. Its sole proprietor is Mike Cuthbertson.

All cash, cheques and credit/debit card transactions paid and received are recorded in an analysed cash book. All sales are subject to VAT at 17.5%. Occasionally Mike Cuthbertson withdraws cash from the ATM for his own use. All ATM withdrawals are therefore treated as drawings.

Task 1

Refer to the paying in slip and the BACS list below.

Write up the receipts and payments sides of the cash book for these items and extract totals, analysing VAT on the cash sales as appropriate. Note that discount of £15.00 was allowed against the receipt from one of the debtors.

DATE 26/2/X3	**bank giro credit**		Please detail cheques/vouchers and cash overleaf		
		NOTES			
		£50	100	00	
Cashier's stamp	Valley Banking Company plc	£20	80	00	
	36 Jayes Street, Wallingford	£10	70	00	
	ACCOUNT	£5	55	00	
	Touchstone Cycles Ltd	£2	16	00	
	PAID IN BY	£1	9	00	
	Mike Cuthbertson	50p	0	00	
		Silver	0	00	
NUMBER OF CHEQUES/ VOUCHERS		Bronze	0	00	
8		TOTAL CASH	330	00	
		Cheques/ vouchers ✛	8,209	54	
	SORT CODE NUMBER ACCOUNT NUMBER	£ 8,539		54	
	80-62-82 17639123				

Valley Banking Company plc
36 Jayes Street, Wallingford

Sort code 80-62-82

BACS Payment Listing

Payment ref:	BACS
Name of customer:	Touchstone Cycles Ltd High St Abingdon OX13 6RT
Account number:	17639123
Date:	25 February 20X3

Authority is hereby given to Valley Banking Company plc to make the following payments by BACS transfer from the account designated above

Payee	Sort code	Account number	Amount £
Tim Collins	63-29-29	78492830	2,390.34
Laura Bagra	28-39-38	10702344	1,293.39
Karen Simpson	39-39-30	84902347	938.39
Total			4,622.12

Please make these payments as soon as possible and debit our account with the total shown above

Authorised signature	Date
MIKE CUTHBERTSON	26/2/X3

CASH BOOK: RECEIPTS

Date	Details	Bank £	Discount allowed £	Sales Ledger Control £	Cash sales £	VAT £	Other £
20X3							
2 Feb	Cheques etc paid in	2,244.27	25.00	1,928.20	269.00	47.07	
6 Feb	Interest paid	54.00					54.00
7 Feb	Cheques etc paid in	3,160.47	19.00	2,298.02	734.00	128.45	
10 Feb	BACS – StraightCall Insurance	200.00					200.00
12 Feb	Cheques etc paid in	1,584.02	14.50	1,290.27	250.00	43.75	
14 Feb	Cheques etc paid in	896.28		896.28			
17 Feb	Cheques etc paid in	3,746.95	65.00	3,291.29	387.80	67.86	
21 Feb	Cheques etc paid in	4,887.27	32.00	4,182.27	600.00	105.00	
23 Feb	Cheques etc paid in	582.33		582.33			
26 - 2	" "	8 539.54		8 209.54	280 85	49.15	
Analysis	Disposals						200.00
	Interest						54.00
							254.00

BPP PUBLISHING

CASH BOOK: PAYMENTS

Date	Details	Cheque No	Bank	Discount received	Purchase Ledger Control	Other
20X3			£	£	£	£
1 Feb	South Oxon Council (rates)	DD	231.50			231.50
1 Feb	Thanet Pension Fund (rent)	DD	500.00			500.00
2 Feb	Drake Bicycles	6295	2,638.39	20.00	2,638.39	
3 Feb	David Lett Shopfitting	6296	4,029.38	55.00	4,029.38	
7 Feb	Sama Newsagents	6297	176.93		176.93	
10 Feb	Mike Cuthbertson - drawings	S/O	3,000.00			3,000.00
11 Feb	Essex Cycles	6298	2,378.49	35.00	2,378.49	
12 Feb	Firebrand Tyres	6299	1,287.35	10.00	1,287.35	
15 Feb	Patrick's Pumps	6300	1,243.66		1,243.66	
16 Feb	South Oxon Council (waste collection)	DD	35.00			35.00
20 Feb	Crutchleys Accountants (fees)	6301	235.00		235.00	
21 Feb	Lurrells & Co (fees)	6302	293.75		293.75	
22 Feb	Heartlands Electric	DD	150.00			150.00
24 Feb	Midland Gas	DD	90.00			90.00
	Analysis:					
	Sales ledger control					
	Staff costs					
	Administration/ overheads					
	Drawings					

Task 2

Refer to the bank statement for the month of February 20X3 and the bank ledger account.

Perform a bank reconciliation as at 28 February 20X3 using the format below.

Bank reconciliation at 28 February 20X3

	£	£

Balance per bank statement at 28/2/X3

Add: outstanding lodgement

Less: unpresented cheques:

Balance per cash book at 28/2/X3

Cash book balance at 1/2/X3
Receipts
Payments

Cash book balance at 28/2/X3
Adjustments to cash book:

Amended cash book balance at 28/2/X3

Valley Banking Company plc

36, Jayes Street, Wallingford

STATEMENT

Account Name: Touchstone Cycles Ltd

Statement no: 19

Account No: 17639123   **Sort code:**   80-62-82

Date	Details	Payments	Receipts	Balance
20X3		£	£	£
1 Feb	Balance brought forward			13,540.12
1 Feb	CC		398.00	13,938.12
1 Feb	DD South Oxon Council	231.50		13,706.62
	DD Thanet Pension Fund	500.00		13,206.62
3 Feb	CC		2,244.27	15,450.89
2 Feb	Cheque issued 6294	7,298.02		8,152.87
5 Feb	Interest paid		54.00	8,206.87
6 Feb	Cheque issued 6295	2,638.39		5,568.48
8 Feb	CC		3,160.47	8,728.95
9 Feb	Cheque issued 6296	4,029.38		4,699.57
9 Feb	Cheque issued 6291	719.71		3,979.86
10 Feb	S/O Mike Cuthbertson	3,000.00		979.86
10 Feb	BACS receipt – StraightCall Insurance		200.00	1,179.86
13 Feb	CC		1,584.02	2,763.88
15 Feb	CC		896.28	3,660.16
16 Feb	DD South Oxon Council	35.00		3,625.16
16 Feb	Cheque issued 6299	1,287.35		2,337.81
18 Feb	CC		3,746.95	6,084.76
20 Feb	Cheque issued 6300	1,243.66		4,841.10
22 Feb	CC		4,887.27	9,728.37
24 Feb	CC		582.33	10,310.70
25 Feb	BACS receipts – Assignia plc		6,283.02	16,593.72
22 Feb	DD Heartlands Electric	150.00		16,443.72
24 Feb	DD Midland Gas	90.00		16,353.72
25 Feb	Cheque returned unpaid – refer to Mr R Handley	352.50		16,001.22
25 Feb	ATM withdrawal	200.00		15,801.22

Key   DD: Direct Debit   BACS: Bankers automated clearing services

        O/D: Overdrawn   ATM – automated teller machine cash withdrawal

Task 3

On the assumption that both Assignia plc and Handley & Co are credit customers, update the receipts and payments side of the cash book as required and calculate the totals.

Task 4

Analyse the 'other' column on the payments side of the cash book.

Task 5

Post from both sides of the cash book to the general ledger accounts below. You do not need to calculate balances except on the bank ledger account.

		ADMINISTRATION/OVERHEADS				
Date	Details	Amount £	Date	Details	Amount £	
20X3			20X3			

		BANK				
Date	Details	Amount £	Date	Details	Amount £	
20X3			20X3			
1/2	Balance b/d	10,542.51				

		DISCOUNT ALLOWED AND RECEIVED				
Date	Details	Amount £	Date	Details	Amount £	
20X3			20X3			

		DISPOSALS				
Date	Details	Amount £	Date	Details	Amount £	
20X3			20X3			

DRAWINGS					
Date	Details	Amount £	Date	Details	Amount £
20X3			20X3		

INTEREST RECEIVED					
Date	Details	Amount £	Date	Details	Amount £
20X3			20X3		

PURCHASE LEDGER CONTROL					
Date	Details	Amount £	Date	Details	Amount £
20X3			20X3		

SALES					
Date	Details	Amount £	Date	Details	Amount £
20X3			20X3		

SALES LEDGER CONTROL					
Date	Details	Amount £	Date	Details	Amount £
20X3			20X3		

STAFF COSTS					
Date	Details	Amount £	Date	Details	Amount £
20X3			20X3		

VAT					
Date	Details	Amount £	Date	Details	Amount £
20X3			20X3		

3 TRURO LEDGER   Assessment

Truro Audio Visual Supplies is a small business hiring out display and training hardware (screens, VCRs, overhead projectors etc) and providing trainers to the business community in the county of Cornwall. It is owned and run by Julian Jones. All sales are credit sales. Truro Audio Visual Supplies is registered for VAT and all sales are standard rated (17.5%). All purchases are made on credit. Expenditure in the day books is analysed into: administration; warehouse overheads; despatch; and marketing. The cash book and the sales and purchase ledgers are not part of the double entry system, and are written up as necessary during the month. The general ledger is only written up at the end of the month.

Task 1

Total the cash book below, and calculate the total values for the day books below.

BPP
PUBLISHING

CASH BOOK: RECEIPTS

Date	Details	Cash	Discount allowed	Sales Ledger Control	Interest
		£	£	£	£
20X5					
1 Jan	Cheques received	3,109.26	45.00	3,109.26	
3 Jan	Cheques received	4,289.20	60.00	4,289.20	
7 Jan	Cheques received	1,901.82		1,901.82	
11 Jan	Cheques received	5,298.20	15.00	5,298.20	
13 Jan	BACS receipt	4,265.26		4,265.26	
17 Jan	Cheques received	2,198.02	11.00	2,198.02	
21 Jan	Cheques received	3,294.11		3,294.11	
25 Jan	BACS receipt	1,278.34	7.00	1,278.34	
30 Jan	Cheques received	7,289.52	65.00	7,289.52	
31 Jan	Interest credited	103.00			103.00

CASH BOOK: PAYMENTS

Date	Details	Cheque No	Cash	Discount received	Purchase Ledger Control	Other
20X5			£	£	£	£
1 Jan	Mr G Formwell	7421	1,910.26	12.00	1,910.26	
4 Jan	Ms S Parker	7422	2,877.46		2,877.46	
8 Jan	Jensen Ltd	7423	7,209.45	52.50	7,209.45	
12 Jan	Norton Motors Ltd (new car)	7425	15,000.00	100.00		15,000.00
12 Jan	Mr J Jones drawings	DD	2,000.00			2,000.00
18 Jan	Tremayne Holdings plc	7426	263.29		263.29	
20 Jan	Kerrier District Council (rates)	DD	350.00		350.00	
24 Jan	Westworld Computers Ltd	7427	638.23		638.23	
29 Jan	Quest plc	7428	2,190.63	32.00	2,190.63	
31 Jan	Salaries	BACS	7,092.87			7,092.87

MONTH ENDED 31 JANUARY 20X5

Purchases Day Book	£
Administration	1,298.02
Warehouse overheads	2,892.19
Despatch	2,817.29
Marketing	3,198.29
VAT	1,786.01
Total value of invoices	

Sales Day Book	£
Sales invoices	20,189.73
VAT	3,533.20
Total value of invoices	

Purchases Returns Day Book	£
Administration	0.00
Warehouse overheads	0.00
Despatch	192.64
Marketing	32.00
VAT	39.31
Total value of credit notes	

Sales Returns Day Book	£
Sales credit notes	200.00
VAT	35.00
Total value of credit notes	

Task 2

Write up the general ledger accounts below as follows for January 20X5.

- Post the cash book to the general ledger.

- Post the January day books to the general ledger.

ADMINISTRATION					
Date	Details	Amount £	Date	Details	Amount £
20X5			20X5		

BPP
PUBLISHING

Practice activities

CASH					
Date	Details	Amount £	Date	Details	Amount £
20X5			20X5		

DESPATCH					
Date	Details	Amount £	Date	Details	Amount £
20X5			20X5		

DISCOUNTS ALLOWED AND RECEIVED					
Date	Details	Amount £	Date	Details	Amount £
20X5			20X5		

DRAWINGS					
Date	Details	Amount £	Date	Details	Amount £
20X5			20X5		

INTEREST RECEIVED					
Date	Details	Amount £	Date	Details	Amount £
20X5			20X5		

MARKETING					
Date	Details	Amount £	Date	Details	Amount £
20X5			20X5		

MOTOR VEHICLES					
Date	**Details**	**Amount** **£**	**Date**	**Details**	**Amount** **£**
20X5			**20X5**		

PURCHASE LEDGER CONTROL					
Date	**Details**	**Amount** **£**	**Date**	**Details**	**Amount** **£**
20X5			**20X5**		
			31/1	Balance b/d	19,140.62

SALARIES					
Date	**Details**	**Amount** **£**	**Date**	**Details**	**Amount** **£**
20X5			**20X5**		

SALES					
Date	**Details**	**Amount** **£**	**Date**	**Details**	**Amount** **£**
20X5			**20X5**		

BPP PUBLISHING

SALES LEDGER CONTROL					
Date	Details	Amount £	Date	Details	Amount £
20X5			20X5		
31/1	Balance b/d	40,363.29			

VAT					
Date	Details	Amount £	Date	Details	Amount £
20X5			20X5		

WAREHOUSE OVERHEADS					
Date	Details	Amount £	Date	Details	Amount £
20X5			20X5		

Task 3

Refer to the balances on the debtors' and creditors' accounts in the subsidiary ledgers below and the further information provided.

- Balance off the relevant control accounts in the general ledger.
- Prepare a debtors' reconciliation and a creditors' reconciliation.

22

Sales ledger	£
Antrobus & Co	2,298.35
Grenfell Brothers	5,238.29
Jeantons	381.11
Land and Field Association	3,182.39
Nelson Ltd	5,178.20
Pristine Engineering Ltd	830.27
Richard Roop Associates	65.00
Tremayne Holdings plc	7,654.02
Varnells Ltd	3,414.41

Purchase ledger	£
Jensen Ltd	239.27
Harrier Ltd	3,189.02
Kerrier District Council (rates)	2,187.19
Westworld Computers Ltd	540.82
Quest plc	1,298.37
Tremayne Holdings plc	5,283.00
Flatscreen Technology	730.27
Robust Engineering plc	2,393.09
Warners Ltd	1,073.52

Further information

An investigation reveals the following errors in the ledgers and day books.

(a) The invoice totals for the sales day book for January was overcast by £900.00.

(b) One invoice for £1,440.00 including VAT was duplicated in the sales day book for January

(c) Cash received of £120.00 from Nelson Ltd was posted to the wrong side of its sales ledger account

(d) The despatch column of the purchase day book for January was undercast by £270.00.

(e) One marketing invoice total for £872.00 including VAT was omitted from the purchase day book in January

(f) An invoice totalling £1,092.35 was posted twice to the purchase ledger account of Harrier Ltd.

(g) A contra of £582.45 was made in the sales and purchase ledger accounts of Tremayne Holdings plc.

Task 4

Prepare a journal to correct the general ledger accounts fully.

Journal

Date 20X5	Account names and narrative	Debit £	Credit £

Task 5

Post the journal to the general ledger, and recalculate the balances on the control accounts.

4   GREEN LEDGER   Assessment

Green's Bottles Ltd is a business which manufactures bottles for the soft drinks industry in the town of Tunbridge Wells in the county of Sussex. It is owned and run by Hana Paritova. All sales are credit sales. Greens's Bottles is registered for VAT and all sales are standard rated (17.5%). All purchases are made on credit. Expenditure in the day books is analysed into: administration and marketing; factory overheads; raw materials. The cash book and the sales and purchase ledgers are not part of the double entry system, and are written up as necessary during the month. The general ledger is only written up at the end of the month.

Task 1

Write up the general ledger accounts below as follows for April 20X1.

- Post the cash book to the general ledger.
- Post the April day books to the general ledger.

CASH BOOK: RECEIPTS

Date	Details	Cash	Discount allowed	Sales Ledger Control	Other
		£	£	£	£
20X1					
2/4	Cheques received	5,290.38	15.00	5,290.38	
4/4	Cheques received	6,209.37	23.00	6,209.37	
5/4	BACS receipt	3,350.00		3,350.00	
7/4	Cheques received	2,182.34	31.00	2,182.34	
10/4	Cheques received	1,192.27		1,192.27	
12/4	Cheques received	7,203.27	154.00	7,203.27	
14/4	BACS receipt	8,023.92		8,023.92	
15/4	BACS receipt	6,390.29	85.00	6,390.29	
19/4	Cresswell Gas Co – refund of factory overheads	123.95			123.95
22/4	Cheques received	2,379.27		2,379.27	
23/4	BACS receipt	10,290.23	300.00	10,290.23	
29/4	Cheques received	9,312.39	45.00	9,312.39	
		61,947.68	653.00	61,823.73	123.95

CASH BOOK: PAYMENTS

Date	Details	Cheque No	Cash	Discount received	Purchase Ledger Control	Other
20X1			£	£	£	£
2 April	Raw Sand Ltd	0816	8,290.38	223.00	8,290.38	
	Metal Fasteners plc	0817	5,353.20	120.00	5,353.20	
	Brundells Lubricants	0818	2,392.39		2,392.39	
	Hana Paritova – drawings	DD	3,000.00			3,000.00
	The Repair Shop	0819	560.28		560.28	
	Pharmco Chemicals Ltd	0820	8,234.20	241.00	8,234.20	
	Cresswell Gas Co	0821	4,209.30	52.00	4,209.30	
	Interest on loan and overdraft	0822	230.00			230.00
	Wages (factory labour)	BACS	7,209.86			7,209.86
	Salaries (admin & marketing)	BACS	5,982.38			5,982.38
			45,461.99	636.00	29,039.75	16,422.24

MONTH ENDED 30 APRIL 20X1

Purchases Day Book	£
Administration and marketing	2,109.28
Factory overheads	1,290.38
Raw materials	9,365.47
VAT	2,183.08
Total value of invoices	14,948.21

Sales Day Book	£
Sales invoices	35,864.86
VAT	6,276.35
Total value of invoices	42,141.21

Purchases Returns Day Book	£
Administration and marketing	0.00
Factory overheads	139.25
Raw materials	984.22
VAT	196.60
Total value of credit notes	1,320.07

Sales Returns Day Book	£
Sales credit notes	2,673.36
VAT	467.83
Total value of credit notes	3,141.19

ADMINISTRATION AND MARKETING					
Date	Details	Amount £	Date	Details	Amount £
20X1			**20X1**		
1/4	Balance b/d	32,290.29			

CAPITAL					
Date	Details	Amount £	Date	Details	Amount £
20X1			**20X1**		
			1/4	Balance b/d	50,000

CASH					
Date	**Details**	**Amount £**	**Date**	**Details**	**Amount £**
20X1			**20X1**		
			1/4	Balance b/d	2,398.20

DISCOUNTS ALLOWED AND RECEIVED					
Date	**Details**	**Amount £**	**Date**	**Details**	**Amount £**
20X1			**20X1**		
1/4	Balance b/d	375.29			

DRAWINGS					
Date	**Details**	**Amount £**	**Date**	**Details**	**Amount £**
20X1			**20X1**		
1/4	Balance b/d	15,000			

FACTORY LABOUR					
Date	**Details**	**Amount £**	**Date**	**Details**	**Amount £**
20X1			**20X1**		
1/4	Balance b/d	43,529.18			

FACTORY OVERHEADS					
Date	**Details**	**Amount £**	**Date**	**Details**	**Amount £**
20X1			**20X1**		
1/4	Balance b/d	28,254.38			

FIXED ASSETS (NBV)					
Date	**Details**	**Amount £**	**Date**	**Details**	**Amount £**
20X1			**20X1**		
1/4	Balance b/d	32,100.10			

BPP PUBLISHING

INTEREST PAID						
Date	**Details**	**Amount** **£**	**Date**	**Details**	**Amount** **£**
20X1			**20X1**		
1/4	Balance b/d	1920.27	1/4	Balance b/d	

LOAN						
Date	**Details**	**Amount** **£**	**Date**	**Details**	**Amount** **£**
20X1			**20X1**		
			1/4	Balance b/d	15,000

PURCHASE LEDGER CONTROL						
Date	**Details**	**Amount** **£**	**Date**	**Details**	**Amount** **£**
20X1			**20X1**		
			1/4	Balance b/d	25,131.14

RAW MATERIALS					
Date	**Details**	**Amount £**	**Date**	**Details**	**Amount £**
20X1			**20X1**		
1/4	Balance b/d	80,265.35			

SALES					
Date	**Details**	**Amount £**	**Date**	**Details**	**Amount £**
20X1			**20X1**		
			1/4	Balance b/d	215,189.19

SALES LEDGER CONTROL					
Date	**Details**	**Amount £**	**Date**	**Details**	**Amount £**
20X1			**20X1**		
1/4	Balance b/d	67,585.12			

STOCK					
Date	**Details**	**Amount** **£**	**Date**	**Details**	**Amount** **£**
20X1			**20X1**		
1/4	Balance b/d	10,198.19			

SUSPENSE					
Date	**Details**	**Amount** **£**	**Date**	**Details**	**Amount** **£**
20X1			**20X1**		

VAT					
Date	**Details**	**Amount** **£**	**Date**	**Details**	**Amount** **£**
20X1			**20X1**		
			1/4	Balance b/d	2,158.26

Task 2

Calculate balances on all the general ledger accounts and draw up an initial trial balance. Enter any imbalance on the initial TB into the suspense ledger account.

Task 3

Refer to the information provided below, and prepare a journal to clear the suspense account.

An investigation reveals the following errors in the ledgers and day books:

- The balance brought down on the factory labour ledger account was miscast. The correct balance is £43,259.18.

- The balance brought down on the purchase ledger control account was miscast. The correct balance is £25,311.14.

- Cash received of £891.20 from Lewis & Co was posted to the wrong side of its sales ledger account.

- One receipt for £1,191.38 was included in the cash book in March but was omitted from the total posted to the sales ledger control account.

Task 4

Post the journal to the general ledger, and recalculate the balances on any accounts affected.

Task 5

Draw up a final TB and prove that it balances.

5 Capital acquisition and disposal

5 FINBAR'S FIXED ASSETS   Assessment

Finbar the Butcher is a retail butcher operating in the town of Hexham. It is owned and run by Finbar O'Hanlon.

The firm prepares and sells a range of meat to wholesalers, restaurants and the general public. Its fixed assets comprise freehold buildings, which are not depreciated, in which there is a butchery, an office and a shop, plus Office and Shop Equipment, Butchery Equipment and Delivery Vehicles. There is a manual fixed asset register showing details of capital expenditure (but not revenue expenditure) incurred in acquiring or enhancing fixed assets, as well as details of depreciation or disposals. For each category of fixed asset the general ledger includes accounts for cost and accumulated depreciation (i.e. the balance sheet accounts). There is one depreciation charge ledger account (i.e. the expense recorded in the profit and loss account) for all classes of fixed asset.

Depreciation rates and methods are as follows:

Office and Shop Equipment	20% p.a. on cost (straight line basis)
Butchery Equipment	20% p.a. on net book value (reducing balance basis)
Delivery Vehicles	25% p.a. on cost (straight line basis)

- A full year's depreciation is charged in the year of an asset's acquisition, regardless of the exact date of acquisition.

- No depreciation is charged in the year of an asset's disposal, regardless of the date of disposal.

- Residual value is assumed to be nil in all cases.

Finbar O'Hanlon authorises all acquisitions and disposals of fixed assets by signing invoices.

Task 1

Finbar O'Hanlon has just handed you the suppliers' invoices below. These refer to the purchase of a new freezer for the Butchery, a new desk for the office and a new computerised till for the Shop.

- Record the acquisitions in the fixed asset register.
- Prepare journals to record the invoices in the general ledger.

INVOICE

Quality Butchery Fittings
4 Smithfield
London E1 5GH

VAT registration:	832 3682 34		
Date/tax point:	31 August 20X4		
Customer:	Finbar the Butcher, 56 Main Street, Hexham		
Description		**Rate**	**Total**
		£	£
1 x 1,200 cubic feet freezer		15,000.00	15,000.00
Delivery and fitting		500.00	500.00
Approved			
Finbar 2/9/X4			
Goods total			15,500.00
VAT		17.5%	2,658.25
Invoice total			18,158.25
2/7, Net 30 days			

INVOICE

JBJ Office Fittings
Yard Square
Newcastle

VAT registration:	638 3349 239		
Date/tax point:	31 August 20X4		
Customer:	Finbar the Butcher, 56 Main Street, Hexham		
Description		**Rate**	**Total**
		£	£
1 x solid beech desk		800.00	800.00
1 x fully computerised till		3,500.00	3,500.00
Approved			
Finbar 2/9/X4			
Goods total			4,300.00
VAT		17.5%	752.50
Invoice total			5,052.50
Net 30 days			

FIXED ASSET REGISTER

Description/serial no	Date acquired	Original cost £	Depreciation £	NBV £	Funding method	Disposal proceeds £	Disposal date
Office and shop equipment							
Depreciation: 20% p.a. on cost (straight line basis)							
Computer	1/9/X1	3,000.00			Cash		
Year ended 31/8/X2			600.00	2,400.00			
Year ended 31/8/X3			600.00	1,800.00			
Printer and photocopier	1/9/X1	2,000.00			Cash		
Year ended 31/8/X2			400.00	1,600.00			
Year ended 31/8/X3			400.00	1,200.00			
Fax machine	30/9/X1	800.00			Cash		
Year ended 31/8/X2			160.00	640.00			
Year ended 31/8/X3			160.00	480.00			
Chiller cabinets	1/4/X2	7,000.00			Cash		
Year ended 31/8/X2			1,400.00	5,600.00			
Year ended 31/8/X3			1,400.00	4,200.00			
Till	1/9/X2	5,000.00			Cash		
Year ended 31/8/X3			1,000.00	4,000.00			
NBV at 31/8/X4 c/f							

BPP PUBLISHING

FIXED ASSET REGISTER

Description/serial no	Date acquired	Original cost £	Depreciation £	NBV £	Funding method	Disposal proceeds £	Disposal date
Office and shop equipment							
Depreciation: 20% p.a. on cost (straight line basis)							
Security shutters	30/9/X1	6,000.00			Cash		
Year ended 31/8/X2			1,200.00	4,800.00			
Year ended 31/8/X3			1,200.00	3,600.00			
NBV at 31/8/X4							
NBV at 31/8/X4 b/f							
NBV at 31/8/X4							

FIXED ASSET REGISTER

Description/serial no	Date acquired	Original cost £	Depreciation £	NBV £	Funding method	Disposal proceeds £	Disposal date
Butchery equipment							
20% p.a. on net book value (reducing balance basis)							
Workbenches (6)	1/9/X1	6,000.00			Cash		
Year ended 31/8/X2			1,200.00	4,800.00			
Year ended 31/8/X3			960.00	3,840.00			
Grinding machine	1/9/X1	3,600.00			Cash		
Year ended 31/8/X2			720.00	2,880.00			
Year ended 31/8/X3			576.00	2,304.00			
Slicer	1/9/X1	2,350.00			Cash		
Year ended 31/8/X2			470.00	1,880.00			
Year ended 31/8/X3			376.00	1,504.00			
Freezer (600 cu ft)	1/9/X2	9,000.00			Cash		
Year ended 31/8/X3			1,800.00	7,200.00			
NBV at 31/8/X4							

BPP PUBLISHING

FIXED ASSET REGISTER

Description/serial no	Date acquired	Original cost £	Depreciation £	NBV £	Funding method	Disposal proceeds £	Disposal date
Delivery vehicles							
25% p.a. on cost (straight line basis)							
Van TY61 CVB	1/4/X2	15,000.00			Cash		
Year ended 31/8/X2			3,750.00	11,250.00			
Year ended 31/8/X3			3,750.00	7,500.00			
Van GH62 UYT	1/5/X3	12,000.00			Cash		
Year ended 31/8/X3			3,000.00	9,000.00			
Van TY72 BNM	1/1/X4	11,500.00			Cash		
NBV at 31/8/X4							

Journal 1

Date 20X4	Account names and narrative	Debit £	Credit £

Task 2

Finbar O'Hanlon tells you that the computerised till that he bought in 20X2 has never functioned properly and has been disposed of for only £200.00. The receipt has been recorded in the cash book but no other entries have been made. There is a balance on the suspense account at 31August of £200.00.

- Write up the fixed asset register for the disposal.
- Prepare a journal to record the disposal in the general ledger.

Journal 2

Date 20X4	Account names and narrative	Debit £	Credit £

Task 3

- In the fixed asset register, calculate and record the relevant amounts of depreciation for the year to 31 August 20X4 on each fixed asset.

- Prepare a journal to record depreciation in the general ledger.

Journal 3

Date 20X4	Account names and narrative	Debit £	Credit £

Task 4

Post the journals you have prepared to the general ledger accounts below, and balance off the fixed asset cost and accumulated depreciation accounts.

BUTCHERY EQUIPMENT (ACCUMULATED DEPRECIATION)

Date	Details	Amount £	Date	Details	Amount £
20X4			20X4		
			31/8	Balance b/d	6,102.00

BUTCHERY EQUIPMENT (COST)

Date	Details	Amount £	Date	Details	Amount £
20X4			20X4		
31/8	Balance b/d	20,950.00			

DELIVERY VEHICLES (ACCUMULATED DEPRECIATION)

Date	Details	Amount £	Date	Details	Amount £
20X4			20X4		
			31/8	Balance b/d	10,500.00

DELIVERY VEHICLES (COST)

Date	Details	Amount £	Date	Details	Amount £
20X4			20X4		
31/8	Balance b/d	38,500.00			

DEPRECIATION CHARGE

Date	Details	Amount £	Date	Details	Amount £
20X4			20X4		

DISPOSALS					
Date	**Details**	**Amount £**	**Date**	**Details**	**Amount £**
20X4			**20X4**		

OFFICE AND SHOP EQUIPMENT (ACCUMULATED DEPRECIATION)					
Date	**Details**	**Amount £**	**Date**	**Details**	**Amount £**
20X4			**20X4**		
			31/8	Balance b/d	8,520.00

OFFICE AND SHOP EQUIPMENT (COST)					
Date	**Details**	**Amount £**	**Date**	**Details**	**Amount £**
20X4			**20X4**		
31/8	Balance b/d	23,800.00			

SUNDRY CREDITORS					
Date	**Details**	**Amount £**	**Date**	**Details**	**Amount £**
20X4			**20X4**		

SUSPENSE					
Date	**Details**	**Amount £**	**Date**	**Details**	**Amount £**
20X4			**20X4**		
			31/8	Balance b/d	200.00

VAT					
Date	Details	Amount £	Date	Details	Amount £
20X4			20X4		

Task 5

Complete the reconciliation below, to ensure that the fixed asset register agrees with the general ledger.

Balances per general ledger accounts:

	Cost £	Accumulated depreciation £	Net book value per fixed asset register £
Butchery equipment			
Office and shop equipment			
Delivery vehicles			

6 NORTHMOOR'S FIXED ASSETS   Assessment

Northmoor Garage is a small garage and repair shop operating in the county of Leicestershire. It is owned and run by Samantha Goodrich. It repairs and services vehicles and sells second hand vehicles to the general public. Its fixed assets comprise freehold buildings, which are not depreciated, in which there is a showroom, an office and a workshop, plus Showroom and Office Equipment, Workshop Equipment and two Breakdown Vehicles. There is a manual fixed asset register showing details of capital expenditure (but not revenue expenditure) incurred in acquiring or enhancing fixed assets, as well as details of depreciation or disposals. For each category of fixed asset the general ledger includes accounts for cost and accumulated depreciation (i.e. the balance sheet accounts). There is one depreciation charge ledger account (i.e. the expense recorded in the profit and loss account) for all classes of fixed asset.

Depreciation rates and methods are as follows.

Showroom and office equipment:	25% p.a. on cost (straight line basis)
Workshop equipment:	20% p.a. on net book value (reducing balance basis)
Breakdown vehicles:	15% p.a. on net book value (reducing balance basis)

A full year's depreciation is charged in the year of an asset's acquisition, regardless of the exact date of acquisition.

No depreciation is charged in the year of an asset's disposal, regardless of the date of disposal.

Residual value is assumed to be nil in all cases.

Samantha Goodrich authorises all acquisitions and disposals of fixed assets by signing invoices. The business is registered for VAT.

Task 1

Samantha Goodrich has just handed you the suppliers' invoices below. These refer to the purchase of a new computer for the Office and a new ramp for the Workshop.

- Record the acquisitions in the fixed asset register.

- Prepare journals to record the invoices in the general ledger.

INVOICE	
Laptop World **Leys Retail Park** **Leicester**	

VAT registration:	783 7289 36		
Date/tax point:	31 March 20X8		
Customer:	Northmoor Garage, Ford Lane, Rickhall, Leicestershire		
Description		Rate	Total
		£	£
1 Dingly Solo Laptop 8927 *Approved* *Samantha 2/3/X8*		1,400.00	1,400.00
Goods total			1,400.00
VAT		17.5%	245.00
Invoice total			1,645.00
Net 30 days			

INVOICE	
Motor Engineering Ltd 70-89 Carshalton Industrial Estate Croydon	

VAT registration:	536 3764 34		
Date/tax point:	31 March 20X8		
Customer:	Northmoor Garage, Ford Lane, Rickhall, Leicestershire		
Description		Rate	Total
		£	£
1 4 metre steel ramp		900.00	900.00
Fitting and testing on your premises		200.00	200.00
Approved *Samantha 2/3/X8*			
Goods total			1,100.00
VAT		17.5%	192.50
Invoice total			1,292.50
Net 30 days			

FIXED ASSET REGISTER

Description/serial no	Date acquired	Original cost £	Depreciation £	NBV £	Funding method	Disposal proceeds £	Disposal date
Showroom and office equipment							
Depreciation: 25% p.a. on cost (straight line basis)							
Display pedestals (5 in total)	1/4/X5	3,000.00			Cash		
Year ended 31/3/X6			750.00	2,250.00			
Year ended 31/3/X7			750.00	1,500.00			
Reception sofas	30/9/X6	2,500.00			Cash		
Year ended 31/3/X7			625.00	1,875.00			
Coffee vending machine	30/9/X6	1,800.00			Cash		
Year ended 31/3/X7			450.00	1,350.00			
Team PC	1/4/X5	3,500.00			Cash		
Year ended 31/3/X6			875.00	2,625.00			
Dingly PC	30/9/X6	4,000.00			Cash		
Year ended 31/3/X7			1,000.00	3,000.00			

FIXED ASSET REGISTER

Description/serial no	Date acquired	Original cost £	Depreciation £	NBV £	Funding method	Disposal proceeds £	Disposal date
Showroom and office equipment							
Depreciation: 25% p.a. on cost (straight line basis)							
Laser printer	30/9/X6	1,500.00			Cash		
Year ended 31/3/X7			375.00	1,125.00			
Photocopier	30/9/X5	2,100.00			Cash		
Year ended 31/3/X6			525.00	1,575.00			
Year ended 31/3/X7			525.00	1,050.00			

FIXED ASSET REGISTER

Description/serial no	Date acquired	Original cost £	Depreciation £	NBV £	Funding method	Disposal proceeds £	Disposal date
Workshop equipment							
20% p.a. on net book value (reducing balance basis)							
Ramp (3 metre)	1/4/X5	500.00			Cash		
Year ended 31/3/X6			100.00	400.00			
Year ended 31/3/X7			80.00	320.00			
Diagnostic machine	1/4/X5	15,000.00			Cash		
Year ended 31/3/X6			3,000.00	12,000.00			
Year ended 31/3/X7			2,400.00	9,600.00			
Service equipment	1/4/X5	21,000.00			Cash		
Year ended 31/3/X6			4,200.00	16,800.00			
Year ended 31/3/X7			3,360.00	13,440.00			

FIXED ASSET REGISTER

Description/serial no	Date acquired	Original cost £	Depreciation £	NBV £	Funding method	Disposal proceeds £	Disposal date
Breakdown vehicles							
15% p.a. on cost (reducing balance basis)							
Tow truck RT21 GHJ	1/4/X5	32,000.00			Cash		
Year ended 31/3/X6			4,800.00	27,200.00			
Year ended 31/3/X7			4,080.00	23,120.00			
Tow truck RT22 DFG	1/5/X5	35,000.00			Cash		
Year ended 31/3/X6			5,250.00	29,750.00			
Year ended 31/3/X7			4,462.50	25,287.50			

Journal 1

Date 20X8	Account names and narrative	Debit £	Credit £

Task 2

Samantha Goodrich has listed the items of equipment in the factory at close of business on 31 March 20X8, and prepared a note about a disposal during the year.

- Compare the list with the details recorded in the fixed asset register, and identify any discrepancies.

- Write up the fixed asset register for the disposal.

- Prepare a journal to record the disposal in the general ledger.

FIXED ASSETS PHYSICALLY PRESENT 31 MARCH 20X8	
Prepared by: Samantha Goodrich **Date: 31 March 20X8**	
Office	Workshop
PC (Dingly)	3 metre ramp
Laptop (Dingly)	4 metre ramp
Laser printer	Diagnostic machine
Photocopier	Service equipment
Showroom	Breakdown vehicles
5 display pedestals	Tow truck RT21 GHJ
Reception sofas	Tow truck RT22 DFG
Coffee machine	

Note

I managed to sell the old Team computer for £1,000.00. I haven't got the cash yet, but should have it any day now. Samantha.

Journal 2

Date 20X8	Account names and narrative	Debit £	Credit £

Task 3

- In the fixed asset register, calculate and record the relevant amounts of depreciation for the year to 31 March 20X8 on each fixed asset.

- Prepare a journal to record depreciation in the general ledger.

Journal 3

Date 20X8	Account names and narrative	Debit £	Credit £

6-11 Final accounts

7   MELANIE LANCTON (55 mins)   **6/96**

Melanie Lancton is considering taking over a small clothing wholesalers which belongs to Rahul Gupta. You have been asked to prepare some figures for Melanie from the records kept for the business.

You are presented with the following.

Rahul Gupta assets and liabilities at 31 May 20X5

	£
Freehold buildings at cost	80,000
Less depreciation to date	16,000
	64,000
Fixtures and fittings at cost	17,500
Less depreciation to date	12,000
	5,500
Stock	33,200
Debtors	39,470
Prepaid general expenses	550
Cash	900
	74,120
Creditors	35,960
Bank overdraft	17,390
	53,350

Summary of the business bank account for the year ended 31 May 20X6

	£		£
Cash sales	147,890	Balance b/d	17,390
From debtors	863,740	To creditors	607,650
Sale proceeds fixtures and			
fittings	1,360	General expenses	6,240
		Salaries	94,170
		Security devices	5,100
		Drawings	28,310
		Balance c/d	254,130
	1,012,990		1,012,990

Other information

(a) The profit margin achieved on all sales is 40%. At the end of the year on 31 May 20X6 the stock was valued at £38,700. However, Rahul Gupta is convinced that various items have been stolen during the year. To prevent further theft the premises were fitted out with various security devices on 31 May 20X6.

(b) Depreciation is calculated on a *monthly* basis as follows.

Premises	2% on cost
Fixtures and fittings	10% on cost

Fixtures and fittings purchased on 1 June 20X0 for £4,000 were sold on 30 November 20X5, the purchaser paying by cheque.

(c) The proceeds of cash sales are held in tills and paid into the bank at the end of the day, apart from a float which is retained on the premises to be used at the start of the following day. During May 20X6 a decision was made to increase the size of the float from the £900 held at the beginning of the year to £1,000.

(d) On 31 May 20X6 creditors amounted to £49,310, debtors £45,400 and £170 was owing for general expenses. During the year bad debts of £2,340 have been written off.

Tasks

1 Draw up a total debtors account (debtors control account) showing clearly the total value of the credit sales for the year ended 31 May 20X6.

2 Calculate the total sales for the year ended 31 May 20X6.

3 Draw up a total creditors account (creditors control account) showing clearly the total purchases for the year ended 31 May 20X6.

4 Calculate the value of the stock stolen during the year.

5 Calculate the profit or loss made from the sale of fixtures and fittings on 30 November 20X5.

6 Calculate the figure for general expenses which would be included in the calculation of profit for the year ended 31 May 20X6.

8 ANDREW HALLGROVE (80 mins)   **12/96**

(a) Andrew Hallgrove decided to open a shop selling cheap alarm systems and security equipment direct to the public. Trading was to start at the beginning of October 20X6. He decided to call the shop and business 'Total Security'.

(b) On 1 September he opened a new bank account and paid in £50,000 of his own money as his investment in the business.

(c) During September he purchased shop fixtures and fittings at £22,500 and stock at £47,300. He paid £9,000 for 6 months' rent covering the period 1 September 20X6 to 28 February 20X7. Insurance of £480 covering the 12 months from 1 September 20X6 was also paid, as were various items of general expenditure totalling £220.

(d) Since it was convenient to make some of the payments in cash he withdrew a lump sum from the bank.

(e) Unfortunately, his £50,000 investment was insufficient to cover all of the expenditure. However, he managed to negotiate a bank loan and all the monies from this were paid into the business's bank account.

(f) The interest rate for the bank loan was fixed at 12% per annum.

(g) At the end of September he had a £10,000 balance remaining in the bank account and £500 in cash.

(h) A summary of the business bank account for October 20X6 is shown below.

	£		£
Balance b/d	10,000	To creditors	20,250
Cash banked	22,000	Drawings	3,500
		General expenses	500
		Stationery	320
		Customer refund	2,000
		Balance c/d	5,430
	32,000		32,000

(i)   The cash banked all came from sales to customers. However, before banking the takings, £2,400 had been paid out as wages. The cash float at the end of October remained at £500.

(j)   In paying his creditors he had been able to take advantage of discounts totalling £1,250. At the end of the month not all creditors had been paid, however, and he calculated that the total of the unpaid invoices amounted to £3,400.

(k)   Depreciation is calculated on the fixtures and fittings at 20% per annum on cost.

(l)   On 31 October 20X6 a customer returned an alarm system which he had decided was not appropriate for his premises. He was given a refund by cheque.

(m) Unsold stock on 31 October was valued at £55,000, but this did not include the returned system. The profit margin on this type of system is 30%.

Tasks

1   Calculate the amount of the bank loan taken out in September, clearly showing your workings.

2   List the business assets as at 30 September 20X6 together with their value. (Depreciation for September should be ignored.)

3   Calculate the value of the purchases made during October 20X6

4   Prepare a draft statement calculating the net profit for the month ended 31 October 20X6.

9   **HIGHBURY STOCKS (15 mins)**   **Assessment**

At Highbury Disks, stocks of compact discs are valued at cost. Cost includes a share of the recording, mastering and production costs as well as any direct overheads attributable to that recording. Stocks as at 31 May 20X5 have not been recorded in the accounting system. The following is an extract of the stock sheets as at 31 May 20X5 along with Anthony Sedgewick's comments.

STOCK SHEETS

Title	Number of discs in stock	Total cost £	Total price to retailers £	Total recom-mended retail price £	Comments
Total b/f from previous pages	4,500	18,000	27,600	39,800	No problems with any of these. We'll be able to make a profit on all of these discs.
Bambino choir of Prague	1,000	3,500	8,500	12,000	This batch of CDs arrived too late for the 20X4 Christmas season. We're keeping them for the 20X5 Christmas season. I think they will sell very well then.
The Joyful Singers sing Wesley	400	2,000	3,600	4,800	We just cannot get rid of these. We'll have to reduce the price to retailers to £3 a disc and recommend that retailers sell them for £5.50 a disc.
Bach at St Thomas's	2,000	7,000	14,000	20,000	This has not sold at all well. We're going to withdraw these discs and repackage them as 'The King of Instruments' and sell them to a chain store for £4 a disc. The repackaging will cost £1.50 per disc.
TOTAL	7,900	30,500	53,700	76,600	

Complete the following table to calculate the value of closing stock for incorporation into the accounts.

Stock sheets	Value £
Total b/f from previous pages	
Bambino choir of Prague	
The Joyful Singers sing Wesley	
Bach at St Thomas's	
VALUE OF STOCK as at 31 May 20X5	

10   JASON BROWN (50 mins)   Pre-assessment

(a)   Jason Brown has a figure for delivery vans of £12,800. This is made up from two vehicles, one costing £6,000 bought on 1 November 20X3 and one costing £6,800 bought on 1 November 20X4. If the first van was now to be sold on 1 May 20X6 for £3,200, then assuming that depreciation is calculated on a monthly basis:

   (i)   What would be the book value of the van at the date of sale?

   (ii)   Show the disposals account as it would appear in the ledger on 31 October 20X6.

MOTOR VANS DISPOSAL ACCOUNT			
	£		£

(b)   Jason Brown intends to launch a new computer consultancy service during 20X7. He is confident that this will bring about a substantial increase in business for his financial year ended 31 October 20X7. A major advertising campaign has been planned for September and October 20X6. What is the argument for including the cost of the campaign in the calculation of profit for the year end 31 October 20X7? Make reference in your answer to the accounting concept or concepts that relate to this matter.

(c)   In Task 4 of Section 1 the following errors, amongst others, were identified.

   (i)   Discounts allowed totalling £125 had been credited to discounts received.

   (ii)   Credit purchases totalling £15,840 had been transferred from the day book into the purchases account as £15,480.

   In correcting each error, would the reported profit be increased or decreased and by what amount?

(d)   Included in Jason Brown's stock are some standard office swivel chairs. At the beginning of October ten chairs each costing £30 were in stock. Stock movements during the month were as follows.

Stock at	1/10/X5	10 at £30
Purchases	10/10/X5	12 at £32
Sales	13/10/X5	2
Sales	18/10/X5	4
Purchases	23/10/X5	10 at £31
Sales	30/10/X5	6

Chairs are sold at £50 each.

Stock is valued on a FIFO basis.

Calculate the value of the following.

  (i)   Sales for October.
  (ii) Cost of goods sold for October.
  (ii) Closing stock at the end of October.

(e) 'Capital expenditure is expenditure on fixed assets which appear in the balance sheet. The cost of a fixed asset does not therefore affect the calculation of profit.' State whether or not you agree with the above statement and briefly explain the reason for your answer.

(f) The total sales figure to be used in the calculation of profit is £246,412.

  (a) Does this figure include or exclude VAT?
  (b) Briefly explain the reason for your answer.

(g) You have received the following note from Jason Brown.

'Thank you for producing the extended trial balance showing key figures for the year. I am concerned about the profitability of the business for next year and I am considering the following changes to improve the profit figure.

  (i)   Running down the stock levels at the end of the financial year. This can be achieved by reducing purchases and a smaller purchases figure will increase profit.

  (ii) Writing off M C Millar's debt this year significantly reduce the profit. If towards the end of next year any large bad debts are identified we should delay writing them off until the following year.

  (iii) We should calculate depreciation on all fixed assets using both the straight line and reducing balance methods. Each year we can then use the method which gives us the highest profit.'

Prepare a memorandum to Jason Brown covering each of the points he has raised.

(h) Some days after preparing the extended trial balance it was discovered that a credit sale for £96.20 had, in error, not been entered into the account of John Pearce Furniture in the sales ledger. Jason Brown is concerned about the control of errors and had contacted you for an explanation.

Write a note to Jason in the form of a memorandum, explaining why the error would not have been detected by drawing up a trial balance and how the existence of such an error would normally be detected by checking the total of the balances in the sales ledger.

11 SUNDRY QUERIES (40 mins)   Pre-assessment

(a) Indicate with a circle the effect on the calculation of profit and on the assets in the balance sheet if capital expenditure is treated as revenue expenditure.

  (i)   Profit would be: Overstated/Understated
  (ii) The value of the assets would be: Overstated/Understated

(b) Explosives makes a credit sale to Dillon Clothes for £600 plus VAT £105. (*Note.* State clearly for each entry the name of the account, the amount and whether debit or credit.)

      (i)   What double entry is made in the general ledger to record the sale?

      (ii)   What double entry is made in the general ledger to record the debtor clearing the debt by cheque?

(c) Expenditure on applied research may be capitalised should a company so wish.

      (i)   State whether or not you agree with the above statement. (Assume the expenditure is not on fixed assets.)

      (ii)   Explain *briefly* the reason for your answer to (a), referring to the relevant statement of standard accounting practice.

(d) Julie Owens is a credit customer of Explosives and currently owes approximately £5,000. She has recently become very slow in paying for purchases and has been sent numerous reminders for most of the larger invoices issued to her. A cheque for £2,500 sent to Explosives has now been returned by Julie Owens' bankers marked 'refer to drawer'. Which accounting concept would suggest that a provision for doubtful debts should be created to cover the debt of Julie Owens?

(e) It is found that cash sales have, in error, been credited to purchases instead of sales. In correcting this error and adjusting the profit, would profit be increased, reduced or stay the same?

(f) At the end of a previous accounting period, a suspense account with a £200 credit balance had been opened to agree the trial balance. It was subsequently found that only one error had been made, which related to cash drawings. Two debit entries had been made for the same amount instead of a debit and a credit. What entries should be passed to correct the error? (*Note.* State clearly for each entry the name of the account, the amount and whether debit or credit.)

(g) You have received the following note from Melanie Lancton.

'I have been looking at the draft final accounts you have produced. In the valuation of the closing stock you have included some of the jeans at less than cost price. The figure you used is net realisable value and this has effectively reduced the profit for the period. The closing stock will be sold in the next financial period and my understanding of the accruals concept is that the revenue from selling the stock should be matched against the cost of that stock. This is not now possible since part of the cost of the stock has been written off in reducing the closing stock valuation from cost price to net realisable value.'

Write a suitable response to Melanie Lancton in the form of a memorandum. Your answer should include references to relevant accounting concepts and to SSAP 9.

10   *Incomplete records*

12   BRAIN HOPE (60 mins)   Assessment

You have been asked to help in preparing the accounts of Brian Hope. Brian started in business in 20X1 doing repair and servicing of electrical equipment and he works in a rented workshop. So far he has not kept proper records of his transactions. His accounts to 31 December 20X1 were prepared for him on the basis of enquiries and the closing position was then shown as follows.

	£	£
Bank balance	190	
Cash in hand	10	
Van	6,000	
Stock of materials	1,210	
Trade debtors and creditors	1,420	2,220
Vehicle repair bill owing		80
Insurance prepaid	340	
Rent prepaid	400	
Capital		7,270
	9,570	9,570

You have started by summarising the bank statements for the year ended 31 December 20X2 as follows.

	£	£
Opening balance		260
Cash paid in		510
Receipts from debtors		21,120
		21,890
Payments to trade creditors (see (g) below)	3,930	
New vehicle (less trade-in)	3,600	
Vehicle running expenses	1,040	
Rent	2,640	
Insurance	960	
Other expenses	1,710	
Hope's drawings	8,000	
		21,880
Closing balance		10

You discover the following information regarding Hope's 20X2 transactions in the year to 31 December 20X2 and the closing position.

(a) He was paid in cash for some of the work done but cannot trace how much. However, you can find sufficient evidence to show that the debtors outstanding at the end of the year totalled £1,120 though £90 of this is probably irrecoverable. Hope does keep copies of all the invoices to his customers and these total £26,720 but he remembers allowing a customer £300 after a charge was disputed.

(b) Outstanding invoices from trade creditors at the end of the year totalled £2,460. Hope says that he is usually allowed a cash discount by one of the suppliers and the total discount for the year is estimated at £200.

(c) The rent was £200 per month until the end of August but was then increased to £240. Hope usually pays two months together in advance and has already paid (in December) for January and February 20X3.

(d) At the end of the year £60 is outstanding for petrol and the insurance has been prepaid by £380.

(e) Hope changed the van at the end of December buying a new one for £8,000 with a trade-in allowance for the old one of £4,400. He thinks he agreed last year to a depreciation charge of 20% per annum on book value (but this would not apply in 20X2 to the new vehicle just purchased).

(f) No adequate records of cash transactions have been kept but as indicated above it is known that customers often paid their accounts in cash and that Hope frequently withdrew cash for his own personal use. He estimates that payments for vehicle running costs of £500 have been made from cash and a similar amount for other expenses. There is no closing balance of cash.

(g) At the beginning of the year there were cheques to trade creditors unpresented at the bank totalling £70 and at the end of the year the unpresented cheques to trade creditors totalled £210.

Tasks

From the above information you are asked to draw up the ledger accounts on page 24 for each of the following showing the balances to be carried forward at the end of the year or the amounts to be transferred to the profit and loss account. (Dates need not be shown in the accounts.)

Trade debtors
Trade creditors
Rent
Vehicles
Vehicle running expenses
Insurance
Cash
Drawings

TRADE DEBTORS			

VEHICLE RUNNING EXPENSES			

TRADE CREDITORS			

INSURANCE			

RENT			

CASH			

VEHICLES			

DRAWINGS			

13   KULDIPA POTIWAL (60 mins)   **12/93**

The suggested time allocation for this incomplete records exercise is 60 minutes.

A friend of yours from Leicester, Kuldipa Potiwal, runs a small computer games retail and mail order business, but she does not keep proper accounting records. She has now been approached by the Inland Revenue for the details of the profit she has earned for the last year. She has provided you with the following bank account summary for the year ended 31 October 20X3.

BANK ACCOUNT SUMMARY

	£
Balance at bank (1 November 20X2)	
Bank overdraft	3,250
Receipts	
Cash paid in	56,000
Cheques from debtors	46,000
Investment income	1,500
Rent received	2,500
Payments	
Payments to trade creditors	78,000
Rent and rates	6,400
Postage and packing costs	2,200
Motor expenses	5,050
Administration expenses	4,600

Additional information was provided as follows.

(a) Kuldipa intends to sell all her computer games at cost plus 50%.

(b) Before paying cash receipts into the bank, Kuldipa used some of the cash received to make a number of payments.

Wages of shop assistant and driver	£350 per week
Drawings	£220 per week
Administration expenses	£750 per annum

All cash is paid into the bank daily.

(c) The investment income was interest on her private investment account.

(d) Other balances were as follows.

	31 October 20X2	*31 October 20X3*
	£	£
Delivery van (valuation)	17,500	12,500
Stock of games	12,200	13,750
Trade creditors	9,000	13,400
Trade debtors	6,000	7,200
Rates paid in advance	500	200
Rent receivable	-	250
Administration expenses owing	175	215

(e) During the year a vanload of games being delivered to credit customers was stolen. The van was recovered, undamaged, but the games have not been recovered. The insurance company has agreed to pay for 50% of the stolen games, but payment has not yet been received.

Kuldipa Potiwal calculated from the copy delivery notes that the selling price value of the games stolen was £6,000.

(f) At Christmas 20X2 Kuldipa Potiwal gave games as presents to her young relatives. The selling price of these games was £480.00.

Task 1

Prepare a detailed calculation of the net profit of the business for the year ended 31 October 20X3.

Task 2

Calculate the balance of Kuldipa's capital account at 31 October 20X3.

14   LYNDA BOOTH (60 mins)   **6/95**

You have been asked to help in preparing the accounts of Lynda Booth who has been trading as a painter and decorator for some years from a rented garage and workshop. Lynda is an excellent painter and decorator but does not have the expertise to maintain a double entry set of records. Your supervisor prepared Lynda's accounts last year and has provided you with a set of working accounts consisting of all accounts with start of year balances. The balances have been entered in the accounts.

You have already spent some time analysing the statements for Lynda's business bank account for the year ended 31 May 20X5 and have the following summary.

	£	£
Opening balance		323
Payments in		
Lottery winnings (see note (a), page 62)	10,000	
Cash takings paid in	2,770	
Receipts from trade debtors	43,210	
		55,980
		56,303
Payments out		
Payments to trade creditors	30,060	
Withdrawn for personal use	12,000	
Purchase of new van	4,800	
Rent and insurance	5,330	
Motor expenses	3,400	
		55,590
		713

Your analysis of the other business documentation kept by Lynda gives you the following additional information as at 31 May 20X5.

(a)   Invoices for work done for customers during the year ended 31 May 20X5 totalled £52,000 (of which £2,000 was unpaid as at 31 May 20X5).

(b)   Unpaid invoices for raw materials purchased from suppliers totalled £4,230.

(c)   Insurance was prepaid by £200.

(d)   Motor expenses were accrued by £209.

Your supervisor has supplied you with the following notes which were made during a meeting with Lynda Booth.

BPP
PUBLISHING

(a)	Lynda was a winner in the National Lottery earlier this year. She was not a jackpot winner and certainly did not win enough to retire. She paid some of her winnings into the business bank account to help with a temporary cash flow problem.
(b)	Lynda thinks that £480 of the amount collectable from customers as at 31 May 20X5 will not be recovered because one of her customers has gone into bankruptcy.
(c)	Lynda buys all her supplies from one supplier who offers 10% discount for prompt settlement. Lynda has been able to take advantage of that discount on all payments made during the year.
(d)	Some customers paid in cash during the year but Lynda has not kept any records. We've estimated that about £600 was paid for motor expenses from these cash receipts. There was £34 in the business safe as at 31 May 20X5.
(e)	Lynda bought the additional motor van on 1 February 20X5 because she thought the price was particularly good. She has used both vans in the business herself but feels that this van will be particularly useful next summer when she expects she will have to employ an assistant. We have agreed that the vans should be written off equally on a month for month basis over an expected life of four years. This is what we did with the first van which was purchased on 1 June 20X3.
(f)	There were materials costing £1,600 unused in the workshop at 31 May 20X5.

Task 1

From the above information reconstruct the ledger accounts provided for the year ended 31 May 20X5 on Pages 63 to 65, showing the balances to be carried forward at the end of the year and/or the amounts to be transferred to the profit and loss account for the year ended 31 May 20X5.

Notes

(a) Dates are not required.

(b) The following accounts are not supplied and need not be shown.

Capital
Work done/sales
Bad debts
Discounts received/allowed

BANK			
	£		£
Balance b/f	323		

CASH			
	£		£
Balance b/f	25		

MOTOR EXPENSES			
	£		£
		Balance b/f	174

MOTOR VAN(S)			
	£		£
Balance b/f	7,500		

RENT AND INSURANCE			
	£		£
Balance (insurance) b/f	180	Balance (rent) b/f	250

MATERIALS USED			
	£		£
Balance b/f	1,530		

TRADE CREDITORS			
	£	Balance b/f	£ 3,650

TRADE DEBTORS			
Balance b/f	£ 1,550		£

DRAWINGS			
	£		£

15 NATASHA (55 mins)   **Assessment**

Natasha inherited some money and an opportunity arose to set up her own business buying and selling stationery. She decided to go ahead with this venture. During October 20X5 she purchased premises costing £74,400, fixtures and fittings at £28,800 and stock at £15,613. The stock was partly bought with her own funds and partly on credit. Her supplier, Carlton Office Supplies Ltd, offered her £10,000 credit and at this point she made full use of the facility. At the end of the month she borrowed £48,000 by way of a loan from the bank at an interest rate of 10% per annum. After these transactions had taken place she had £1,220 of surplus funds remaining and on 1 November, the date the business opened, this sum was paid into a business bank account.

All of Natasha's sales were for cash and all were at a mark up of 25% on cost. Unfortunately Natasha did not appreciate the importance of recording sales despite the fact that she had bought a computer on 1 November with the intention of using it to record business transactions. It is estimated that the computer will be used for three years after which time it will have a residual value of £250. Depreciation should be calculated on a monthly basis for the computer and for other fixed assets. (Any depreciation for October should, however, be ignored.)

During November, Natasha took out from the takings any money she needed for her own use but, again, without recording the sums involved. The following amounts were also paid out of the cash and the remainder of the takings were then deposited in the bank.

Postages	£43
Cash purchases	£187
Sundry expenses	£52

Apart from the cash purchases, all other purchases of stock during November were made on credit from Carlton Office Supplies Ltd. Natasha's summarised business bank account for the period appeared as follows.

	Discount £	Bank £		Discount £	Bank £
Balance b/d		1,220	Purchase of the computer		1,402
Takings		30,408	Carlton Office Supplies	200	9,800
			Sundry expenses		61
			Insurance		384
			Carlton Office Supplies	250	12,250
			Balance c/d		7,731
		31,628		450	31,628

The insurance payment covered the period 1 November 20X5 to 31 October 20X6. On 30 November an invoice received from Carlton Office Supplies Ltd for £8,600 was still outstanding and this sum was therefore owed to the company. On the same date Natasha's stock was valued at £11,475. This, however, included £275 for a new electronic diary supplied for trial purposes on a sale or return basis. The £275 had not been included in any of the invoices received.

Depreciation is to be calculated at 2% per annum on cost for the premises and at 10% per annum on cost for the fixtures and fittings.

Tasks

1   Calculate Natasha's original capital sum introduced into the business.

2   Draw up the account for Carlton Office Supplies Ltd showing clearly the total purchases made on credit from the company during October and November.

3   Calculate the value of the total purchases made up to the end of November, including the purchase of the initial stock.

4   Prepare a draft statement calculating the net profit for the month ended 30 November 20X5 and clearly showing the total sales for the period.

5   Prepare the cash account for November showing clearly the total drawings made by Natasha during the month.

---

16   RICHARD FAIRLEY (70 mins)   **6/98**

Richard Fairley, has been watching Caroline's growing success and is tempted also to set up business on his own. He has found a small newsagent which would be ideal. The current owner of the business, Babek Assidian, is equally keen to sell the business and has therefore very kindly given Richard Fairley some information which he could use to asses the viability of the business.

Unfortunately, the information provided is incomplete, so Richard Fairley has passed the information to you so that you can calculate some of the necessary figures.

The following is the information provided.

Assets as at 31 December 20X6

	£	£
Fixtures and fittings at cost	17,500	
Less provision for depreciation	12,250	
		5,250
Motor vehicle at cost	12,500	
Less provision for depreciation	6,250	
		6,250
Stock		15,750
Debtors		630
Insurance prepayment		495
Cash		355
		28,730
Creditors	4,750	
Bank overdraft	3,490	
		8,240
		20,490

Other information

(a)   The normal gross profit margin on all sales is 30%. Babek Assidian has no idea what the value of the stock is at 31 December 20X7. However, he does know that he has taken stock which has a cost price of £270 for his own private use.

(b)   Depreciation is calculated as follows.

Fixture and fittings	10% on cost
Motor vehicle	25% on cost

(c) The proceeds of cash sales and receipts from debtors for credit sales are all paid into the bank account at the end of the day, apart from the float which is retained on the premises to be used at the start of the following day.

(d) On 31 December 20X7, the creditors amounted to £7,400 and the debtors amounted to £290.

(e) Also, on 31 December 20X7, it was discovered that there was £260 owing for electricity costs and the buildings insurance had not yet been paid. The insurance should have been paid in November 20X7 to provide cover from 1 December 20X7 for the following twelve months, but Babek Assidian forgot to pay until mid-January 20X8. The annual insurance premium was £600.

(f) A summary of the business bank account for the year ended 31 December 20X7 showed:

	£		£
Receipts from sales	126,790	Balance b/d	3,490
		To creditors	83,410
		General expenses	16,060
		Salaries	5,110
		Drawings	17,500
		Balance c/d	1,220
	126,790		126,790

Note. General expenses includes electricity and insurance.

Tasks

1 Calculate the total sales for the year ended 31 December 20X7.

2 Calculate the total purchases for the year ended 31 December 20X7.

3 Calculate the total cost of sales for the year ended 31 December 20X7.

4 Calculate the value of the closing stock as at 31 December 20X7.

5 Calculate the figure for general expenses which would be included in the calculation of profit for the year ended 31 December 20X7.

6 Calculate the figure for net profit for the year ended 31 December 20X7.

17 SHEENA GORDON (60 mins) 12/98

Sheena Gordon, has been trading for just over twelve months as a dressmaker. She has kept no accounting records at all, and she is worried that she may need professional help to sort out her financial position. Knowing that Donald Johnson runs a successful business, Sheena Gordon approached him for advice. He recommended that you, his bookkeeper, should help Sheena Gordon.

You meet with Sheena Gordon and discuss the information that you require her to give you. Sometime later, you receive a letter from Sheena Gordon providing you with the information that you requested, as follows.

(a) She started her business on 1 October 20X7. She opened a business bank account and paid in £5,000 of her savings.

(b) During October she bought the equipment and the stock of materials that she needed. The equipment cost £4,000 and the stock of materials cost £1,800. All of this was paid for out of the business bank account.

(c) A summary of the business bank account for the twelve months ended 30 September 20X8 showed the following.

	£		£
Capital	5,000	Equipment	4,000
Cash banked	27,000	Opening stock of materials	1,800
		Purchases of materials	18,450
		General expenses	870
		Drawings	6,200
		Balance c/d	680
	32,000		32,000

(d) All of the sales are on a cash basis. Some of the cash is paid into the bank account while the rest is used for cash expenses. She has no idea what the total value of her sales is for the year, but she knows that she has spent £3,800 on materials and £490 on general expenses. She took the rest of the cash not banked for her private drawings. She also keeps a cash float of £100.

(e) The gross profit margin on all sales is 50%.

(f) She estimates that all the equipment should last for five years. You therefore agree to depreciate it using the straight line method.

(g) On 30 September 20X8, the creditors for materials amounted to £1,400.

(h) She estimates that the cost of stock of materials that she had left at the end of the year was £2,200.

Tasks

1   Calculate the total purchases for the year ended 30 September 20X8.

2   Calculate the total cost of sales for the year ended 30 September 20X8.

3   Calculate the sales for the year ended 30 September 20X8.

4   Show the entries that would appear in Sheena Gordon's cash account.

5   Calculate the total drawings made by Sheena Gordon throughout the year.

6   Calculate the figure for net profit for the year ended 30 September 20X8.

11 Club accounts and manufacturing accounts

18 PAT HALL (60 mins) 12/98

Pat Hall owns a small manufacturing business, Hall Products, which makes and supplies some of the furniture for The Pine Warehouse. The financial year for Hall Products ends on 30 November and Pat Hall asks you to produce some information from the following figures for the year ended November 20X8.

(a) *Stocks*   £

Stock of raw material at 1 December 20X7	4,300
Raw materials purchased	95,600
Stock of raw materials at 30 November 20X8	9,400
Stock of finished goods at 1 December 20X7	10,360
Stock of finished goods at 30 November 20X8	12,510

Note. Work in progress can be ignored.

(b) *Staff costs*

Furniture production wages	38,000
Factory supervisory wages	28,000
Office wages	16,000

(c) *Business fixed assets*

Factory premises at cost 1 December 20X0	80,000
Office premises at cost 1 December 20X0	30,000
Factory machinery at cost 1 December 20X5	20,000
Office equipment at cost 1 December 20X6	10,000

(d) *Depreciation*

Premises: 2% per annum straight line method
Machinery and equipment: 10% per annum straight line method

(e) *Other expenses*

Factory overheads	12,500
Office expenses	8,300

(f) *Debtors and creditors for stock*

Debtors at 1 December 20X7	22,200
Debtors at 30 November 20X8	24,500
Creditors at 1 December 20X7	12,100
Creditors at 30 November 20X8	13,300
Received from debtors during the year	294,700

Note. All payments and receipts pass through the business bank account.

Task 1

Calculate the prime cost of the goods produced by Hall Products during the year ended 30 November 20X8.

Task 2

Calculate the total production cost of the goods made by Hall Products during the year ended 30 November 20X8.

Task 3

Calculate the total sales made by Hall Products during the year ended 30 November 20X8.

Task 4

Calculate the gross profit made by Hall Products during the year ended 30 November 20X8.

Task 5

The opening balance of Hall Products' bank account on 1 December 20X7 was an overdraft of £3,600. Calculate the closing balance of the bank account on 30 November 20X8.

19   ANANDA CARVER (50 mins)   6/99

Ananda Carver is the treasurer of the City Fields Tennis Club. As treasurer he needs to prepare some financial statements and asks you to provide assistance.

The following information is available at the year end on 31 December 20X8.

BANK ACCOUNT SUMMARY

	£		£
Balance b/d (1 January 20X8)	1,200	Purchase of refreshments	10,600
Subscriptions	30,000	Club staff wages	28,000
Sale of refreshments	15,260	Electricity	1,780
Donations	500	Sundry expenses	1,820
Loan	6,000	Repairs to tennis courts	800
		Clubhouse improvements	6,400
		Rent of land	3,400
		Balance c/d (31 December 20X8)	160
	52,960		52,960

(a)   *Balances at 1 January 20X8:*   £

Stock of refreshments	120
Creditors for refreshments	860
Clubhouse at cost	24,000
Provision for depreciation – clubhouse	7,200
Subscriptions in advance	400

(b)   *Balances at 31 Decmeber 20X8*

Stock of refreshments	230
Creditors for refreshments	780
Subscriptions in advance	550

(c)   Depreciation on the clubhouse is calculated at the rate of 5% of cost at the end of the financial year.

(d)   15% of wages relate to refreshments, 85% to other activities.

(e)   20% of electricity relates to refreshments, 80% to other activities.

(f)   The loan was taken out on 30 June 20X8 at a rate of interest of 10% per annum.

(g)   Club rules state that donations over £1,000 should be capitalised.

Task 1

List separately the opening assets and liabilities of the club at 1 January 20X8 and calculate the accumulated fund at that date.

Task 2

Calculate the subscriptions figure to be used in the calculation of the surplus or deficit for the year ended 31 December 20X8.

Task 3

Calculate the purchases of refreshments for the year ended 31 December 20X8.

Task 4

Prepare a statement calculating the profit or loss on refreshments for the year ended 31 December 20X8.

Task 5

By listing the various items of income and expenditure, prepare a statement calculating the surplus or deficit of income over expenditure for the year ended 31 December 20X8.

12   *Extended trial balance*

20   CLEGG AND CO (70 mins)   **Assessment**

Below is an alphabetical list of balances taken from the ledger of Clegg and Co as at 31 May 20X9, which operates an integrated cash book but memorandum sales and purchase ledgers, plus some additional information.

	£
Administration costs	72,019.27
Bank overdraft	8,290.12
Capital	50,000.00
Loan	100,000.00
Depreciation charge	12,000.00
Drawings	36,000.00
Fixed assets: Cost	120,287.00
Fixed assets: Depreciation	36,209.28
Interest payable	12,182.26
Interest receivable	21.00
Labour	167,302.39
Raw materials	104,293.38
Stock as at 1/6/X8	25,298.30
Purchase ledger control	42,190.85
Sales	481,182.20
Sales ledger control	156,293.00
VAT	4,938.20

Task 1

Enter the balances in the format trial balance provided below. Set up a suspense account if necessary.

BPP PUBLISHING

	Trial balance		Adjustments		Profit and loss account		Balance sheet	
	£	£	£	£	£	£	£	£

Task 2

With reference to the additional information below, clear the suspense account.

(a) The debit side of the journal to record depreciation expense of £15,000.00 for the second six months of the period has been omitted.

(b) An examination of administration costs shows that there is a prepayment for insurance of £320.00 and an accrual for electricity of £480.00.

(c) One page of the sales returns day book was left out of the total posted to the sales ledger control account, although it was included in the other totals posted. The total value of credit notes on this page was £6,092.35.

(d) Invoices totalling £6,283.38 have not been recorded in the purchase ledger accounts.

(e) The payment by BACS of wages in May of £14,248.40 has not been posted to the labour account, and nor has the purchase in May of a fixed asset for £4,000.00 been posted. This asset should be depreciated at a rate of 25% straight line, with a full year's depreciation being charged in the year of purchase.

(f) A cash receipt of £10,000.00 was recorded in the cash book but, as it was not identified, it has not yet been posted. It has now been clarified that this represents additional capital from the proprietor.

(g) Interest due of £650.00 on the loan needs to be accrued.

(h) At 31 May 20X9 stock on hand was valued at £32,125.28.

Task 3

With reference to the additional information above, make whatever other adjustments to the trial balance as are necessary.

Task 4

(a) Extended trial balance
(b) Total all columns of the trial balance.
(c) Make entries to record the net profit or loss for the year ended 31 May 20X9.

21 **SADIE PET PRODUCTS (60 mins)**   **Assessment**

Sadie Pet Products makes luxury hutches of a standard size for guinea pigs, rabbits and rats, which are sold to high quality garden centres. It is owned and run by Chris Betts, who employs two staff to help make the hutches. Chris maintains all the accounts, posting all the day books each month, and does all the other administration. The business is registered for VAT and all sales are charged at the standard rate of 17.5%.

Stock consists of raw materials and finished goods.

(a) Raw materials consist of metre lengths of pine wood valued on a first-in-first-out (FIFO) basis, and of miscellaneous items (including wire mesh) valued on an actual cost basis.

(b) Finished goods stock consists of finished hutches. The cost of producing the hutches includes direct labour, raw materials, overheads and depreciation of workshop equipment.

Practice activities

Task 1

Balance off the general ledger accounts below and draw up a trial balance.

ADMINISTRATION					
Date	**Details**	**Amount £**	**Date**	**Details**	**Amount £**
20X3			**20X3**		
1/11	Balance b/d	4,209.38			
30/11	PDB	456.87			

CAPITAL					
Date	**Details**	**Amount £**	**Date**	**Details**	**Amount £**
20X3			**20X3**		
			1/11	Balance b/d	5,000.00

CASH					
Date	**Details**	**Amount £**	**Date**	**Details**	**Amount £**
20X3			**20X3**		
30/11	Cash book	5,209.38	1/11	Balance b/d	1,278.39
			30/11	Cash book	4,152.37

DEPRECIATION ON WORKSHOP EQUIPMENT					
Date	**Details**	**Amount £**	**Date**	**Details**	**Amount £**
20X3			**20X3**		
30/11	Charge for the year	1,500.00	30/11	Balance c/d	1,500.00

76

DRAWINGS					
Date	**Details**	**Amount** £	**Date**	**Details**	**Amount** £
20X3			**20X3**		
1/11	Balance b/d	11,000.00			
30/11	Cash book	1,000.00	30/11	Balance c/d	12,000.00

FIXED ASSETS (COST)					
Date	**Details**	**Amount** £	**Date**	**Details**	**Amount** £
20X3			**20X3**		
1/11	Balance b/d	15,000.00	30/11	Balance c/d	15,000.00

FIXED ASSETS (ACCUMULATED DEPRECIATION)					
Date	**Details**	**Amount** £	**Date**	**Details**	**Amount** £
20X3			**20X3**		
			1/11	Balance b/d	9,000.00
			30/11	Charge for the year	1,500.00

INTEREST PAID					
Date	**Details**	**Amount** £	**Date**	**Details**	**Amount** £
20X3			**20X3**		
1/11	Balance b/d	1,100.00			
30/11	Cash book	100.00			

LABOUR

Date	Details	Amount £	Date	Details	Amount £
20X3			20X3		
1/11	Balance b/d	16,683.33			
30/11	Cash book	1,516.67			

LOAN

Date	Details	Amount £	Date	Details	Amount £
20X3			20X3		
			1/11	Balance b/d	15,000.00

PURCHASE LEDGER CONTROL

Date	Details	Amount £	Date	Details	Amount £
20X3			20X3		
30/11	Cash book	1,535.70	1/11	Balance b/d	2,954.06
			30/11	PDB	4,621.67

RAW MATERIALS

Date	Details	Amount £	Date	Details	Amount £
20X3			20X3		
1/11	Balance b/d	19,972.05			
30/11	PDB	2,821.07			

SALES					
Date	**Details**	**Amount £**	**Date**	**Details**	**Amount £**
20X3			**20X3**		
			1/11	Balance b/d	49,306.52
			30/11	SDB	5,205.19

SALES LEDGER CONTROL					
Date	**Details**	**Amount £**	**Date**	**Details**	**Amount £**
20X3			**20X3**		
1/11	Balance b/d	5,251.29	30/11	Cash book	5,209.38
30/11	SDB	6,116.09			

STOCK (RAW MATERIALS)					
Date	**Details**	**Amount £**	**Date**	**Details**	**Amount £**
20X2			**20X2**		
1/12	Balance b/d	3,093.84			
20X3			**20X3**		

VAT					
Date	**Details**	**Amount £**	**Date**	**Details**	**Amount £**
20X3			**20X3**		
30/11	PDB	688.33	1/11	Balance b/d	980.29
			30/11	SDB	910.90

WORKSHOP OVERHEADS					
Date	Details	Amount £	Date	Details	Amount £
20X3			**20X3**		
1/11	Balance b/d	7,209.37			
30/11	PDB	655.40			

	£																									
Balance sheet	£																									
	£																									
Profit and loss account	£																									
	£																									
Adjustments	£																									
	£																									
Trial balance	£																									

BPP PUBLISHING

Task 2

Calculate any relevant accruals, prepayments and adjustments for bad debts from the information below.

- Four months business rates have been paid in advance. The annual amount due is £4,500.

- Annual insurance from 1 October 20X3 of £676.80 has been paid..

- The last phone bill received and paid was for the three months to the end of September. It was for £210.00 excluding VAT. The business has equal monthly usage of the phone.

- There is a debt of £600.00 on the sales ledger which Chris does not expect to be paid.

Task 3

Details of Sadie Pet Products' closing stocks are given below.

- Calculate the value of closing stocks of raw materials.

- Prepare a manufacturing account in order to calculate the value of closing stock of finished goods at 30 November 20X3 for inclusion in the trial balance.

STOCK AT 30 NOVEMBER 20X3

Stocks were counted at close of business on 30 November 20X3. Details are summarised below:

Raw materials – pine wood

The business had 380 metres of pine wood, which was purchased and used in production as follows:

Date		metre	Cost per metre £
9 November	Purchase	1,000.00	4.95
12 November	Taken to production	(600.00)	
13 November	Purchase	300.00	5.20
15 November	Purchase	1,000.00	5.40
18 November	Taken to production	(1,200.00)	
22 November	Taken to production	(290.00)	
26 November	Purchase	170.00	4.80
In stock at 30 November 20X3		380.00	

Raw materials – miscellaneous items

	Cost £	Net realisable value £
Nails and screws	349.28	250.00
Wire mesh	927.27	1,200.00
Waterproof sheeting	582.39	400.00

All this stock was in good condition and it is estimated that most of it has now been used in production.

Finished goods

There were 9 finished hutches in stock at the year end. 250 hutches were made in the year.

Task 4

On the face of the ETB format:

(a) Make adjustments for the accruals and prepayments calculated above.

(b) Make adjustments for the closing stock calculated above.

Task 5

Extend the trial balance as follows.

(a) Total all columns.

(b) Make entries to record the net profit or loss for the year ended 30 November 20X3.

22 PINE WAREHOUSE (70 mins)   (12/98)

Pat Hall is the proprietor of The Pine Warehouse, a business which buys, repairs and supplies pine furniture.

• You are employed by Pat Hall to assist with the bookkeeping.

• The business currently operates a manual system consisting of a general ledger, a sales ledger and a purchases ledger.

• Double entry takes place in the general ledger and the individual accounts of debtors and creditors are therefore regarded as memoranda accounts.

• Day books consisting of a purchases day book, a sales day book, a purchases returns day book and a sales returns day book are used. Totals from the various columns of the day books are transferred periodically into the general ledger.

At the end of the financial year, on 30 November 20X8, the balances were extracted from the general ledger and entered into an extended trial balance as shown on page 85.

Task 1

Make appropriate entries in the adjustment columns of the extended trial balance on page 85 to take account of the following.

(a) Stock was initially valued on 30 November 20X8 at £136,000. However, it was later found that this figure included some pine chairs which had been valued at selling price rather than at cost. The selling price valuation of the chairs was £9,600 and the profit mark-up for the chairs was 50%.

(b) Depreciation calculated on a monthly basis is to be provided as follows.

Motor vehicles - 20% per annum straight line method
Machinery - 10% per annum reducing balance method
Equipment - 10% per annum reducing balance method

Note. The machinery figure shown in the extended trial balance includes some new machinery purchased on 31 May 20X8 at a cost of £6,000.

(c) The advertising figure includes £7,200 paid for 3 newspaper adverts each costing the same amount and due to appear on:

10 August 20X8
10 October 20X8

10 December 20X8

(d) Rent payable by the business is £2,460 per month.

(e) An invoice relating to goods received by The Pine Warehouse on 1 November 20X8 has been lost and no entries have therefore been made. The goods supplied cost £1,800 plus £315 VAT and have been included in the valuation of the closing stock on 30 November 20X8.

(f) A standing order has been set up to transfer £3,000 on the 28th day of each month from the business bank account into Pat Hall's private bank account. The transfer for 28 November 20X8 has not been entered into the accounts of the business.

(g) The provision for bad debts is to be adjusted to a figure representing 5% of debtors.

Task 2

After the preparation of the extended trial balance the following errors, which had caused the opening of the suspense account, were found. Prepare journal entries to record the correction of all the errors using the blank journal on page 316. Dates and narratives are not required.

(a) Sales of £10,810 had been transferred from the total column of the sales day book into the debtors' control account as £10,180.

(b) The VAT column of the purchases day book had been overcast by £500.

(c) The net column of the sales day book had been overcast by £4,450.

(d) A cheque for £1,200 received from a debtor had been entered into the cash book but not into the relevant control account.

(e) Discounts allowed of £40 had been credited to the discounts received account.

Extended trial balance

DESCRIPTION	LEDGER BALANCES		ADJUSTMENTS	
	Dr	Cr	Dr	Cr
	£	£	£	£
Sales		1,240,600		
Purchases	826,400			
Debtors' control account	93,340			
Creditors' control account		70,870		
Bad debts	8,750			
Provision for bad debts		4,010		
Motor vehicles (MV) at cost	80,500			
Provision for depreciation (MV)		15,760		
Machinery (Mach) at cost	24,000			
Provision for depreciation (Mach)		2,000		
Equipment (Equip) at cost	27,400			
Provision for depreciation (Equip)		5,850		
Drawings	33,000			
Cash	3,000			
Bank		12,500		
Lighting and heating	3,250			
Insurance	1,020			
Advertising	10,620			
VAT (credit balance)		13,600		
Stock at 1 December 20X7	125,560			
Motor expenses	8,670			
Discounts allowed	4,200			
Discounts received		1,200		
Salaries and wages	120,650			
Rent	24,600			
Capital		32,030		
Suspense	3,460			
Prepayments				
Depreciation				
Closing stock - P&L				
Closing stock - balance sheet				
Provision for bad debts - adjustment				
Accrued expenses				
	1,398,420	1,398,420		

JOURNAL		
Details	DR £	CR £

23 CREATIVE CATERING (80 mins)   Assessment

Jane Sutton is the proprietor of Creative Catering, a firm that provides catering services for a variety of events and functions. Creative Catering's premises are located in Bristol and most of the firm's customers can be found in the west of England.

(a) You are employed by Jane Sutton to assist with the bookkeeping.

(b) The business currently operates a manual system consisting of a general ledger, a sales ledger and a purchases ledger.

(c) Double entry takes place in the general ledger and the individual accounts of debtors and creditors are therefore regarded as memoranda accounts.

(d) Day books consisting of a purchases day book, a sales day book, a purchases returns day book and a sales returns day book are used. Totals from the various columns of the day books are transferred periodically into the general ledger.

At the end of the financial year on 30 April 20X8, the balances were extracted from the general ledger and entered into an extended trial balance as shown on page 88.

Task 1

Make appropriate entries in the adjustment columns of the extended trial balance to take account of the following.

(a) The stock consists of food and drink and has been valued on 30 April 20X8 at £6,240. This figure includes some frozen food that had cost £860 but will have to be thrown out due to a problem with a freezer. Although the Polar Insurance Company has agreed to pay for the full cost of the food, no money has yet been received. Also included in the stock valuation figure are 20 bottles of wine. These had originally cost £8.50 each but since they are not popular they are to be sold off at £6.50 per bottle.

(b) Depreciation calculated on a monthly basis is to be provided as follows.

Motor vehicles - 20% per annum straight line method
Equipment - 10% per annum reducing balance method

(c) The sum of £20,000 was invested in the bank deposit account on 1 May 20X7. The interest rate is fixed at 7% per annum.

(d) Rent payable by the business is as follows.

Up to 31 October 20X7   £1,200 per month
From 1 November 20X7   £1,300 per month

(e) The provision for bad debts is to be adjusted to a figure representing 5% of debtors.

(f) On 29 April 20X8 Jane Sutton withdraw £5,000 from the bank account for her own use. The entries made were:

Dr   Cash   £5,000
Cr   Bank   £5,000

(g) A series of adverts were broadcast during April 20X8 by Western Radio at a cost to Creative Catering of £2,750. The invoice has yet to be received from Western Radio and no entries have been made.

87

Extended Trial Balance at 30 April 20X8

CREATIVE CATERING	Trial balance		Adjustments	
Account	Debit	Credit	Debit	Credit
	£	£	£	£
Sales		620,700		
Purchases	410,650			
Purchases returns		390		
Salaries and wages	90,820			
Rent	16,300			
Debtors control account	51,640			
Creditors control account		33,180		
Bad debts	6,550			
Provision for bad debts		3,100		
Motor vehicles (cost)	60,700			
Motor vehicles (prov for depreciation)		12,600		
Equipment (cost)	24,200			
Equipment (prov for depreciation)		6,300		
Drawings	28,500			
Cash	7,000			
Bank	6,250			
Lighting and heating	2,100			
Insurance	760			
Advertising	3,470			
VAT (credit balances)		8,400		
Stock at 1 May 20X7	5,660			
Motor expenses	4,680			
Bank deposit amount	20,000			
Bank interest received		700		
Capital		54,010		
Polar Insurance Company				
Depreciation				
Closing stock (P&L)				
Closing stock (B/S)				
Provision for bad debts (adjustment)				
Deposit account interest owing				
Prepayments / accruals				
Subtotal	739,380	739,380		
Profit for the year				
TOTAL	739,380	739,380		

Note. Only the above columns of the extended trial balance are required for this central assessment.

The bank statement shown below was received by Creative Catering on 1 June 20X8 and was compared with the bank account section of the cash book also shown below.

MIDWEST BANK LTD

Bank statement

Creative Catering   **Account Number: 60419776**

Date 20X8		Detail	Debit £	Credit £	Balance £
May	14	Balance			6,300
	14	Cheque 606842	120		6,180
	14	Bank Giro Credit		230	6,410
	15	Credit		320	6,730
	18	Cheque 606844	260		6,470
	19	Cheque 606843	440		6,030
	20	Credit		375	6,405
	21	Credit		2,650	9,055
	22	Cheque 606846	1,100		7,955
	22	Credit		860	8,815
	26	Cheque 606848	1,650		7,165
	27	Cheque	470		6,695
	28	Credit		1,950	8,645

Bank account

Date		Detail	£	Date		Detail		£
May	15	Balance b/d	5,800	May	16	J Champion	845	620
	18	P Donald	175		16	Catering Services	846	1,100
	18	Mayes Ltd	200		20	Witworth Drinks	847	490
	19	A Palmer	230		20	K J Foods	848	1,650
	19	Rugby Club	1,260		22	D Andrews	849	470
	20	Town Institute	1,390		26	Catering Services	850	260
	22	P Whelan	860		27	Days Bakery	851	320
	25	P Whitehead	1,950		29	K J Foods	852	1,400
	28	Tennis Club	1,810		29	Balance c/d		7,365
			13,675					13,675

Task 2

Prepare a statement reconciling the £5,800 opening balance of the cash book with the £6,300 opening balance of the bank statement.

Task 3

Prepare a bank reconciliation statement as at 29 May 20X8.

24 ELECTRONICS WORLD (75 mins) (6/97)

The company Electronics World Ltd operates out of offices and a warehouse located in Wales. The company purchases hi-fi systems, televisions and other electronic goods from manufacturers world-wide. Customers are mainly UK based shops specialising in electronic items.

- You are employed by Electronics World Ltd to assist with the bookkeeping.

- The company is relatively new and is still considering an appropriate computerised accounting system.

- The manual system currently in use consists of a general ledger, a sales ledger and a purchases ledger.

- Double entry takes place in the general ledger and the individual accounts of debtors and creditors are therefore regarded as memoranda accounts.

- Day books consisting of a purchases day book, a sales day book, a purchases returns day book and a sales returns day book are used. Totals from the various columns of the day books are transferred periodically into the general ledger.

The following balances were extracted by a colleague from the general ledger on 24 May 20X7, one week before the end of the financial year, which is on 31 May 20X7.

	£
Share capital	600,000
Premises	360,000
Fixtures and fittings (F and F) at cost	140,000
Provision for depreciation (F and F)	65,000
Purchases	972,140
Sales	1,530,630
Salaries	206,420
Sales returns	23,200
Purchases returns	17,350
General expenses	74,322
Insurance	16,390
Bad debts	7,506
Provision for bad debts	6,000
Debtors control account	237,855
Creditors control account	121,433
Stock at 1 June 20X6	188,960
Bank	65,200
Bank deposit account	150,000
Bank interest received	3,750
Motor vehicles (MV) at cost	22,400
Provision for depreciation (MV)	3,800
VAT (credit balance)	24,720
Profit and loss	91,710

During the last week of the financial year a number of transactions took place and these are summarised below.

Purchases day book	*Total*	*VAT*	*Net*
	£	£	£
	23,970	3,570	20,400

Sales day book	*Total*	*VAT*	*Net*
	£	£	£
	35,955	5,355	30,600

Sales returns day book	*Total*	*VAT*	*Net*
	£	£	£
	1,410	210	1,200

Cheques issued	£
Payable to various creditors in settlement of debts	5,000

Task 1

Complete the table below to show the double entry which would have to be carried out in order to update the balances extracted on 24 May 20X7, to take account of the summarised transactions shown above.

DOUBLE ENTRY TO UPDATE BALANCES EXTRACTED ON 24 MAY 20X7		
Names of accounts	*Dr* £	*Cr* £
Entries from purchases day book		
Entries from sales day book		
Entries from sales returns day book		
Entries from cheques issued		

Task 2

Enter the updated balances into the first two columns of the extended trial balance provided on Page 93. Total the two columns ensuring that the two totals agree.

Note. It is the *updated* balances that should be used taking into account the effects of the entries prepared for Task 1.

Task 3

Make appropriate entries in the adjustment columns of the extended trial balance to take account of the following.

(a)   Depreciation is to be provided as follows.

Motor vehicles: 20% per annum on cost
Fixtures and fittings: 10% per annum reducing balance method

No depreciation is charged on assets in their year of purchase or in their year of sale. On 12 November 20X6 new fixture and fittings costing £6,000 had been purchased.

(b)   The £150,000 was invested in the bank deposit account on 30 November 20X6 at a fixed rate of interest of 6% per annum.

(c) The general expenses figure includes the sum of £2,400 paid to a company to clean the offices of Electronics World Ltd during the period 1 April 20X7 to 30 September 20X7.

(d) Stock has been valued on 31 May 20X7 at £198,650. This figure excludes a television which was damaged beyond repair and had to be scrapped (no sale proceeds). Regis Insurance has agreed to cover the loss incurred in writing off the television.

   Cost price of television: £420
   Sales price of television: £630

(e) A cheque for £60 was issued at the beginning of May 20X7 to pay for insurance cover which expired on 31 May 20X7. A bank statement showed that the cheque was paid on 20 May. As yet no entries have been made in the books of Electronics World Ltd.

(f) The provision for bad debts is to be adjusted to a figure representing 5% of debtors.

ELECTRONICS WORLD	Trial balance		Adjustments	
Account	Debit	Credit	Debit	Credit
	£	£	£	£
Share capital				
Premises				
Fixtures & fittings at cost				
Fixtures & fittings (prov for depreciation)				
Purchases				
Sales				
Salaries				
Sales returns				
Purchases returns				
General expenses				
Insurance				
Bad debts				
Provision for bad debts				
Debtors control account				
Creditors control account				
Stock at 1 June 20X6				
Bank				
Bank deposit account				
Bank interest received				
Motor vehicles (cost)				
Motor vehicles (prov for depreciation)				
VAT: Credit balance				
Profit and loss				
Depreciation				
Regis Insurance				
Closing stock (P&L)				
Closing stock (B/S)				
Provision for bad debts (adjustment)				
Bank interest owing				
Prepayments				
Subtotal				
Profit for the year				
TOTAL				

25   DREW INSTALLATIONS (75 mins)   **12/97**

Colin Drew is the proprietor of Drew Installations, a firm specialising in the supply and installation of kitchens and bathrooms. The showroom, warehouse and offices are located in London and most of the work carried out by the business is in the London area.

(a) You are employed by Colin Drew to assist with the bookkeeping.

(b) The business currently operates a manual system consisting of a general ledger, a sales ledger and a purchases ledger.

(c) Double entry takes place in the general ledger and the individual accounts of debtors and creditors are therefore regarded as memoranda accounts.

(d) Day books consisting of a purchases day book, a sales day book, a purchases returns day book and a sales returns day book are used. Totals from the various columns of the day books are transferred periodically into the general ledger.

At the end of the financial year on 31 October 20X7, the balances were extracted from the general ledger and entered into an extended trial balance as shown on page 96.

Unfortunately in preparing the extended trial balance it was found that the total of the debit column did not agree with the total of the credit column. A suspense account was opened as a temporary measure.

Task 1

Make appropriate entries in the adjustment columns of the extended trial balance on page 96 to take account of the following.

(a) Depreciation calculated on a monthly basis is to be provided as follows:

Motor vehicles - 20% per annum straight line method
Equipment - 10% per annum reducing balance method

On 30 April 20X7 a new motor vehicle costing £12,000 had been purchased.

(b) The bank loan had originally been taken out on 30 April 20X6 when the sum of £60,000 had been borrowed, repayable by six annual repayments of £10,000. The first repayment had been made as agreed on 30 April 20X7. Interest is charged on the loan at 8% per annum.

(c) Rent payable by the business is as follows:

Showroom and offices - £3,000 per month
Warehouse - £2,000 per month

(d) The motor vehicle expenses include a payment of £260 paid out of the business bank account to service Colin Drew's family car which is not used in the business.

(e) Insurance includes an annual buildings policy which runs from 1 August 20X7. The premium paid was £2,400.

(f) The provision for bad debts is to be adjusted to a figure representing 8% of debtors.

(g) Stock has been valued at cost on 31 October 20X7 at £107,300. However, this includes some discontinued kitchen cabinets the details of which are as follows:

Cost £2,300
Normal selling price £3,500
Net realisable value £1,800

Task 2

Subsequent to the preparation of the extended trial balance the following errors were found, some of which had caused the opening of the suspense account. Prepare journal entries to record the correction of the errors using the blank journal on Page 97. Dates and narratives are not required.

(a) The VAT column of the sales returns day book had been overcast by £200.

(b) Motor vehicle expenses of £40 had been debited to Motor Vehicles (any adjustment to depreciation can be ignored).

(c) Sales returns of £160 had been credited to purchases returns. The VAT element of the returns had been entered correctly.

(d) Purchases of £2,340 had been transferred from the rent column of the day book and into the purchases account as £2,430.

(e) A cheque for £2,450 paid to Ashwood Kitchens, a credit supplier, had been entered in the cash book but not in the relevant control account.

| DREW INSTALLATIONS | Trial balance | | Adjustments | |
Account	Debit	Credit	Debit	Credit
	£	£	£	£
Purchases	339,500			
Sales		693,000		
Purchases returns		6,320		
Sales returns	1,780			
Carriage inwards	8,250			
Salaries and wages	106,200			
Bad debts	4,890			
Provision for bad debts		4,500		
Debtors control account	46,800			
Creditors control account		28,760		
Stock at 1 November 20X6	113,450			
Motor vehicles expenses	5,780			
Motor vehicles (cost)	86,000			
Motor vehicles (prov for depreciation)		12,800		
Equipment (cost)	24,500			
Equipment (prov for depreciation)		6,700		
Rent	58,000			
Drawings	32,900			
Insurance	5,720			
Bank	8,580			
Bank loan account		50,000		
Bank interest paid	2,400			
VAT (credit balance)		12,400		
Capital		32,750		
Suspense account	2,480			
Depreciation				
Closing stock (P&L)				
Closing stock (B/S)				
Provision for bad debts (adjustment)				
Loan interest owing				
Subtotal	847,230	847,230		
Profit for the year				
TOTAL	847,230	847,230		

Note. Only the above columns of the extended trial balance are required for this exercise.

JOURNAL		
Details	DR £	CR £

26 TULIPS (85 mins)   12/98

Donald Johnson is the proprietor of Tulips, a business which specialises in the growing, buying and selling of flowers. The growing of the flowers take places in greenhouses, which are large glass buildings specially designed for this purpose.

(a) You are employed by Donald Johnson as the bookkeeper.

(b) The business currently operates a manual system consisting of a general ledger, a sales ledger and a purchases ledger.

(c) Double entry takes place in the general ledger and the individual accounts of debtors and creditors are therefore regarded as memoranda accounts.

(d) Day books consisting of a purchases day book, a sales day book, a purchases returns day book and a sales returns day book are used. Totals from the various columns of the day books are transferred periodically into the general ledger.

The following list of balances had been extracted from the general ledger on 30 November 20X8, which is the financial year end for Tulips.

	£
Sales	313,746
Sales returns	971
Purchases	186,574
Purchases returns	714
Stock	25,732
Wages	40,000
Rent and rates	18,608
Light and heat	11,940
Office expenses	9,530
Greenhouse running expenses	11,290
Motor expenses	4,782
Sundry expenses	5,248
Motor vehicles (cost)	25,810
Motor vehicles (provision for depreciation) at 1 December 20X7	5,162
Greenhouses (cost)	25,500
Greenhouses (provision for depreciation) at 1 December 20X7	7,650
Cash	100
Bank current account (debit balance)	3,020
Bank loan	30,000
Debtors' control account	6,860
Creditors' control account	4,720
Capital account	21,112
Drawings	11,000
VAT account (credit balance)	3,587
Suspense account (credit balance)	274

After all the above balances had been extracted from the books of Tulips, the following additional information became available.

(a) For one month only, the drawings for Donald Johnson had been posted, in error, to the wages account. The drawings had amounted to £1,000.

(b) A cheque received from a debtor, J Willis, had been credited, in error, to the creditors' control account. The amount of the cheque was £280.

(c) In one month, the total of the columns in the sales returns day book for £560, net of VAT, had been correctly treated in the sales returns account, and the debtors' control account had been correctly posted with the gross amount. However, the VAT element had not been posted to the VAT account.

(d) In August 20X8, the total of the columns in the purchase returns day book showed net £480, VAT £84 and total £564. Although the net amount and the VAT amount had been correctly treated in the general ledger, the total amount had been credited to the creditors' control account.

(e) A receipt of £1,500 had been shown in the bank statement in November 20X8. Originally, you had not known what this was for, so an entry was made in the bank account and in the suspense account. On investigation, you discovered that one of the greenhouses had been sold in November 20X8, and the £1,500 represented the proceeds from that disposal. The greenhouse had cost £2,500 and its accumulated depreciation on 1 December 20X7 amounted to £750. The business has a policy of not depreciating an asset in the year of disposal.

Task 1

Prepare the journal entries to record the correction of the errors and omissions listed on Page 100. Use the blank journal on page 305. Dates and narratives are not required.

Note. Your journal should include the completion of the disposal account with the transfer to the profit or loss on disposal.

Task 2

Enter the updated account balances into the first two columns of the extended trial balance provided on page 101. Total the two columns.

Note. It is the updated balances that should be used, ie after taking into account the effect of the journal entries prepared in Task 1.

Task 3

Make appropriate entries in the adjustment columns of the extended trial balance to take account of the following.

(a) Depreciation is to be provided as follows:

Motor vehicles - 20% per annum straight line method
Greenhouses - 10% per annum straight line method

(b) On reviewing the debtors on 30 November 20X8, it was decided that a provision for doubtful debts should be made. This provision is to be 5% of the outstanding debtors.

(c) Closing stock was valued at cost at £24,895.

(d) Rent is paid quarterly in advance on 1 January, 1 April, 1 July and 1 October each year. The instalment due on 1 October 20X8 was overlooked and a cheque, for £4,500, was not raised until 10 December 20X8.

Practice activities

Task 1

JOURNAL		
Details	DR £	CR £

Tasks 2 and 3

DESCRIPTION	LEDGER BALANCES		ADJUSTMENTS	
	Dr	Cr	Dr	Cr
	£	£	£	£
Sales				
Sales returns				
Purchases				
Purchases returns				
Stock at 1 December 20X7				
Wages				
Rent and rates				
Light and heat				
Office expenses				
Greenhouse running expenses				
Motor expenses				
Sundry expenses				
Motor vehicle (MV) at cost				
Provision for depreciation MV				
Greenhouses (GH) at cost				
Provision for depreciation GH				
Cash				
Bank current account				
Bank loan				
Debtors' control account				
Creditors' control account				
Capital account				
Drawings account				
VAT account				
Suspense account				
Profit or loss on disposal of fixed asset				
Depreciation				
Provision for doubtful debts - P&L				
Provision for doubtful debts - balance sheet				
Closing stock - P&L				
Closing stock - balance sheet				
Accrual				

Note. Only the above columns of the extended trial balance are required for this exercise.

BPP PUBLISHING

27 **AUTOMANIA (80 mins)**   **6/99**

Ananda Carver is the proprietor of Automania, a business which supplies car parts to garages to use in servicing and repair work.

(a) You are employed by Ananda Carver to assist with the bookkeeping.

(b) The business currently operates a manual system consisting of a general ledger, a sales ledger and a purchases ledger.

(c) Double entry takes place in the general ledger and the individual accounts of debtors and creditors are therefore regarded as memoranda accounts.

(d) Day books consisting of a purchases day book, a sales day book, a purchases returns day book and a sales returns day book are used. Totals from the various columns of the day books are transferred into the general ledger.

At the end of the financial year, on 30 April 20X9, the balances were extracted from the general ledger and entered into an extended trial balance as shown on Page 103.

Task 1

Make appropriate entries in the adjustments columns of the extended trial balance to take account of the following.

(a) Rent payable by the business is as follows.

For period to 31 July 20X8:	£1,500 per month
From 1 August 20X8:	£1,600 per month

(b) The insurance balance includes £100 paid for the period 1 May 20X9 to 31 May 20X9.

(c) Depreciation is to be calculated as follows.

Motor vehicles:	20% per annum straight line method
Fixtures and fittings:	10% per annum reducing balance method

(d) The provision for bad debts is to be adjusted to a figure representing 2% of debtors.

(e) Stock has been valued at cost on 30 April 20X9 at £119,360. However, this figure includes old stock, the details of which are as follows.

Cost price of old stock:	£3,660
Net realisable value of old stock:	£2,060

Also included is a badly damaged car door which was to have been sold for £80 but will now have to be scrapped. The cost price of the door was £60.

(f) A credit note received from a supplier on 5 April 20X9 for goods returned was filed away with no entries having been made. The credit note has now been discovered and is for £200 net plus £35 VAT.

Extended Trial Balance at 30th April 20X9

DESCRIPTION	Ledger balances		Adjustments	
	Dr	Cr	Dr	Cr
	£	£	£	£
Capital		135,000		
Drawings	42,150			
Rent	17,300			
Purchases	606,600			
Sales		857,300		
Sales returns	2,400			
Purchases returns		1,260		
Salaries and wages	136,970			
Motor vehicles (M.V.)at cost	60,800			
Provision for depreciation (M.V)		16,740		
Fixtures and fittings (F&F) at cost	40,380			
Provision for depreciation (F&F)		21,600		
Bank		3,170		
Cash	2,100			
Lighting and heating	4,700			
VAT		9,200		
Stock at 1 May 20X8	116,100			
Bad debts	1,410			
Provision for bad debts		1,050		
Debtors control account	56,850			
Creditors control account		50,550		
Sundry expenses	6,810			
Insurance	1,300			
Accruals				
Prepayments				
Depreciation				
Provision for bad debts - Adjustment				
Closing stock - P&L				
Closing stock - Balance sheet				
Totals	1,095,870	1,095,870		

28 FUTON ENTERPRISES (80 mins)   6/94

Jason Sarmiento, trading as Futon Enterprises, is a sole trader assembling and selling futons. A futon is a Japanese-style bed, consisting of a slatted wooden frame and a mattress. Jason buys in the pre-cut timber and the mattresses and assembles the futons for sale through his retail shop in Lincoln and by mail order.

The assembly takes place in a small workshop to the rear of the shop and is carried out by a full-time assembler. The business also employs a driver, a secretary and you, the accounts clerk. Jason spends most of his time in the shop and dealing with the mail order side of the business.

The business accounts are currently operated using a manual system, though Jason is actively engaged in investigating computerised accounting systems.

A very simple sales ledger is operated and the purchase ledger contains about 20 accounts. There are few cash transactions. Any that do occur are handled through a traditional petty cash book. A £50 cash float is maintained and at weekly intervals the expenditure is posted to the nominal ledger and the float replenished.

Accounting policies

1   *Manufacturing*

Purchases of raw materials are posted to a materials account. The assembler's wages are posted to the production wages account. No separate production overheads account is maintained.

It has been agreed that finished goods stocks should be valued at a standard cost of production, calculated as follows per futon.

	£
Materials	36.00
Production wages	7.00
Overheads	5.00
	48.00

2   *Depreciation*

Rates:	Assembling machinery	10% per annum straight line
	Delivery van	30% per annum reducing balance
	Furniture and fittings	20% per annum straight line

Depreciation is charged a full year in the year of purchase and is not charged in the year of sale. Zero scrap values are assumed.

3   *Mark-up*

The company normally marks up all its products at 75% on standard production costs.

Fixed asset information

	Date of purchase	Cost	
		£	£
Assembling machinery	1.6.X0		3,650
Delivery van (see note (b)(i) below)	1.8.X3		12,400
Furniture and fittings			
Shop fittings	1.6.X0	7,200	
Office furniture	1.6.X0	2,350	
Reception (materials only)			
(see note (b)(ii) below)	1.9.X3	1,240	
			10,790

Data

(a)   Listed below is the company's trial balance at 31 May 20X4.

FUTON ENTERPRISES
TRIAL BALANCE AS AT 31 MAY 20X4

	Dr £	Cr £
Delivery vans (cost)	12,000	
Delivery vans (provision for depreciation)		7,884
Assembling machinery (cost)	3,650	
Assembling machinery (provision for depreciation)		1,095
Furniture and fittings (cost)	10,790	
Furniture and fittings (provision for depreciation)		5,730
Raw materials stock	1,320	
Finished goods stock	1,440	
Sales ledger total	1,860	
Bank		320
Cash	50	
Purchase ledger total		4,265
Sales		120,240
Materials	35,465	
Production wages	12,480	
Driver's wages	11,785	
Salaries	22,460	
Employer's national insurance	4,365	
Motor expenses	2,160	
Rent	3,930	
Sundry expenses	3,480	
VAT		1,220
Inland Revenue		1,365
Drawings	12,400	
Capital		7,516
Suspense	10,000	
	149,635	149,635

(b) Adjustments need to be made for the following.

(i) A new delivery van was purchased for £12,400 on 1 August 20X3. The old delivery van, originally purchased for £12,000 on 1 August 20X0, was given in part exchange; the balance of £10,000 was paid for by cheque and debited to Suspense Account.

(ii) The reception area was re-built in the first week of September 20X3. This work was carried out by the assembler as business was rather slack at that time. He spent the whole of the first week in September on this task; his pay is £12,480 per annum.

(iii) Jason gave two futons as Christmas presents in December 20X3. An account was opened in the sales ledger to record these transactions.

(c) The following additional information needs to be taken into account.

(i) Depreciation for the year ended 31 May 20X4 is to be provided for.

(ii) The stocktake at 31 May 20X4 has revealed the following.

Stock of timber, mattresses and sundry materials = £1,526
23 fully completed futons were in stock

There was no work in progress.

(iii) The electricity bill for £180 covering the February, March, April 20X4 quarter had been received on 15 May and entered into the purchase ledger. Electricity usage is relatively even throughout the year. Electricity is included within sundry expenses.

(iv) On 12 May the delivery van was involved in an accident, suffering minor damage. The repairs, costing £164, have been carried out and the cost included in motor expenses. A letter has been received today from the Mercury Insurance Company agreeing to compensate for all but the first £50 of the repair costs.

(v) A customer, T Young, who bought two futons at the regular price in July 20X3, has disappeared without paying. It has been decided to write off the amount owing.

(vi) The rent of £3,144 per annum is paid annually in advance on 1 September.

Task 1

Prepare journal entries for the transactions listed in (b) above. Narratives are required. Use the blank journal form on Page 107.

Task 2

Enter all the account balances, including those adjusted in Task 1 above, in the first two columns of the extended trial balance. Use the blank ETB on Page 108.

Task 3

Make appropriate entries in the adjustments columns of the extended trial balance. Create additional accounts as required.

Task 4

Extend the figures into the extended trial balance columns for profit and loss account and balance sheet. Total all columns, transferring the balance of profit or loss as appropriate.

JOURNAL		
Details	DR £	CR £

FUTON ENTERPRISES

Account	Trial balance Debit £	Trial balance Credit £	Adjustments Debit £	Adjustments Credit £	Profit and Loss a/c Debit £	Profit and Loss a/c Credit £	Balance Sheet Debit £	Balance Sheet Credit £
Delivery vans (cost)								
Assembling machine (costs)								
Furniture and fittings (cost)								
Delivery vans (prov for depreciation)								
Assembling machine (prov for depreciation)								
Furniture and fittings (prov for depreciation)								
Stock : raw materials								
Stock : finished goods								
Sales ledger total								
Bank								
Cash								
Purchase ledger total								
Sales								
Materials								
Production wages								
Driver's wages								
Salaries								
Employer's NI								
Motor expenses								
Rent								
Sundry expenses								
VAT								
Inland Revenue								
Drawings								
Capital								
Depreciation: Delivery vans								
Depreciation: assembling machine								
Depreciation: furniture and fittings								
Subtotal								
Profit for the year								
TOTAL								

BPP PUBLISHING

29   KIDDITOYS (80 mins)   12/94

Kidditoys is a retail shop which specialises in the sale of unusual toys, games and other baby products. The business was started in December 20W7 and is owned and run by Sophie Stewart.

About half the sales of the business are cash sales through the shop, the remainder being on mail order. Mail order customers pay cash with order.

Sophie employs one sales assistant and one packing assistant.

Her present manual system of bookkeeping comprises a purchase ledger with approximately 30 active accounts, a nominal ledger and a petty cash book. A petty cash float of £50 is maintained for sundry expenses and is replenished as required. A further cash float of £50 is maintained in the sales till. All cash receipts are banked daily.

You are an accounting technician who is helping Sophie to prepare the business's accounts up to the trial balance stage.

Fixed asset information

	Date of purchase	*Cost* £	*Expected useful economic life (years)*
Motor van	07.08.X3	12,640	5
Shop fittings	10.12.W7	3,240	10
Office equipment	08.04.X1	4,250	5

All fixed assets are depreciated on a straight line basis using the expected useful economic lives, above, and zero-estimated residual values.

Depreciation is charged a full year in the year of purchase and is not charged for in the year of sale.

Other information

Average mark up is 100%.

The VAT rate is 17.5%.

Data

(a) The following list of balances has been extracted from the nominal ledger at the business's year end, 30 November 20X4.

	£
Sales	392,182
Sales returns	1,214
Purchases	208,217
Purchase returns	643
Stock	32,165
Wages	50,000
Rent	27,300
Rates	8,460
Light and heat	2,425
Office expenses	3,162
Selling expenses	14,112
Motor expenses	14,728
Sundry expenses	6,560
Motor vans (cost)	12,640
Motor vans (provision for depreciation) at 1.12.X3	2,528
Shop fittings (cost)	3,240
Shop fittings (provision for depreciation) at 1.12.X3	1,944
Office equipment (cost)	4,250
Office equipment (provision for depreciation) at 1.12.X3	2,550
Cash	100
Bank current account (debit balance)	4,420
Bank investment account	68,340
Interest received	3,280

	£
Purchase ledger total	27,683
Capital	22,145
VAT (credit balance)	6,420
Suspense (see note (b)(ii))	1,958

(b) After extracting the balances listed in (a), the following six errors and omissions were discovered.

(i) Credit purchases of £954 had been correctly posted to the purchases account, but had been debited in the supplier's account (T Ditton).

(ii) The shop had been entirely re-fitted during the year. The old fittings had been sold off to the local Boy Scouts for £50. This had been debited in the bank account, but had been credited in the suspense account.

The invoice for the new shop fittings, for £9,620, had been received from Kingston Displays Ltd on 15 November. This invoice had not yet been entered into the accounts. Sophie intended to pay the invoice in January after the Christmas sales period. The new shop fittings are expected to have a useful economic life of 10 years.

(iii) Sophie paid herself a 'wage' of £2,000 per calendar month which she debited to wages account.

(iv) During the year an invoice for £843 (for zero-rated supplies) had been received from a supplier (E Molesey). When payment was made, Sophie accidentally made out the cheque for £840. Sophie noticed this error and contacted E Molesey who told her to ignore such a small sum of money. No adjustment has yet been made for this discrepancy.

(v) During the year Sophie gave away a number of toys from the shop as presents to relatives and friends. She kept a record of these, which came to £640 at selling price, including VAT, but has not so far entered the transactions into the accounts.

(vi) The company's current bank account statement arrived on 30 November 20X4. This showed interest received for the month of November at £9. This has not yet been entered into the accounts.

(c) The following additional matters need to be taken into account.

(i) Depreciation for the year ended 30 November 20X4 is to be provided for.

(ii) The stock in the shop at 30 November 20X4 was valued at £42,120 at selling price.

(iii) Rent was £2,100 per month payable in advance. The rent for December 20X4 had already been paid.

(iv) Business rates are paid half yearly on 1 May and 1 November. The business rates bill for the period 1 April 20X4 - 31 March 20X5 amounted to £6,240.

(v) The electricity bill for £318 covering the July, August and September quarter had been received on 15 October. This had been entered into the purchase ledger and duly paid. Electricity usage can be considered to be relatively even throughout the year.

Task 1

Prepare journal entries for the transactions listed in (b). Narratives are required. Use the journal voucher on the next two pages.

Task 2

Enter all the account balances, including those adjusted in Task 1 above, in the first two columns of the extended trial balance shown on Page 114. Note that some of the balances have already been filled in for you. Create additional accounts as required.

Task 3

Make appropriate entries in the adjustments columns of the extended trial balance on page 114. Create additional accounts as required.

Do not extend the figures in the extended trial balance into the profit and loss account and balance sheet columns.

Note. All final workings should be clearly shown in your finished answers.

JOURNAL		
Details	DR £	CR £

JOURNAL		
Details	DR £	CR £

BPP PUBLISHING

Practice activities

KIDDITOYS

Account	Trial balance Debit £	Trial balance Credit £	Adjustments Debit £	Adjustments Credit £
Sales				
Sales returns				
Purchases				
Purchase returns				
Stock				
Wages				
Rent				
Rates				
Light and heat				
Office expenses				
Selling expenses				
Motor expenses				
Sundry expenses				
Motor vans (cost)				
Shop fittings (cost)				
Office equipment (cost)				
Motor vans (prov for depreciation)				
Shop fittings (prov for depreciation)				
Office equipment (prov for depreciation)				
Cash				
Bank current account				
Bank investment account				
Interest received				
Capital				
VAT				
Subtotal				
Profit for the year				
TOTAL				

Practice devolved assessments

Practice devolved assessment
1 Reggie Stir

Performance criteria

The following performance criteria are covered in this Devolved Assessment.

Element 5.1: Maintain records and accounts relating to capital acquisition and disposal

1   Relevant details relating to capital expenditure are correctly entered in the appropriate records

3   All acquisition and disposal costs and revenues are correctly identified and recorded in the appropriate records

6   Profit or loss on disposal is correctly calculated and recorded in the appropriate records

7   The organisation's policies and procedures relating to the maintenance of capital records are adhered to

Notes on completing the Assessment

This Assessment is designed to test your ability to record capital transactions in the journal, the fixed assets register and the ledger.

You are provided with data (Page 118) which you must use to complete the tasks on Page 119.

You are allowed **two hours** to complete your work.

A high level of accuracy is required. Check your work carefully.

Correcting fluid should not be used. Errors should be crossed out neatly and clearly. You should write in ink and not in pencil.

BPP
PUBLISHING

PRACTICE DEVOLVED ASSESSMENT 1: REGGIE STIR

Data

Reggie Stir Ltd is a small company producing many different kinds of jugs. Skilled craftsmen make the jugs on a potter's wheel. They are then fired in a kiln and distributed by van to various gift shops.

You are Fletcher Clink, an accounting technician and your boss is Nick McKay, the financial controller. Mr McKay is concerned that the records relating to fixed assets should be kept up to date.

The company, which operates from rented premises, does not have a large number or turnover of fixed assets, the main ones being three potter's wheels, four kilns, one pugmill (a long tube for turning the clay), three delivery vans and various items of furniture, all of which were bought some time ago and are fully depreciated.

The firm keeps a manual fixed assets register, the relevant pages of which are reproduced below.

					PLANT AND EQUIPMENT				
Ref	Description	Date of purchase	Cost £	Depreciation period	Accumulated depreciation 31 Dec 20X4 £	Date of disposal	Net book value 31 Dec 20X4 £	Sale/scrap proceeds £	Loss/ profit £
1/K	Kiln	1 Jan 20X3	1,200	6 years	400		800		
1/P	Pugmill	1 July 20X4	300	4 years	75		225		
2/K	Kiln	1 Mar 20X2	600	6 years	300		300		
3/K	Kiln	20 Aug 20X1	750	6 years	500		250		
1/W	Wheel	31 Mar 20X3	400	4 years	200		200		
2/W	Wheel	1 Feb 20X2	400	4 years	300		100		
4/K	Kiln	1 Sep 20X2	900	6 years	450		450		
3/W	Wheel	1 Mar 20X4	420	4 years	105		315		
Totals			4970		2330		2640		

					MOTOR VEHICLES				
Ref	Description	Date of purchase	Cost £	Depreciation type	Accumulated depreciation 31 Dec 20X4 £	Date of disposal	Net book value 31 Dec 20X4 £	Sale/scrap proceeds £	Loss/ profit £
1/V	Van reg G249 NPO	1 Feb 20X0	4000	Reducing balance 25%	3051		949		
2/V	Van reg K697 JKL	1 June 20X3	6000	Reducing balance 25%	2625		3375		
3/V	Van reg M894 TMG	30 Sep 20X4	8000	Reducing balance 25%	2000		6000		
Totals			18000		7676		10324		

It is the firm's policy to charge a full year's depreciation in the year of purchase and none in the year of sale. Plant and equipment are depreciated on a straight line basis over the periods shown on the register. Motor vehicles are all depreciated at a rate of 25% using the reducing balance method.

During 20X5 the following transactions in fixed assets took place.

(a) On 3 August an old kiln (ref. 1/K) was traded in at Cumere Oven Ltd and a new one (ref. 5/K) purchased for £1,600 from the same supplier. A trade-in allowance of £500 was given for the old kiln, the balance to be settled at a later date. An invoice (no. 35X42) was raised by the supplier for the amount in question.

(b) On 5 September, a new potter's wheel (ref. 4/W) was purchased for £500 cash.

(c) On 10 October the oldest delivery van (ref. 1/V) was traded in for a new one (ref. 4/V), registration N583 MNO, costing £9,000. The supplier, Van Guard Ltd, gave a trade-in allowance of £1,000 on the old van and raised an invoice (no. Z/2643) for the difference.

It is now 31 December 20X5 and you have been asked to help prepare the year-end accounts.

Tasks

(a) Record the above transactions and the year-end provisions for depreciation in:

  (i)   The journal
  (ii)   The ledger accounts
  (iii) The fixed assets register

(b) Produce an extract from the year-end balance sheet showing the following.

  (i)   Plant and equipment (cost)
  (ii)   Motor vehicles (cost)
  (iii) Plant and equipment (provision for depreciation)
  (iv)   Motor vehicles (provision for depreciation)

All workings should be to the nearest £.

The relevant ledger accounts, journal pages and fixed assets register page are attached for you to complete.

Tutorial note. In practice you would post from the journal to the ledger accounts, but in this exercise you may find it helpful to do the opposite in order to calculate any profit or loss on disposal of fixed assets.

BPP PUBLISHING

JOURNAL

Page 50

Date	Details	Folio Ref	£	£

	JOURNAL			Page 51
Date	Details	Folio Ref	£	£

BPP PUBLISHING

LEDGER ACCOUNTS

PLANT AND EQUIPMENT

	£		£
Date		*Date*	
20X5		*20X5*	
1 Jan Balance b/f	4,970		

PLANT AND EQUIPMENT: PROVISION FOR DEPRECIATION

	£		£
		Date	
		20X5	
		1 Jan Balance b/f	2,330

PLANT AND EQUIPMENT: DISPOSALS

	£		£

MOTOR VEHICLES

	£		£
Date			
20X5			
1 Jan Balance b/f	18,000		

MOTOR VEHICLES: PROVISION FOR DEPRECIATION

	£		£
		Date	
		20X5	
		1 Jan Balance b/f	7,676

MOTOR VEHICLES: DISPOSALS

	£		£

PLANT AND EQUIPMENT									
Ref	Description	Date of purchase	Cost £	Depreciation period	Accumulated depreciation 31 Dec 20X5 £	Date of disposal	Net book value 31 Dec 20X5 £	Sale/scrap proceeds £	Loss/ profit £
1/K	Kiln	1 Jan 20X3	1200	6 years					
1/P	Pugmill	1 July 20X4	300	4 years					
2/K	Kiln	1 Mar 20X2	600	6 years					
3/K	Kiln	20 Aug 20X1	750	6 years					
1/W	Wheel	31 Mar 20X3	400	4 years					
2/W	Wheel	1 Feb 20X2	400	4 years					
4/K	Kiln	1 Sep 20X2	900	6 years					
3/W	Wheel	1 Mar 20X4	420	4 years					
Totals									
Disposals									
Totals c/f									

MOTOR VEHICLES									
Ref	Description	Date of purchase	Cost £	Depreciation type	Accumulated depreciation 31 Dec 20X5 £	Date of disposal	Net book value 31 Dec 20X5 £	Sale/scrap proceeds £	Loss/ profit £
1/V	Van reg G249 NPO	1 Feb 20X0	4000	Reducing balance 25%					
2/V	Van reg K697 JKL	1 June 20X3	6000	Reducing balance 25%					
3/V	Van reg M894 TMG	30 Sep 20X4	8000	Reducing balance 25%					
Totals									
Disposals									
Totals c/f									

(b) EXTRACTS FROM YEAR-END BALANCE SHEET

	Cost £	Accumulated depreciation £	NBV £

Practice devolved assessment
2 Booths

Performance criteria

The following performance criteria are covered in this Devolved Assessment.

Element 5.1: Maintain records and accounts relating to capital acquisition and disposal

1   Relevant details relating to capital expenditure are correctly entered in the appropriate records

Element 5.2: Record income and expenditure

1   All income and expenditure is correctly identified and recorded in the appropriate records

2   Relevant accruals and prepaid income and expenditure are correctly identified and adjustments are made

3   The organisation's policies, regulations, procedures and timescales are observed in relation to recording income and expenditure

Notes on completing the Assessment

This Assessment is designed to test your ability to post transactions correctly to the ledger accounts and the trial balance.

You are provided with data (Pages 126 to 135) which you must use to complete the tasks on Page 135.

You are allowed **two hours** to complete your work.

A high level of accuracy is required. Check your work carefully.

Correcting fluid should not be used. Errors should be crossed out neatly and clearly. You should write in ink and not in pencil.

PRACTICE DEVOLVED ASSESSMENT 2: BOOTHS

Data

You are acting as the temporary bookkeeper at Booths Ltd, a builder's merchant. The financial year end, 30 June 20X7, is approaching. During the day of 30 June 20X7, several primary documents are passed to you for posting to the ledger accounts.

All sales and all purchases are made on credit. All other expenses are paid *immediately* on receipt of a bill.

The ledger accounts appear as follows at the end of 29 June 20X7.

ADVERTISING					
20X7			20X7		
29 June Balance b/f	288	91			

ACCOUNTANCY FEES					
20X7			20X7		
29 June Balance b/f	1,500	00			

BANK ACCOUNT					
20X7			20X7		
29 June Balance b/f	19,330	65			

DOUBTFUL DEBT PROVISION

20X7			20X7		
			29 June Balance b/f	1,242	94

ELECTRICITY

20X7			20X7		
29 June Balance b/f	1,733	84			

FIXTURES AND FITTINGS

20X7			20X7		
29 June Balance b/f	11,893	55			

GAS

20X7			20X7		
29 June Balance b/f	1,161	20			

INSURANCE

20X7			20X7		
29 June Balance b/f	658	38	30 June P and L account	658	38

INTEREST

20X7			20X7		
29 June Balance b/f	1,141	31			

MAINTENANCE					
20X7			20X7		
29 June Balance b/f	3,807	43			

MOTOR EXPENSES					
20X7			20X7		
29 June Balance b/f	606	19			

MOTOR VEHICLES					
20X7			20X7		
29 June Balance b/f	43,675	07			

PROFIT AND LOSS ACCOUNT					
20X7			20X7		
			29 June Balance b/f	27,225	92

PURCHASES					
20X7			20X7		
29 June Balance b/f	76,648	31			

PURCHASE LEDGER CONTROL A/C

20X7			20X7		
			29 June Balance b/f	9,554	93

PRINT, POSTAGE & STATIONERY

20X7			20X7		
29 June Balance b/f	117	29			

RENT

20X7			20X7		
29 June Balance b/f	9,250	00			

SHARE CAPITAL

20X7			20X7		
			29 June Balance b/f	10,000	00

ACCUMULATED DEPRECIATION

20X7			20X7		
			29 June Balance b/f	27,241	12

BPP PUBLISHING

Practice devolved assessments

SALES					
20X7			20X7		
			29 June Balance b/f	180,754	17

SALES LEDGER CONTROL A/C					
20X7			20X7		
29 June Balance b/f	19,356	30			

SUNDRY EXPENSES					
20X7			20X7		
29 June Balance b/f	1,427	70			

OPENING STOCK					
20X7			20X7		
29 June Balance b/f	37,321	56			

TELEPHONE			20X7		
20X7					
29 June Balance b/f	3,879	09			

UNIFORM BUSINESS RATE			20X7		
20X7					
29 June Balance b/f	4,917	94			

VAT CONTROL A/C					
20X7			20X7		
			29 June Balance b/f	6,719	19

WAGES					
20X7			20X7		
29 June Balance b/f	21,575	63			

WATER RATES					
20X7			20X7		
29 June Balance b/f	2,447	92			

The documents which have been passed to you are as follows:

BPP PUBLISHING

Invoice 1

BOOTHS LTD

62 Maple St
NO7 3PN
Tax point 30.06.X7
VAT No. 3171156327

MP Price & Co A/C No. 01729	Q	£
Standard bricks	400	504.00
TOTAL		504.00
VAT 17.5%		88.20
		£592.20

Invoice 2

BOOTHS LTD

62 Maple St
NO7 3PN
Tax point 30.06.X7
VAT No. 3171156327

H Contractors A/C No. 02147	Q	£
Cement bags	10	67.00
Trowel	1	5.50
Spirit Level	1	17.95
TOTAL		90.45
VAT 17.5%		15.83
		£106.28

Invoice 3

BOOTHS LTD

62 Maple St
NO7 3PN
Tax point 30.06.X7
VAT No. 3171156327

NP Plumbers A/C No. 01227	Q	£
Piping: 1 metre length	40	210.00
Piping: 0.5 metre length	40	102.00
'A' type fittings	25	30.75
TOTAL		342.75
VAT 17.5%		59.98
		402.73

Invoice 4

BOOTHS LTD

62 Maple St
NO7 3PN
Tax point 30.06.X7
VAT No. 3171156327

CR Harris & Co A/C No. 03994	Q	£
Standard bricks	500	630.00
White bricks	50	100.00
TOTAL		730.00
VAT 17.5%		127.75
		857.75

LARKIN LUMBER LTD

The Mill
Park Lane
NO4 INQ

55321194   Tax point: 30 06 X7

To Booths Ltd

                                        £

3" Timber   1,320.00
4" Timber   1,975.00
                                3,295.00

VAT 17.5%   576.63
                                3,871.63

30 days net   VAT No. 371 1942 678

Tax point	Inv. no.
3006X7	X371172L

PLUMBING SUPPLIES LTD
Unit 17 Park Estate No7 1ZR

To Booths Ltd

4cm piping   20m   486.23
6cm piping   30m   1,049.82

TOTAL   1,536.05
VAT   268.81
Amount due   1,804.86

VAT No. 442 1986 883   30 days net

Post Office Counters Ltd
Tax point: 30 06 X7

To Booths Ltd

Franking services
01 March 20X7 to 31 May 20X7

869   1st   208.56
942   2nd   169.56

                               378.12

HALFWAY INVESTMENTS LIMITED

To Booths Ltd   Tax point 29 June 20X7
                          VAT 497 3328 679

RENT

QUARTER TO
29 September 20X7   £2,312.50

BPP PUBLISHING

WOODLEY GAZETTE
37 Half Lane
NO7 9RP

INV 21737
Tax point: 30/6/X7

VAT No. 113 4279 179

Booths Ltd Wednesday 5th June Half page ad.	33.50
VAT @ 17.5%	5.86
Total	39.36

007321

M Able & Co
Insurance Brokers
9 Green Lane
NO3 4PW

Tax point
30.06.20X7

To Booths Ltd
62 Maple St

Motor vehicle
insurance
per attatched

£1,437.50

Year to 31 May 20X8. Sorry
for the delay - you have
still been covered

Pratts Garage
114 Lark Road
NO1 1NR

S14117
Tax point: 30/6/X7

VAT No. 172 1173 499

BOOTHS LTD A/C 4173

Petrol and oil to 30 June 20X7	317.42
VAT @ 17.5%	55.55
	372.97

1134734

To: Booths Ltd
62 Maple St
NO7 3PN

IRT DEALERS
4 The Forecourt

VAT 147 3321 198
Tax point: 30/6/X7

Executive Car XZ3i Reg J172 BNC	12,600.00
Road Tax	100.00
Extras	542.75
	13,242.75 2,299.98
VAT £13,142.75 @ 17.5%	15,542.73

```
┌─────────────────────────────────────────────────────────────────────────────┐
│  ╱╲    NATIONAL                                                                │
│ ╱──╲   ELECTRICITY                                                             │
│ ┌──────────────────────────────────────────┬──────────────────────────────┐  │
│ │ YOUR CUSTOMER SERVICES OFFICE IS:          │ YOU CAN PHONE US ON:         │  │
│ │ POWER ROAD LONDON E2 9AJ                    │ 020 7123 1234               │  │
│ ├────────────────────────────────────────────┴──────────────────────────────┤│
│ │ BOOTHS LTD                                   WHEN TELEPHONING               ││
│ │ 62 MAPLE STREET                              We have a call queuing         ││
│ │ N07 3PN                                      system. When you hear          ││
│ │                                              the ringing tone please        ││
│ │                                              wait for a reply as calls       ││
│ │                                              are answered in strict         ││
│ │                                              rotation.                      ││
│ │                                              BUSY TIMES                     ││
│ │                                              Please try to avoid            ││
│ │                                              9-30AM - 10-30 AM              ││
│ │                                              and 2 PM to 3 PM               ││
│ └────────────────────────────────────────────────────────────────────────────┘│
└─────────────────────────────────────────────────────────────────────────────┘
```

METER READING		UNITS USED	UNIT PRICE (pence)	V.A.T code	AMOUNT £
PRESENT	PREVIOUS				
31946E	29587	2359	17.470	1	412.12
STANDING CHARGE				1	217.50
TOTAL CHARGE (EXCLUDING VAT)					629.62
VAT 1 629.62 @ 17.5% COMMERCIAL					110.18

MAKE YOUR BILLS EASIER TO SWALLOW - SEE PAGE 4 OF 'SOURCE'

DIRECT DEBIT
THE EASY WAY TO PAY

E=Estimated reading. Please read carefully the advice given on the back of this bill
C=Your own reading

BALANCE TO PAY			739.80
VAT CHARGE THIS BILL			110.18
YOUR ACCOUNT NUMBER	BILL DATE/TAX POINT	READING DATE	NON-DOMESTIC USE
34721193672	29.06.X7	29.06.X7	100%

You have also received the following information.

(a) Bank interest of £67.48 has been charged on the company's bank account but has not yet been posted.

(b) The gross wages cost for June, paid on 30 June 20X7, amounted to £2,169.52.

Tasks

(a) Post the transactions shown above to the ledger accounts.

(b) Balance and close off the ledger accounts. You should balance off the revenue and expenditure accounts (as well as the asset and liability accounts), but there is no need to post the balances to the profit and loss account.

(c) Post the balances in the ledger accounts to the trial balance provided overleaf. Add up the trial balance to check that it balances. Investigate any discrepancies.

Note. For (a) to (c) ignore accruals and prepayments.

(d) Identify any accruals and prepayments which would require adjustment in the *extended* trial balance.

Practice devolved assessments

Folio	Account	Ref	Trial balance	
			Debit	Credit
			£	£
	TOTAL			

Practice devolved assessment
3 Lakeland Catering

Performance criteria

The following performance criteria are covered in this Devolved Assessment.

Element 5.1: Maintain records and accounts relating to capital acquisition and disposal

1   Relevant details relating to capital expenditure are correctly entered in the appropriate records

4   Depreciation charges and other necessary entries and adjustments are correctly calculated and recorded in the appropriate records

Element 5.2: Record income and expenditure

4   Incomplete data is identified and either resolved or referred to the appropriate person

Element 5.4: Prepare the extended trial balance

1   Totals from the general ledger or other records are correctly entered on the ETB

2   Adjustments not dealt with in the ledger accounts are correctly entered on the ETB

4   An agreed valuation of closing work is correctly entered on the ETB

7   The ETB is accurately extended and totalled

Notes on completing the Assessment

This Assessment is designed to test your ability to record capital transactions, prepare accounts from incomplete records and prepare the extended trial balance.

You are provided with data (Pages 138 to 140) which you must use to complete the tasks on Pages 138 and 139.

You are allowed **four hours** in total to complete your work.

A high level of accuracy is required. Check your work carefully.

Correcting fluid should not be used. Errors should be crossed out neatly and clearly. You should write in ink and not in pencil.

PRACTICE DEVOLVED ASSESSMENT 3: LAKELAND CATERING

Background information

Lakeland Catering is an organisation established by David Newsome in the early 19X0s and which specialises in two main trading activities as follows:

1   Day to day catering operated through a shop and restaurant
2   Specialist catering for functions and banquets

The business which started in a small way has expanded quite rapidly and now employs 18 staff on either a full time or a part time basis.

David has been finding it increasingly difficult to find time to deal with the day to day paperwork and bookkeeping and has appointed you (Caroline Carter) to help him keep day to day control of the organisation's finances and produce some of the necessary financial year end figures for the organisation's accountant.

It is now 31 January 20X7 and the firm's year end is 31 December.

In order to complete the tasks you will find attached the following items.

Shop and restaurant

1   Memorandum from David relating to the shop and restaurant
2   List of balances as at 1 January 20X6
3   Cash book information for 20X6
4   Statement of affairs proforma
5   Closing cash position proforma
6   Control account proformas
7   Trading and profit and loss account proforma
8   Balance sheet proforma

Specialist catering

1   Memorandum from David relating to vans
2   Depreciation methods memorandum proforma
3   Straight line depreciation calculation proforma
4   Reducing balance depreciation calculation proforma
5   Note from David relating to the extended trial balance as at 31 December 20X6
6   Extended trial balance proforma

Tasks

Shop and restaurant

(a)   Prepare an opening statement of affairs as at 1 January 20X6 clearly identifying the Capital account balance at 1 January 20X6.

(b)   Calculate the cash position as at 31 December 20X6.

(c)   Prepare the following control accounts.

     (i)   Trade debtors (credit sales only)
     (ii)   Trade creditors
     (iii)   Rent
     (iv)   Wages
     (v)   Electricity

(d) Prepare the trading and profit and loss account for the period ended 31 December 20X6 on the proforma on page 145.

(e) Prepare the balance sheet as at 31 December 20X6 on page 146.

Specialist catering

(f) Refer to the memo from David on page 147 and write a short note to David on the attached proforma, explaining the difference between straight line and reducing balance methods of depreciation.

(g) Calculate the fixed asset records for the van using the proforma and the straight line method of depreciation using the schedule on page 149.

(h) Calculate the fixed asset records for the van using the proforma and, as an alternative, a reducing balance of 40% method of depreciation using the schedule on page 149.

(i) Refer to the memo on page 150 and extended trial balance on page 151 and extend the trial balance, calculate the profit or loss, and balance the extended trial balance.

MEMORANDUM

To: Caroline
From: David
Date: 31 January 20X7

Shop and restaurant

As you are aware I have had some difficulty keeping up to date with all the necessary records and bookkeeping and so unfortunately I have not kept a complete set of records.

I have managed though to put together some information which I am enclosing as follows.

(a) Balances at 1 January 20X6
(b) Cash book information for 20X6

Shop and restaurant

List of balances 1 January 20X6

	£
Stock	6,000
Debtors	200
Creditors	1,100
Vehicle (NBV)	5,800
Restaurant fittings (NBV)	3,900
Rent owing	250
Wages owing	610
Electricity prepayment	150
Cash at bank	350

BPP
PUBLISHING

Practice devolved assessments

Cash book information for 20X6

	£		£
Balance 1 January 20X6	350	Payments to trade creditors	17,850
Receipts from debtors	4,910	Telephone	570
Cash sales	27,060	Restaurant maintenance	710
		Insurance	312
		Rent	745
		Wages	8,090
		Electricity	640

All cash and cheques had been banked.

The following needs to be taken into account.

(a) At 31 December 20X6 £250 was owing for electricity and £60 rent was paid in advance.

(b) Fittings are depreciated at 20% and the vehicle at 30%, both on a reducing balance basis.

(c) Balances at 31 December 20X6 were as follows:

	£
Debtors	615
Creditors	840
Stock	5,400

Shop and restaurant

For task (a)

Statement of affairs as at 1 January 20X6

	£	£

Assets

Less: liabilities

BPP
PUBLISHING

For task (b)

Closing cash position as at 31 December 20X6

	£	£
Receipts		
Payments		
Closing cash book balance		

For task (c)

Control accounts

TRADE DEBTORS

	£		£

TRADE CREDITORS

	£		£

RENT

	£		£

WAGES

	£		£

ELECTRICITY

	£		£

For task (d)

Shop and restaurant
Trading and profit and loss account for the period ended 31 December 20X6

£ £

BPP
PUBLISHING

For task (e)

Shop and restaurant
Balance sheet as at 31 December 20X6

	£	£	£

MEMORANDUM

To: Caroline
From: David
Date: 31 January 20X7

Specialist catering - vans

I have recently been reviewing the use of vans for our specialist catering division. I do not really understand depreciation but our accountant tells me that we should change our depreciation method from straight line to reducing balance, whatever that means.

The current van we use in the specialist catering division was bought on 1 January 20X6 for £10,000 and it was estimated that it would have a useful life of six years, at the end of which it could be sold for £460. Depreciation was to be provided on a straight line basis.

The accountant informs me that the same van, if depreciated on a reducing balance basis would now have a different value in the business. This I do not understand.

For task (f)

MEMORANDUM

To: David
From: Caroline
Date: 31 January 20X7

Depreciation methods

MEMORANDUM (cont'd)

MEMORANDUM (cont'd)

For task (g)

Van depreciation - straight line method

Depreciation charge $= \dfrac{10,000 - 460}{6} = 1,590$

		Depreciation charge for year £	Book value £
End of year	1		
	2		
	3		
	4		
	5		
	6		

For task (h)

Van depreciation - reducing balance method

Cost $= £10,000$

		Calculation of depreciation charge £	Depreciation charge for year £	Book value £
End of year	1			
	2			
	3			
	4			
	5			
	6			

BPP PUBLISHING

MEMORANDUM

To: Caroline
From: David
Date: 31 January 20X7

Extended trial balance

Please can you complete the extended trial balance for the specialist catering division. I've made a start on it, but I know the following adjustments have still got to be put through.

(a) Vehicle depreciation   £1,590

(b) Fittings depreciation   £250

(c) Electricity owing   £100

(d) Rent prepayment   £250

(e) An invoice of £50 has been charged to insurance when it should have been charged to telephone.

(f) Closing stock at 31 December 20X6 of £3,000.

LAKELAND CATERING - SPECIALIST CATERING DIVISION

Description	Trial balance Debit £	Trial balance Credit £	Adjustments Debit £	Adjustments Credit £	Profit and Loss a/c Debit £	Profit and Loss a/c Credit £	Balance Sheet Debit £	Balance Sheet Credit £
Sales		38,500						
Purchases	19,250							
Opening stock	4,000							
Wages	10,100							
Electricity	750							
P/L Depn								
- fittings								
- vehicles								
Telephone	600							
Insurance	450							
Rent	950							
Fixtures -								
cost	5,000							
depn		2,500						
Vehicle -								
cost	10,000							
dep'n								
Stock -								
bal sheet								
trading a/c								
Debtors	700							
Creditors		1,200						
Cash in hand	100							
Bank overdraft		1,400						
Capital		8,300						
Prepayments								
Accruals								
Net profit								
	51,900	51,900						

Practice devolved assessment
4 Cut Price Electricals

Performance criteria

The following performance criteria are covered in this Devolved Assessment.

Element 5.1: Maintain records and accounts relating to capital acquisition and disposal

1 Relevant details relating to capital expenditure are correctly entered in the appropriate records

4 Depreciation charges and other necessary entries and adjustments are correctly calculated and recorded in the appropriate records

6 Profit or loss on disposal is correctly calculated and recorded in the accounts

Element 5.2: Record income and expenditure

4 Incomplete data is identified and either resolved or referred to the appropriate person

Element 5.4: Prepare the extended trial balance

1 Totals from the general ledger or other records are correctly entered on the ETB

3 Adjustments not dealt with in the ledger accounts are correctly entered on the ETB

4 An agreed valuation of closing work is correctly entered on the ETB

7 The ETB is accurately extended and totalled

Notes on completing the Assessment

This Assessment is designed to test your ability to record capital transactions, prepare accounts from incomplete records and prepare the extended trial balance.

You are provided with data (Pages 154 to 156) which you must use to complete the tasks on Pages 154 and 155.

You are allowed **four hours** in total to complete your work.

A high level of accuracy is required. Check your work carefully.

Correcting fluid should not be used. Errors should be crossed out neatly and clearly. You should write in ink and not in pencil.

BPP
PUBLISHING

PRACTICE DEVOLVED ASSESSMENT 4: CUT PRICE ELECTRICALS

Background information

Cut Price Electricals is a medium sized organisation in the North of England specialising in two major areas of activity:

(a) Electrical products - wholesaling and retailing
(b) Electrical installation and contracting

The two aspects of the business are treated as separate for accounting purposes although both parts belong to the same business organisation.

The business was established in the mid 19X0s by Ian McFarland who retired around 5 years ago leaving the day to day control of the business to his niece Karen Wiggans.

The business has been expanding rapidly over the last few years and Karen has increasingly needed to spend time away from the business attending trade fairs and negotiating contracts. In view of this, and given the significant amount of work which needs doing in establishing and maintaining the financial controls and systems within the organisation, she has recently appointed you (Peter Phillips) as an Accounting Technician to help her with the bookkeeping and the accounting.

It is now 30 November 20X6 and the company's year end is 31 October.

Karen is extremely busy and has just left for a three week tour of major trade fairs in the South of England. She has had to leave you alone to put together some of the adjustments and records needed in preparing the accounts for the year ended 31 October 20X6. You have been supplied with a certain amount of information which will help you with the more immediate tasks.

In order to complete the tasks, you will find attached the following items:

Retailing Division

(a) Memorandum from Karen Wiggans relating to the Retailing Division
(b) Proforma for opening capital statement
(c) Control account proformas
(d) Bank Reconciliation proforma
(e) Memorandum from Karen Wiggans relating to depreciation of vans
(f) Proforma for van depreciation and fixed asset disposal

Installation and contracting

(a) Memorandum from Karen Wiggans relating to the trial balance as at 31 October
(b) Extended trial balance proforma

Tasks

Retail Division

(a) Prepare a statement of opening capital for the Retail Division, as at 1 November 20X5, in the form of a Trial Balance.

(b) Prepare the following control accounts

    (i)   Wages
    (ii)   Rent
    (iii)   Rates
    (iv)   Advertising
    (v)   Insurance
    (vi)   Debtors (trade) - not to include cash sales
    (vii)   Creditors (trade) - not to include cash purchases

(c) Prepare a bank reconciliation statement for Mrs Wiggans on the proforma on page 160.

(d) Refer to the memo from Karen on page 161 and complete the asset register for Van number 2 given.

(e) Complete the following accounts for the disposal of Van number 1 given on page 162.

    (i)   Van account
    (ii)   Van depreciation account
    (iii)   Asset disposal account

Installation and Contracting Division

(f) Refer to the memo from Karen on page 163 and enter the balances as at 31 October 20X6 onto the extended trial balance on page 164.

(g) Make any adjustments necessary, referring the memorandum from Karen Wiggans, onto the trial balance.

(h) Extend the trial balance, calculate the profit or loss, and balance the extended trial balance.

MEMORANDUM

To: Peter Phillips
From: Karen Wiggans
Date: 30/11/X6

Retailing Division

Welcome to Cut Price Electricals!

I am sorry that I have to leave you alone so soon after joining Cut Price Electricals but as you know, I am on a three week tour of the major trade fairs in the South of England.

There are several urgent tasks which need doing in connection with our Retailing Division to help prepare the necessary books and records prior to completion of our annual accounts.

I have managed to gather some information which should help you with these tasks and this I set out below.

(a)   The following balances are available

		1 November 20X5	*31 October 20X6*
		£'000	£'000
Premises:	cost	100	100
	depreciation	20	20
Fixtures:	cost	85	85
	Depreciation	15	15
Stock		36	46
Debtors (trade)		20	14
Creditors (trade)		16	27
Vans:	cost	20	20
	Depreciation	10	10
Wages in advance		2	5
Rent in advance		7	3

BPP PUBLISHING

Rates in arrears	6	2
Insurance - in advance	6	-
Insurance - in arrears	-	3
Advertising - in arrears	5	8

(b) A summary of the cash book shows the following for the year ended 31/10/X6

£'000

Receipts

Debtors	212
Cash sales	37

Payments

Bank overdraft - 1/11/X5	5
Creditor payments (trade)	104
Cash purchases	12
Wages	79
Rent	17
Rates	14
Advertising	8
Insurance	16
Miscellaneous	24

All cash is banked at the earliest opportunity.

(c) Mr Shah, our bank manager, has told me that we were significantly overdrawn on 31/10/X6. I have looked at our cash book and checked it against the bank statement and the differences seem to be as follows.

(i) Income not yet credited to bank statement but in cash book is £17,000.

(ii) Cheques paid out of our cash book figures but not yet charged to our account:

101202	£900
101206	£1,100
101209	£650

There was no cash in hand at the year end because I ensured that it was all banked as soon as it was received.

For Task (a)

Cut Price Electricals Retail Division
Opening Capital Statement as at 1 November 20X5

	Debit £'000	*Credit* £'000

For task (b)

Control accounts - Retail division

WAGES

£'000	£'000

RENT

£'000		£'000

RATES

£'000		£'000

ADVERTISING

£'000		£'000

For task (b) (continued)

INSURANCE

£'000	£'000

TRADE DEBTORS

£'000	£'000

TRADE CREDITORS

£'000	£'000

BPP PUBLISHING

For Task (c)

**Cut Price Electricals
Bank Reconciliation Statement**

£

Balance as per bank statement

Unlodged credits

Uncleared cheques

Balance as per cash book

MEMORANDUM

To: Peter Phillips

From: Karen Wiggans

Date: 30/11/X6

Depreciation of Vans

The Retailing Division has 2 vans, details of which are set out below.

Figures have been rounded and at the end of 20X4/X5, the combined NBV of both vans was £10,000. Depreciation needs adding for both vans for 20X5/X6. The depreciation rate for both vans will be 20% straight-line basis assuming no residual value.

You will not be aware that I have been considering selling van number 1 and the offer I received of £3,500 just before the year end I have now accepted. There was no estimated residual value for this van.

Retailing Division
Van Records

Van no	Purchased	Cost	Depreciation to 31/10/X5	NBV
		£	£	£
1	20X2/X3	10,000	(6,000)	4,000
2	20X3/X4	10,000	(4,000)	6,000

For Task (d)

Fixed asset register as at 31 October 20X6
Van number 2

Cost	Depreciation to 31/10/X5	Depreciation for year ended 31/10/X6	Net book value at 31/10/X6
£	£	£	£

For task (e)

Van number 1

VAN ACCOUNT

	£'000		£'000

VAN DEPRECIATION ACCOUNT

	£'000		£'000

ASSET DISPOSAL ACCOUNT

	£'000		£'000

MEMORANDUM

To: Peter Phillips

From: Karen Wiggans

Date: 30/11/X6

Installation and Contracting

I have managed to obtain the attached list of balances for the Installation and Contracting Division as at 31/10/X6. You will need to take account of the following adjustments.

(a)   Closing stock at 31/10/X6 following the stocktaking was £14,000.

(b)   Depreciation needs providing as follows.

  (i)   Vans - straight line method at 30% with no estimated residual value
  (ii) Fixtures - straight line method at 4% with no estimated residual value

(c)   I would like to make a provision of £2,000 to cover possible bad debts.

(d)   Rent on the garage includes a payment for the next financial year of £1,000.

(e)   An invoice for £3,000 which has been charged to van expenses should have been charged to travel expenses.

(f)   There is an outstanding advertising invoice for £2,000 for the year to 31/10/X6.

Installation and contracting
Balances as at 31 October 20X6

	£'000
Sales	109
Purchases	64
Stock (1/11/X5)	11
Wages	57
Van expenses	14
Travel expenses	3
Garage rent	6
Insurance	2
Tools allowance	5
Advertising	8
Miscellaneous expenses	4
Vans - cost	20
Vans - depreciation	12
Fixtures - cost	75
Fixtures - depreciation	60
Capital	100
Debtors	36
Creditors	21
Cash in hand	6
Bank overdraft	9

For tasks (f), (g), (h)

CUT PRICE ELECTRICALS - INSTALLATION AND CONTRACTING DIVISION

Description	Trial balance		Adjustments		Profit and Loss a/c		Balance Sheet	
	Debit £	Credit £	Debit £	Credit £	Debit £	Credit £	Debit £	Credit £

Trial run devolved assessment

TRIAL RUN DEVOLVED ASSESSMENT

INTERMEDIATE STAGE - NVQ/SVQ3

Unit 5

Maintaining Financial Records

and

Preparing Accounts

The purpose of this Trial Run Devolved Assessment is to give you an idea of what a Devolved Assessment could be like. It is not intended as a definitive guide to the tasks you may be required to perform.

The suggested time allowance for this Assessment is four hours. Extra time may be permitted in a real Devolved Assessment. Breaks in assessment may be allowed, but it must normally be completed in one day.

Calculators may be used but no reference material is permitted.

**DO NOT OPEN THIS PAPER UNTIL YOU ARE READY TO START
UNDER TIMED CONDITIONS**

Performance criteria

The following performance criteria are covered in this Simulation.

*Covered
in task(s)*

Element 4.1 Maintain records relating to capital expenditure and disposal

1	Relevant details relating to capital expenditure are correctly entered in the appropriate records.	3
2	The organisation's records agree with the physical presence of capital items.	4
3	All acquisition and disposal costs and revenues are correctly identified and recorded in the appropriate records.	3,4
4	Depreciation charges and other necessary entries and adjustments are correctly calculated and recorded in the appropriate records.	5
5	The records clearly show the prior authority for capital expenditure and disposal and indicate the approved method of funding and disposal.	4
6	Profit and loss on disposal is correctly calculated and recorded in the appropriate records.	4
7	The organisation's policies and procedures relating to the maintenance of capital records are adhered to.	3, 4, 5
8	Lack of agreement between physical items and records are identified and either resolved or referred to the appropriate person.	4
9	When possible, suggestions for improvements in the way the organisation maintains its capital records are made to the appropriate person.	4

Element 4.2 Record income and expenditure

1	All income and expenditure is correctly identified and recorded in the appropriate records.	1
2	Relevant accrued and prepaid income and expenditure is correctly identified and adjustments are made.	10
3	The organisation's policies, regulations, procedures and timescales in relation to recording income and expenditure are observed.	1
4	Incomplete data is identified and either resolved or referred to the appropriate person.	2

Element 4.3 Collect and collate information for the preparation of final accounts

1	Relevant accounts and reconciliations are correctly prepared to allow the preparation of final accounts.	1, 6
2	All relevant information is correctly identified and recorded.	1, 6
3	Investigations into business transactions are conducted with tact and courtesy.	2
4	The organisation's policies, regulations, procedures and timescales relating to preparing final accounts are observed.	All
5	Discrepancies and unusual features are identified and either resolved	2

BPP
PUBLISHING

Covered in task(s)

or referred to the appropriate person.

6   The trial balance is accurately prepared and, where necessary, a   8
     suspense account is opened and reconciled.

Element 4.4 Prepare the extended trial balance

1   Totals from the general ledger or other records are correctly entered   8
     on the extended trial balance.

2   Material errors disclosed by the trial balance are identified, traced   Not
     and referred to the appropriate authority.   covered

3   Adjustments not dealt with in the ledger accounts are correctly   10
     entered on the extended trial balance.

4   An agreed valuation of closing stock is correctly entered on the   9
     extended trial balance.

5   The organisation's policies, regulations, procedures and timescales in   All
     relation to preparing extended trial balances are observed.

6   Discrepancies, unusual features or queries are identified and either   Not
     resolved or referred to the appropriate person.   covered

7   The extended trial balance is accurately extended and totalled.   11

Trial run devolved assessment Semiotix Associates

Instructions

This simulation is designed to let you show your ability to maintain financial records and prepare accounts.

The Situation is provided on page 172. The tasks you are required to complete are set out on pages 173 -176.

The simulation is divided into 11 tasks. **You are advised to look through the whole simulation first to gain a general appreciation of your tasks.**

You are allowed four hours to complete your work.

A high level of accuracy is required. Check your work carefully before handing it in.

Correcting fluid may be used but should be used in moderation. Errors should be crossed out neatly and clearly. You should write in black ink, but not pencil.

Write your answers in the answer booklet provided. If you require additional answer pages, ask the person in charge.

You may pull apart and rearrange your booklets if you wish to do so, but you must put them back in their original order before handing them in.

You are reminded that you should not bring any unauthorised material, such as books or notes, into the simulation. If you have any such material in your possession, you should surrender it to the assessor immediately.

Any instances of misconduct will be brought to the attention of the AAT, and disciplinary action may be taken.

Coverage of performance criteria and range statements

It should be recognised that it is not always possible to cover all performance criteria and range statements in a simulation; some may be more appropriate and entirely natural in the workplace and others may not be practicable within the scope of a particular simulation. Where performance criteria and range statements are not covered they must be assessed by other means by the assessor before the candidate can be deemed competent.

On pages 167 - 170, you will find an indication of the performance criteria coverage for this simulation and also flags up the need to ensure that all areas of the range statement are covered.

BPP PUBLISHING

Semiotix Associates

THE SITUATION

Your name is Ronnie Hall. You are accounts assistant to Semiotix Associates.

*   Semiotix Associates is owned and managed in partnership by Alex Beech and Bridget Meadows.

*   It has operated for several years from premises in Cardiff rented on a short lease.

*   The business manufactures specialist signs made from a specialist high strength plastic material, tungstra.

You are the only full time member of accounts staff employed by the business.

*   You report directly to Alex Beech and Bridget Meadows. Each is authorised to sign for the other.

*   You maintain all the accounting records, but both partners have access to them and occasionally make entries.

*   The annual accounts are prepared by a local firm of certified accountants, Sarsfield & Co, who require an extended trial balance by Friday 22 July 20X3.

This simulation relates to the accounting year ended 30 June 20X3.

Accounting System

Semiotix Associates maintains a full general ledger system of manual ledger accounts in alphabetical order. There are separate memorandum sales (debtors) and purchases (creditors) ledgers, for which there are control accounts in the general ledger. There is also a manual fixed asset register. Day books consist of an analysed cash book, a sales day book, a sales returns day book, a purchases day book, a purchases returns day book and a journal. There are no separate sales returns and purchases returns ledger accounts.

TASKS TO BE COMPLETED

Today's date is Wednesday 20 July 20X3.

Part 1 Recording income and expenditure

Background information

All cash and cheques paid and received are recorded in an analysed cash book, which is then posted to the bank current account in the general ledger, and other relevant ledger accounts. When performing bank reconciliations in previous months you have found that a number of items of income and expenditure have appeared on the bank statement for which you can find no information. Alex Beech and Bridget Meadows have told you to credit or debit such items to a suspense account in the general ledger.

Task 1

Refer to the bank statement on Page 177 of this booklet, the receipts and payments sides of the cash book for the month of June 20X3 on Page 186 of the answer booklet, and the bank ledger account on Page 189 of the answer booklet.

- Perform a bank reconciliation as at 30 June 20X3. Set out your reconciliation on Page 183 of the answer booklet.

- Update the receipts and payments side of the cash book on Page 186 of the answer booklet as required, analysing any receipts or payments not so far recorded to the suspense ledger account.

- Post from the cash book to the general ledger accounts on Pages 188-196 of the answer booklet (note that all receipts from debtors and payments to creditors have already been posted to the individual accounts in the sales and purchases ledgers).

Task 2

Refer to the suspense account in the general ledger on Page 196 of the answer booklet.

- Draft a response to the memo from Alex Beech on Page 182 of this booklet, describing how you will account for the balance in the suspense account, and suggesting any relevant improvements that could be made to the information given to you during the year. Use Page 197 of the answer booklet.

- As far as you are able, prepare a journal to clear the suspense account in the general ledger using Page 198 of the answer booklet. (Note that you will not be able to clear it all until later in the assessment.)

Part 2 Accounting for fixed assets

Background information

The partnership owns factory equipment, office equipment (computers) and motor vehicles which are still being depreciated. The manual fixed asset register shows details of capital expenditure (but not revenue expenditure) incurred in acquiring or enhancing fixed assets, as well as details of depreciation or disposals. For each category of fixed asset the general ledger includes accounts for cost and accumulated depreciation (ie the balance sheet accounts). There is one depreciation charge ledger account (ie the expense recorded in the profit and loss account) for all classes of fixed asset.

Depreciation rates and methods are as follows.

Factory equipment   15% pa on net book value (reducing balance basis)
Office equipment   25% pa on cost (straight line basis)
Motor vehicles   20% pa on cost (straight line basis)

- Residual value is assumed to be nil in all cases.

- A full year's depreciation is charged in the year of an asset's acquisition, regardless of the exact date of acquisition.

- No depreciation is charged in the year of an asset's disposal, regardless of the date of disposal.

Alex Beech and Bridget Meadows authorise all acquisitions and disposals of fixed assets by signing invoices.

Task 3

Alex Beech has just handed you the suppliers' invoices on Pages 178 and 179 of this booklet. These refer to the purchase of a new jig for the factory and a new motor vehicle.

- Record the acquisitions in the fixed asset register on Pages 199 to 202 of the answer booklet.

- Prepare journals to record the invoices in the general ledger using Page 198 of the answer booklet. You will need to refer to the suspense account on Page 196 of the answer booklet.

Task 4

Bridget Meadows has listed the items of equipment in the factory at close of business on 30 June 20X3. Her list is on Page 180 of this booklet, together with a note about a disposal during the year.

- Compare this list with the details recorded in the fixed asset register, and identify the asset disposed of during the year.

- Write up the fixed asset register for the disposal.

- Prepare a journal to record the disposal in the general ledger using Page 198 of the answer booklet.

- Draft a memo to Alex Beech and Bridget Meadows setting out what records should be kept to show their prior authority for both capital expenditure and disposal, and the funding and disposal methods approved. Use Page 203 of the answer booklet.

Task 5

- In the fixed asset register, calculate and record the relevant amounts of depreciation for the year to 30 June 20X3 on each item of factory equipment and office equipment, and on each motor vehicle.

- Prepare a journal to record depreciation in the general ledger using Page 198 of the answer booklet.

Part 3 Collecting and collating information and preparing a trial balance

Background information: Sales and purchases

All sales are credit sales. Semiotix Associates is registered for VAT and all sales are standard rated (17.5%). All purchases are made on credit. Expenditure in the day books is analysed into: administration; assemblies; factory overheads; and raw materials.

Task 6

Write up the general ledger accounts on Pages 188 – 196 of the answer booklet as follows for June 20X3.

- Post the journals that you have prepared in Tasks 2, 3, 4 and 5 to the general ledger. (*Note.* This will enable you to calculate any profit or loss on disposal.)

- Post the June day book totals on Page 181 of this booklet to the general ledger (the subsidiary ledger accounts have already been updated for all income and expenditure).

Note that the fixed asset invoices from Task 3 were *not* included in the June totals because they were not received until after the period end.

Task 7

Refer to the balances on the debtors' and creditors' accounts in the subsidiary ledgers on Page 204 of the answer booklet.

- Balance off the relevant control accounts in the general ledger.

- Prepare a creditors reconciliation on Page 204 of the answer booklet and a debtors reconciliation on Page 204 of the answer booklet.

- Identify any discrepancies and resolve them by reference to the memo on Page 182 of this booklet

- Prepare a journal on Page 202 of the answer booklet to correct the general ledger accounts fully, and post the journal to the general ledger.

Task 8

It is now time to prepare the trial balance.

- Bring down a balance as at 30 June 20X3 on each account in the general ledger.

- Enter the balances in the first two columns of the trial balance (Page 205 in the answer booklet).

Part 4 Preparing the Extended Trial Balance

Background information: Stock

Stock consists of raw materials, assemblies and finished goods.

- Raw materials consist of sheets of tungstra, valued on a first-in-first-out (FIFO) basis, and of miscellaneous items valued on an actual cost basis.

- Assemblies consist of bought-in frames for signs, valued at actual cost.

- Finished goods stock consists of finished signs. The cost of producing the signs includes, assemblies, depreciation of factory equipment, direct labour, factory overheads and raw materials.

Task 9

Details of Semiotix Associates ' closing stocks are given on Pages 183 of this booklet.

- Calculate the value of closing stocks of raw materials and assemblies on Page 206 of the answer booklet.

- Prepare a manufacturing account in order to calculate the value of closing stock of finished goods at 30 June 20X3 for inclusion in the trial balance. Use the proforma on Page 207 of the answer booklet for your answer. Note that as well as the ledger account balances on the trial balance you will also need to refer to the journal for depreciation that you prepared in Task 5.

Task 10

It is now time to adjust the trial balance.

- Make adjustments for the closing stock calculated in Task 9.

- Make adjustments for the accruals and prepayments listed on Page 184 of this booklet.

Task 11

Extend the trial balance as follows:

- Total all columns of the trial balance

- Make entries to record the net profit or loss for the year ended 30 June 20X3.

ROYAL WEST WALES BANK
Bank Buildings, High St, Cardiff C25 9GH

STATEMENT

Account Name: Mr A Beech and Miss B Meadows (trading as Semiotix Associates)

Statement no: 26

Account No: 76839029   **Sort code:**   03-39-20

Details	Date	Payments	Receipts	Balance
	20X3	£	£	£
Balance forward	1 Jun			5,391.85
CC	2 Jun		8,189.00	13,580.85
ATM cash withdrawal	7 Jun	1,500.00		12,080.85
8390	8 Jun	6,290.83		5,790.02
8391	9 Jun	7,268.26		1,478.24 OD
CC	10 Jun		9,309.39	7,831.15
Debit card payment	12 Jun	5,000.00		2,831.15
8393	15 Jun	1,092.03		1,739.12
CC	17 Jun		3,387.03	5,126.15
BACS receipt	17 Jun		7,829.03	12,955.18
BACS receipt - Midlands Development Agency	18 Jun		8,930.93	21,886.11
ATM cash withdrawal	20 Jun	1,500.00		20,386.11
8394	22 Jun	736.99		19,649.12
CC	27 Jun		5,114.56	24,763.68
8395	28 Jun	738.83		24,024.85
BACS – ref salaries	30 Jun	13,095.98		10,928.87

Key   S/O: Standing order   DD: Direct Debit   CC: Cash and/or cheques
BACS: Bankers automated clearing services   O/D: Overdrawn   ATM –
automated teller machine cash withdrawal

BPP
PUBLISHING

Semiotix Associates
MEMO

Date: 19 July 20X3
To: Ronnie Hall
From: Alex Beech
Re: Suspense account

This memo is intended to confirm that both Bridget and I have have withdrawn, in cash from the local ATM, £1,500.00 per calendar month from July 20X2 to June 20X3 as drawings.

I also got a phone call from Oonagh Shops that they had authorised a BACS payment to us on 17 June in settlement of their overdue account. I received a remittance advice for the amount of £7,829.03, but as this was not the full amount I didn't pass the remittance on to you, but simply updated the sales ledger myself and then got on the phone to try and get the balance out of them.

I hope this information helps with the suspense account.

Alex

INVOICE
Horton Manufacturing Jigs Ltd
Caernarvon Road
Monmouth C45 8UY

T: 01783 728938	**F: 01783 767392**	
VAT registration:	33 72 33 647 364	
Date/tax point:	30 June 20X3	
Customer:	Semiotix Associated, Priory Road, Cardiff C6 8DF	
Description	**Rate**	**Total**
	£ 3,000.00	£ 3,000.00
1 all purpose Setup Master jig, delivered and installed 25 June 20X2 **Approved** **Bridget 18/7/X3**		
Goods total		3,000.00
VAT	17.5%	525.00
Invoice total		3,525.00
Net 30 days		

INVOICE

FinLease Co Ltd
Johnson Street
Cardiff C6 9SD

T: 01652 678392	F: 01652 678253
VAT registration:	02 38 37 847 363
Date/tax point:	12 June 20X3
Customer:	Semiotix Associated, Priory Road, Cardiff C6 8DF

Description	Total
	£
Mercedes Mark 7 car registration JH58 YTK, fully taxed on the road price inc VAT of £4,468.08	30,000.00
Deposit received by debit card 12 June 20X3	(5,000.00)
Ronnie *I meant to hand this to you sooner. No doubt you have spotted the deposit payment on the bank statement by now! Please make sure we pay June's instalment as soon as possible.* *Bridget 18/7/X3*	
Amount to be paid in 35 equal monthly instalments of £695.00, with the 36th payment being £675.00.	25,000.00
Interest of £125.00 per month is also due. The first instalment of £820.00 is due by 30 June 20X3.	

FIXED ASSETS PHYSICALLY PRESENT 30 JUNE 20X3
Prepared by: Bridget Meadows
Date: 30 June 20X3

Factory

Frame machine – large
Cutter
Jig
Print machine (colour)
Lifter
Laminator

Office
Laser printer
Photocopier
PC (Velox)
Laptop (Velox)

Motor vehicles
Delivery van JH54 HJK
Delivery van JH56 ADF
Mercedes 7 JH58 YTK

Note
The asset that we got the insurance payout of £1,750.00 for back in April is still on the premises – we haven't yet managed to find anyone to take away the charred remains! I believe this amount was credited to suspense from the cash book

MONTH ENDED 30 JUNE 20X3

Purchases day book	£
Administration	785.56
Assemblies purchases	6,417.09
Factory overheads	1,019.94
Raw materials purchases	9,249.50
VAT	3,057.61
Total value of invoices	20,529.70
Sales day book	£
Sales invoices	28,120.93
VAT	4,921.16
Total value of invoices	33,042.09
Purchases returns day book	£
Administration	0.00
Assemblies purchases	207.50
Factory overheads	0.00
Raw materials purchases	1,098.76
VAT	228.59
Total value of invoices	1,534.85
Sales returns day book	£
Sales credit notes	6,015.42
VAT	1,052.69
Total value of credit notes	7,068.11

BPP
PUBLISHING

Semiotix Associates
MEMO

Date: 19 July 20X3
To: Ronnie Hall
From: Alex Beech
Re: Purchase day book

While I was going through my papers I found a page of the June purchases day book which had got mixed up in them. The entries have been ticked off to show they were posted to the purchases ledger, but no totals were calculated so I feel sure they've not been included in the general ledger. The amounts are as follows:

Raw materials purchases:	£1,208.45
Assemblies purchases	£542.33
Factory overheads	£105.00
Administration	£189.62
VAT	£357.94

Please make the necessary adjustments.

Alex

STOCK AT 30 JUNE 20X3

Stocks were counted at close of business on 30 June 20X3. Details are summarised below.

Raw materials – tungstra

The business had 375kg of tungstra, which was purchased and used in production as follows:

Date		Kg	Cost per kg £
9 June	Purchase	1,000.00	25.00
12 June	Taken to production	(750.00)	
13 June	Purchase	200.00	30.00
15 June	Purchase	850.00	27.50
18 June	Taken to production	(500.00)	
22 June	Taken to production	(600.00)	
26 June	Purchase	175.00	32.00
In stock at 30 June 20X3		375.00	

Raw materials – miscellaneous items

	Cost £	Net realisable value £
Ink	2,019.82	2,781.92
Laminate	274.62	150.00
Fixings	728.10	920.35

All this stock was in good condition and it is estimated that most of it has now been used in production.

Assemblies

	Cost £	Net realisable value £
Small frames	1,000.00	600.00
Large frames	2,500.00	3,000.00
Extra large frames	3,800.00	4,000.00

Finished goods

The only finished goods in stock at 30 June 20X3 were as follows.

	In stock at 30 June 20X3	Quantity made in year	Percentage of factory costs in year
Small signs	2	55	10%
Large signs	4	110	50%
Extra large signs	3	60	40%

BPP
PUBLISHING

ACCRUALS AND PREPAYMENTS AT 30 JUNE 20X3

All calculations are made to the nearest month.

Only two items are expected to give rise to material accruals or prepayments:

Insurance

During May, Semiotix Associates paid general insurance premiums of £945, covering the six months to 31 October 20X3.

Rent

On 28 June, the business paid rent of £3,000.00 on its offices for the three months to 31 May 20X3. The next payment, for the three months to 31 August 20X3, is not due until mid-September.

TRIAL RUN DEVOLVED ASSESSMENT

Maintaining Financial Records

and

Preparing Accounts

ANSWER BOOKLET

ANSWERS (Task 1)

CASH BOOK: RECEIPTS

Date	Details	Bank	Sales Ledger Control	Suspense
		£	£	£
20X3				
1 June	Balance bfwd	7,290.02		
7 June	Cheques banked	9,309.39	9,309.39	
14 June	Cheques banked	3,387.03	3,387.03	
15 June	BACS receipt	8,930.93	8,930.93	
24 June	Cheques banked	5,114.56	5,114.56	
28 June	Cheques banked	648.93	648.93	
		27,390.84	27,390.84	

CASH BOOK: PAYMENTS

Date	Details	Cheque No	Bank	Purchase Ledger Control	Other
20X3			£	£	£
7 June	Plastika Inc	8391	7,268.26	7,268.26	
8 June	Jensen Plastics	8392	2,004.87	2,004.87	
12 June	MetalFramer Ltd	8393	1,092.03	1,092.03	
13 June	Welsh Water Authority				
	– water usage	8394	736.99		736.99
20 June	Lentril Inks Ltd	8395	738.83	738.83	
27 June	Signmakers' Guild				
	– annual subscription	8396	93.00		93.00
27 June	Salaries	BACS	13,095.98		13,095.98
27 June	Orbitol Ltd	8397	373.49	373.49	
			25,403.45	11,477.48	13,925.97
	Analysis:				
	Direct labour				
	Administration				
	Factory overheads				
	Suspense				

ANSWERS (Task 1, continued)

Bank reconciliation at 30 June 20X3

	£	£
Cash book balance at 1/6/X3		
Receipts		
Payments		
		_____
Cash book balance at 30/6/X3		
		_____
Amended cash book balance at 30/6/X3		
		════════
Balance per bank statement at 30/6/X3		
Add outstanding lodgement		
Less unpresented cheques:		
	_____	
		_____
Amended cash book balance at 30/6/X3		
		════════

ANSWERS (Tasks 1, 6, 7 and 8)

GENERAL LEDGER

ADMINISTRATION					
Date	**Details**	**Amount £**	**Date**	**Details**	**Amount £**
20X3			20X3		
1/6	Balance b/d	8,543.09			

ASSEMBLIES PURCHASES					
Date	**Details**	**Amount £**	**Date**	**Details**	**Amount £**
20X3			20X3		
1/6	Balance b/d	64,319.05			

ASSEMBLIES STOCK					
Date	**Details**	**Amount £**	**Date**	**Details**	**Amount £**
20X3			20X3		
1/6	Balance	6,930.83			

ANSWERS (Tasks 1, 6, 7 and 8, continued)

GENERAL LEDGER

BANK					
Date	Details	Amount £	Date	Details	Amount £
20X3			20X3		
1/6	Balance	7,290.02			

CAPITAL					
Date	Details	Amount £	Date	Details	Amount £
20X3			20X3		
			1/6	Balance	70,000.00

DEPRECIATION CHARGE					
Date	Details	Amount £	Date	Details	Amount £
20X3			20X3		

BPP PUBLISHING

GENERAL LEDGER

DIRECT LABOUR					
Date	Details	Amount £	Date	Details	Amount £
20X3			20X3		
1/6	Balance	142,086.56			

DISPOSALS					
Date	Details	Amount £	Date	Details	Amount £
20X3			20X3		

DRAWINGS					
Date	Details	Amount £	Date	Details	Amount £
20X3			20X3		

ANSWERS (Tasks 1, 6, 7 and 8, continued)

GENERAL LEDGER

FACTORY EQUIPMENT: ACCUMULATED DEPRECIATION					
Date	Details	Amount £	Date	Details	Amount £
20X3			20X3		

FACTORY EQUIPMENT: COST					
Date	Details	Amount £	Date	Details	Amount £
20X3			20X3		

FACTORY OVERHEADS					
Date	Details	Amount £	Date	Details	Amount £
20X3			20X3		
1/6	Balance	17,683.35			

ANSWERS (Tasks 1, 6, 7 and 8, continued)

GENERAL LEDGER

	FINISHED GOODS STOCK				
Date	**Details**	**Amount £**	**Date**	**Details**	**Amount £**
20X3			**20X3**		
1/6	Balance	13,645.86			

	HIRE PURCHASE CREDITOR				
Date	**Details**	**Amount £**	**Date**	**Details**	**Amount £**
20X3			**20X3**		

	INTEREST EXPENSE				
Date	**Details**	**Amount £**	**Date**	**Details**	**Amount £**
20X3			**20X3**		
1/6	Balance	1,100.00			

	MOTOR VEHICLES: ACCUMULATED DEPRECIATION				
Date	**Details**	**Amount £**	**Date**	**Details**	**Amount £**
20X3			**20X3**		
			1/6	Balance	12,150.00

ANSWERS (Tasks 1, 6, 7 and 8, continued)

GENERAL LEDGER

	MOTOR VEHICLES: COST				
Date	**Details**	**Amount** **£**	**Date**	**Details**	**Amount** **£**
20X3			**20X3**		
1/6	Balance	36,750.00			

	OFFICE EQUIPMENT: ACCUMULATED DEPRECIATION				
Date	**Details**	**Amount** **£**	**Date**	**Details**	**Amount** **£**
20X3			**20X3**		
			1/6	Balance	2,912.50

	OFFICE EQUIPMENT: COST				
Date	**Details**	**Amount** **£**	**Date**	**Details**	**Amount** **£**
20X3			**20X3**		
1/6	Balance	8,650.00			

BPP PUBLISHING

ANSWERS (Tasks 1, 6, 7 and 8, continued)

GENERAL LEDGER

PURCHASE LEDGER CONTROL					
Date	**Details**	**Amount £**	**Date**	**Details**	**Amount £**
20X3			**20X3**		
			1/6	Balance	21,548.55

RAW MATERIALS PURCHASES					
Date	**Details**	**Amount £**	**Date**	**Details**	**Amount £**
20X3			**20X3**		
1/6	Balance	95,476.98			

RAW MATERIALS STOCK					
Date	**Details**	**Amount £**	**Date**	**Details**	**Amount £**
20X3			**20X3**		
1/6	Balance	15,019.86			

ANSWERS (Tasks 1, 6, 7 and 8, continued)

GENERAL LEDGER

SALES					
Date	**Details**	**Amount** **£**	**Date**	**Details**	**Amount** **£**
20X3			20X3		
			1/6	Balance	408,243.67

SALES LEDGER CONTROL					
Date	**Details**	**Amount** **£**	**Date**	**Details**	**Amount** **£**
20X3			20X3		
1/6	Balance b/d	52,754.01			

SUNDRY CREDITORS					
Date	**Details**	**Amount** **£**	**Date**	**Details**	**Amount** **£**
20X3			20X3		

ANSWERS (Tasks 1, 6, 7 and 8, continued)

GENERAL LEDGER

	SUSPENSE				
Date	**Details**	**Amount** **£**	**Date**	**Details**	**Amount** **£**
20X3			20X3		
1/6	Cash book	33,000.00	30/4	Cash book	1,750.00

	VAT				
Date	**Details**	**Amount** **£**	**Date**	**Details**	**Amount** **£**
20X3			20X3		
			1/6	Balance	7,268.02

ANSWERS (Task 2)

Semiotix Associates

MEMO

Date:

To:

From:

Re:

BPP PUBLISHING

ANSWERS (Tasks 2, 3, 4, 5 and 6)

JOURNAL

Journal number	Date 20X3	Account names and narrative	Debit £	Credit £

ANSWERS (TASKS 3, 4 AND 5)
FIXED ASSET REGISTER

Description/serial no	Date acquired	Original cost £	Depreciation £	NBV £	Funding method	Disposal proceeds £	Disposal date
Factory equipment							
Depreciation: 15% pa reducing balance							
High tensile cutter	1/7/X0	5,500.00			Cash		
Year ended 30/6/X1			825.00	4,675.00			
Year ended 30/6/X2			701.25	3,973.75			
Small frame machine	1/7/X0	2,500.00			Cash		
Year ended 30/6/X1			375.00	2,125.00			
Year ended 30/6/X2			318.75	1,806.25			
Large frame machine	31/12/X0	6,000.00			Cash		
Year ended 30/6/X1			900.00	5,100.00			
Year ended 30/6/X2			765.00	4,335.00			

ANSWERS (TASKS 3, 4 AND 5, CONTINUED)
FIXED ASSET REGISTER

Description/serial no	Date acquired	Original cost £	Depreciation £	NBV £	Funding method	Disposal proceeds £	Disposal date
Factory equipment							
Depreciation: 15% pa reducing balance							
Colour print machine	1/7/X0	7,500.00			Cash		
Year ended 30/6/X1			1,125.00	6,375.00			
Year ended 30/6/X2			956.25	5,418.75			
Lifting machine	1/7/X0	1,750.00			Cash		
Year ended 30/6/X1			262.50	1,487.50			
Year ended 30/6/X2			223.12	1,264.38			
Laminator	1/1/X2	4,500.00			Cash		
Year ended 30/6/X2			675.00	3,825.00			

ANSWERS (TASKS 3, 4 AND 5, CONTINUED)
FIXED ASSET REGISTER

Description/serial no	Date acquired	Original cost £	Depreciation £	NBV £	Funding method	Disposal proceeds £	Disposal date
Office equipment *Depreciation: 25% pa straight line*							
Velox Pentium III PC	1/7/X1	2,000.00			Cash		
Year ended 30/6/X2			500.00	1,500.00			
Velox Pentium III laptop	1/7/X1	2,650.00			Cash		
Year ended 30/6/X2			662.50	1,987.50			
Photocopier	1/7/X0	3,000.00			Cash		
Year ended 30/6/X1			750.00	2,250.00			
Year ended 30/6/X2			750.00	1,500.00			
Laser printer	1/7/X1	1,000.00			Cash		
Year ended 30/6/X2			250.00	750.00			

ANSWERS (TASKS 3, 4 AND 5, CONTINUED)
FIXED ASSET REGISTER

Description/serial no	Date acquired	Original cost £	Depreciation £	NBV £	Funding method	Disposal proceeds £	Disposal date
Motor vehicles							
Depreciation: 20% pa straight line							
High sided delivery van JH54 HJK	1/7/X0	24,000.00			Hire purchase (30 months)		
Year ended 30/6/X1			4,800.00	19,200.00			
Year ended 30/6/X2			4,800.00	14,400.00			
Delivery van JH56 ADF	1/5/X2	12,750.00			Cash		
Year ended 30/6/X2			2,550.00	10,200.00			

ANSWERS (Task 4, continued)

Semiotix Associates

MEMO

Date:

To:

From:

Re:

ANSWERS (Task 7)

Debtors' reconciliation

	£
Addlestone Town Council	7,930.84
Friary Shopping Mall	3,074.83
Granville Leisure Park	2,039.72
Highways Agency	2,928.03
Midlands Development Agency	15,920.39
Oonagh Shops Ltd	4,037.49
Pinewood plc	3,904.04
Warrington Town Council	3,672.78

Creditors' reconciliation

	£
Adams Adhesives Ltd	4,920.37
Ericson plc	5,309.48
Jensen Plastics	253.39
Lentril Inks Ltd	1,028.39
MetalFramer Ltd	13,290.03
Orbitol Ltd	892.02
Plastika Inc	2,539.30
Tendrils plc	3,236.28

JOURNAL

Journal number	Date 20X3	Account names and narrative	Debit £	Credit £

ANSWERS (Tasks 8, 10 and 11)

EXTENDED TRIAL BALANCE AT 30 JUNE 20X3

Ledger account name	Balance at 30/6/X3 £	£	Adjustments £	£	Profit and loss account £	£	Balance sheet £	£
Administration								
Assemblies purchases								
Assemblies opening stock								
Assemblies closing stock								
Bank								
Capital								
Depreciation charge								
Direct labour								
Disposals								
Drawings								
Factory equipment: accumulated depreciation								
Factory equipment: cost								
Factory overheads								
Finished goods opening stock:								
Finished goods closing stock								
Hire purchase creditor								
Interest expense								
Motor vehicles: accumulated depreciation								
Motor vehicles: cost								
Office equipment: accumulated depreciation								
Office equipment: cost								
Purchase ledger control								
Raw materials purchases								
Raw materials closing stock								
Raw materials opening stock								
Sales								
Sales ledger control								
Sundry creditors								
VAT								
Total								

ANSWERS (Task 9)

STOCK VALUATION AT 30 June 20X3

Raw materials

Assemblies

ANSWERS (Task 9, continued)

Finished goods

MANUFACTURING ACCOUNT FOR THE YEAR ENDED 30 JUNE 20X3

	£	£
Raw material stock at 1 July 20X2		
Assemblies stock at 1 July 20X2		
Purchases: raw materials		
assemblies		
	————	
Raw material stock at 30 June 20X3		
Tungstra		
Miscellaneous items		
	————	
		————
Direct labour		
		————
Prime cost		
Factory overheads		
Depreciation of factory equipment		
	————	
		————
Factory cost of finished goods produced		
		════

Factory cost of signs made	Total costs £	Quantity made	Unit cost per sign £	Quantity in closing stock	Valuation £
Small signs					
Large signs					
Extra large signs	————				————
	════				════

AAT sample simulation

AAT SAMPLE SIMULATION

INTERMEDIATE STAGE - NVQ/SVQ3

Unit 5

Maintaining Financial Records

and Preparing Accounts

(AAT Sample)

This Sample Simulation is the AAT's Sample Simulation for Unit 5. Its purpose is to give you an idea of what an AAT simulation looks like. It is not intended as a definitive guide to the tasks you may be required to perform.

The suggested time allowance for this Assessment is four hours. Up to 30 minutes extra time may be permitted in an AAT simulation. Breaks in assessment will be allowed in the AAT simulation, but it must normally be completed in one day.

Calculators may be used but no reference material is permitted.

**DO NOT OPEN THIS PAPER UNTIL YOU ARE READY TO START
UNDER TIMED CONDITIONS**

INSTRUCTIONS

This Simulation is designed to test your ability to maintain financial records and prepare accounts.

The situation is provided on **Page 213**.

The tasks you are to perform are set out on **Page 214 and 215**.

You are provided with data which you must use to complete the tasks.

Your answers should be set out in the answer booklet on **Pages 223 to 241** using the documents provided.

You are allowed **four hours** to complete your work.

A high level of accuracy is required. Check your work carefully.

Correcting fluid may be used in moderation. Errors should be crossed out neatly and clearly. You should write in black ink, not pencil.

You are advised to read the whole of the Simulation before commencing as all of the information may be of value and is not necessarily supplied in the sequence in which you might wish to deal with it.

THE SITUATION

Your name is Val Denning and you are an accounts assistant working for Branson & Co, a partnership business owned by two partners called Amy Brandreth and Sanjay Sondin. You report to the firm's Accountant, Jenny Holden.

Branson is a manufacturing business, purchasing raw materials and producing a finished product called a mendip. The manufacturing process is very simple, involving the assembly of just two bought-in parts and a small amount of finishing work. The firm's stocks consist of raw materials (the bought-in parts) and finished mendips; work in progress is negligible in value at any time.

Books and records

Branson maintains a full system of ledger accounts in manual format. Money coming in and going out is recorded in a manual cash book which serves both as a book of prime entry and a ledger account.

Branson also maintains a manual fixed assets register. This includes details of capital expenditure (but not revenue expenditure) incurred in acquiring or enhancing fixed assets, as well as details of depreciation and disposals.

Accounting policies and procedures

Branson is registered for VAT and all of its sales are standard-rated.

Branson classifies its fixed assets into three categories: company cars, plant and equipment, and other fixed assets. For each category the nominal (general) ledger includes accounts relating to cost, depreciation charge (ie the profit and loss expense), accumulated depreciation (ie the balance sheet provision), and disposals.

Company cars are depreciated at a rate of 45% per annum on the reducing balance. Plant and equipment and other fixed assets are depreciated at 25% per annum straight line, assuming nil residual value. In the year of an asset's acquisition a full year's depreciation is charged, regardless of the exact date of acquisition. In the year of an asset's disposal, no depreciation is charged. Company car running costs are recorded in the firm's accounts as an administration overhead. Branson is not able to recover input VAT on the purchase of company cars. Similarly, the firm is not required to account for output VAT when company cars are disposed of.

Authorisation for the acquisition and disposal of fixed assets, and for the method of finance, derives from the partners and is communicated to you by means of a memo from the firm's Accountant at the beginning of each month in which an acquisition or disposal is planned. In the month of March 20X8 one acquisition and one disposal took place; these are referred to in the memo on Page 138.

The simulation

In this simulation you will be required to perform a number of tasks leading up to the preparation of an extended trial balance for the year ended 31 March 20X8.

TASKS TO BE COMPLETED

In the answer booklet on Pages 223 to 241 complete the tasks outlined below. Data for this assessment is provided on Pages 216 to 221.

1   Refer to the memo on Page 216 and the supplier's invoice on Page 217. This refers to the purchase of a new company car and the trade-in of an existing company car. Record the acquisition and the trade-in in the fixed assets register (see Pages 224 and 225 in the answer booklet) and in the nominal (general) ledger (see Pages 226-235 in the answer booklet). You are reminded that Branson is *not* able to recover VAT on the acquisition of company cars.

2   By reference to the fixed assets register, calculate the depreciation for the year on each of the company cars and on each item of plant and equipment. You should record the relevant amounts in the fixed assets register and in the nominal (general) ledger. You should also calculate the depreciation for the year on 'other fixed assets' by reference to the relevant account in the nominal (general) ledger and record the amount in the nominal (general) ledger.

3   A member of staff has listed the company cars actually present on Branson's premises at close of business on 31 March 20X8. His list is on Page 218. Compare this list with the details recorded in the fixed assets register and describe any discrepancies in a memo to the firm's Accountant. Use the memo form on Page 236 of the answer booklet.

4   The nominal (general) ledger already includes sales and purchases transactions up to 28 February 20X8. The sales and purchases day books have been totalled for March 20X8 and the totals are displayed on Page 218. Post these totals to the nominal (general) ledger. Note that the invoice from Task 1 was *not* included in the March totals because it was not received until April.

5   Refer to the business bank statement and the business cash book on Pages 219 and 220. Perform a bank reconciliation as at 31 March 20X8. Set out your reconciliation on Page 237 of the answer booklet.

6   Post from the business cash book to the nominal (general) ledger for the month of March 20X8.

7   Bring down a balance as at 1 April 20X8 on each account in the nominal (general) ledger and enter the balances in the first two columns of the trial balance (see Page 238 of the answer booklet). The totals of the two columns will not be equal. You should establish why, and make the appropriate addition to the trial balance.

8   The debit entry in the suspense account (£750) represents a cheque made out on the business bank account earlier in the year. The payee is not known to you as a supplier or employee of Branson. Describe how you would ascertain the nature of this payment so that you can account for it correctly. Set out your answer on Page 239 of the answer booklet.

    (*Note: once you have completed this task you should turn to the answer to Task 8 for an explanation of what the payment represents. You will need this information to complete Task 9*).

9   The credit entry on the suspense account is the proceeds on disposal of a fixed asset included in the category 'other fixed assets'. No other entries have been made in the nominal ledger in respect of this disposal. The asset originally cost £2,317.69, and its accumulated depreciation at 31 March 20X7 was £946.23. Draft journal entries,

dated 31 March 20X8, to clear the balance on the suspense account. Set out your entries, with full narrative, on Page 240 of the answer booklet. (**Note**; you are *not* required to adjust the nominal (general) ledger accounts in the light of this transaction.)

10 Details of Branson's closing stocks are given on Page 221. Calculate the value of closing stock of raw materials and finished goods at 31 March 20X8 for inclusion in the trial balance. Use the blank Page 241 of the answer booklet for your answer. Note that to calculate the value of finished goods stock you will need to prepare a manufacturing account for the year ended 31 March 20X8.

11 On the trial balance, make appropriate adjustments in respect of the following matters.

(a) The journal entries prepared in Task 9

(b) Closing stock calculated in Task 10

(c) Accruals and prepayments. For details of these see Page 221.

12 Extend the trial balance. This includes totalling all columns of the trial balance and making entries to record the net profit or loss for the year ended 31 March 20X8.

BPP
PUBLISHING

DATA

MEMO

To: Val Denning

From: Jenny Holden

Subject: Fixed asset acquisitions/disposals in March 20X8

Date: 2 March 20X8

Only one fixed asset acquisition is planned for the month of March. Our salesman, Andy Noble, will trade in his old car (registration M104PTY) and purchase a new one. The new one will be financed partly by the trade-in value agreed at £1,850), and partly by cash.

SALES INVOICE

HYLEX MOTORS
BLANKTON

VAT registration: 318 1627 66

Extines Road, Blankton

Telephone: 01489 22514   Fax: 01489 56178

Date/tax point: 27 March 20X8

Invoice to:

Invoice number: 42176

Branson & Co

Unit 6 Chalmers Industrial Estate

Blankton

BT3 4NY

Registration: R261 GHT   Registration date: 27/3/X8 Stock number: Q4510

Chassis no: TWQQAW 66780   Engine no: ER43218   Sales person: M Easton

	£
Ford Mondeo	
List price	10,900.10
VAT at 17.5%	1,907.50
	12,807.50
Vehicle excise duty (12 months)	140.00
Total due	12,947.50
Less: part-exchange (M104 PTY)	1,850.00
Balance to pay	11,097.50

Terms: net, 30 days

BPP
PUBLISHING

Company cars on the premises, 31 March 20X8

P321 HDR - in yard

N33 FGY - in yard

R261 GHT - in yard

Sales day book totals, March 20X8

	£
Total value of invoices	36,514.59
Sales value	31,076.25
VAT	5,438.34

Purchases day book totals, March 20X8

	£
Total value of invoices	9,133.18
Administration overheads	991.24
Factory overheads	1,451.09
Purchases	4,871.22
Selling and distribution overheads	524.87
VAT	1,294.76

Northern Bank plc

26 High Street, Blankton BT1 6FG

Account: Branson & Co

Account no: 28771243

STATEMENT

45-32-20

Statement no: 192

Details	Payments £	Receipts £	Date	Balance £
			20X8	
Balance forward			1-Mar	1,912.90
19328	1,105.36		3-Mar	807.54
CC		4,227.18	4-Mar	5,034.72
19332	365.11		10-Mar	4,669.61
CC		4,265.77	11-Mar	8,935.38
19331	1,192.45		12-Mar	7,742.93
19333	2,651.08		16-Mar	5,091.85
CC		5,931.20	18-Mar	11,023.05
19335	299.52		23-Mar	10,723.53
19334	3,006.12		24-Mar	7,717.41
CC		3,773.81	25-Mar	11,491.22
19340	10,480.05		30-Mar	1,011.17
19336	2,561.29		31-Mar	1,550.12 O/D

AAT sample simulation

Key	S/O Standing order	DD Direct debit	CC Cash and/or cheques	CHGS Charges
		BACS Bankers automated clearing services	O/D Overdrawn	

RECEIPTS

Date 20X8	Details	Total £	Sales ledger control £	Other £
01-Mar	Balance b/f	5,034.72		
06-Mar	Cash and cheques banked	4,265.77	4,265.77	
13-Mar	Cash and cheques banked	5,931.20	5,931.20	
20-Mar	Cash and cheques banked	3,773.81	3,773.81	
27-Mar	Cash and cheques banked	6,071.88	6,071.88	
31-Mar	Cash and cheques banked	5,512.67	5,512.67	
		30,590.05	25,555.33	
01-Apr	Balance b/d	8,806.42		

PAYMENTS

Date 20X8	Details	Cheque no	Total £	Purchases ledger control £	Other £
03-Mar	Hanway plc	19331	1,192.45	1,192.45	
05-Mar	Peters Limited	19332	365.11	365.11	
09-Mar	Wright & Parkin	19333	2,651.08	2,651.08	
16-Mar	Westcott Limited	19334	3,006.12	3,006.12	
17-Mar	Sidlow & Morris	19335	299.52	299.52	
24-Mar	Harper John & Co	19336	2,561.29	2,561.29	
24-Mar	Paul Darby plc	19337	278.01	278.01	
27-Mar	Brandreth: drawings	19338	500.00		500.00
27-Mar	Sondin: drawings	19339	450.00		450.00
27-Mar	Wages and salaries (see analysis below)	19340	10,480.05		10,480.05
31-Mar	Balance c/d		8,806.42		
			30,590.05	10,353.58	11,430.05

Wages and salaries analysis

	£
Direct labour	6,014.73
Admin overhead	1,105.69
Factory overhead	1,931.75
Sell and dist overhead	1,427.88
	10,480.05

Stock at 31 March 20X8

Raw materials

	Cost	Net realisable value
	£	£
Material X	3,417.22	3,817.66
Material Y	5,441.08	4,719.33

Finished mendips

A total of 25,613 units were produced in the year ended 31 March 20X8, of which 3,117 units remained in stock at the year end.

Accruals and prepayments at 31 March 20X8

Branson & Co do not attempt to calculate accruals and prepayments for immaterial amounts, defined as being anything less than £200.

The only two items which may amount to more than this are included in administration overheads, as follows.

- Office rental of £3,250 was paid in December 20X7 in respect of the six months ending 30 June 20X8.

- Telephone and fax charges amount to about £630 per quarter. At 31 March 20X8 these charges had already been paid for the quarter ended 31 January 20X8, but the invoice for the subsequent quarter is not expected to arrive until May 20X8.

AAT SAMPLE SIMULATION

Maintaining Financial Records and Preparing Accounts

ANSWER BOOKLET

ANSWERS (Task 1,2)

Description/serial no	Location	Date acquired	Original cost £	Enhance-ments £	Total £	Depreciation £	NBV £	Funding method	Disposal proceeds £	Disposal date £
Plant and equipment										
Milling machine 45217809	Factory	20/6/X4	3,456.08		3,456.08			Cash		
Year ended 31/3/X5						864.02	2,592.06			
Year ended 31/3/X6						864.02	1,728.04			
Year ended 31/3/X7						864.02	864.02			
Lathe 299088071	Factory	12/6/X5	4,008.24		4,008.24			Cash		
Year ended 31/3/X6						1,002.06	3,006.18			
Year ended 31/3/X7						1,002.06	2,004.12			
Drill assembly 51123412	Factory	12/2/X6	582.44		582.44			Cash		
Year ended 31/3/X6						145.61	436.83			
Year ended 31/3/X7						145.61	291.22			
Punch drive 91775321	Factory	12/2/X6	1,266.00		1,266.00			Cash plus trade in		
Year ended 31/3/X6						316.50	949.50			
Year ended 31/3/X7						316.50	633.00			
Winding gear 53098871	Factory	13/3/X6	1,082.68		1,082.68			Cash		
Year ended 31/3/X6						270.67	812.01			
Year ended 31/3/X7				341.79	1,153.80	384.60	769.20			
Plant and equipment										
Tender press 44231809	Factory	8/8/X6	4,256.04		4,256.04			Cash		
						1,064.01	3,192.03			

ANSWERS (Task 1,2, continued)

EXTRACTS FROM FIXED ASSETS REGISTER

Description/serial no	Location	Date acquired	Original cost £	Enhance-ments £	Total £	Depreciation £	NBV £	Funding method	Disposal proceeds £	Disposal date £
Company cars										
M412 RTW	Yard	25/8/X4	8,923.71		8,923.71			Lease		
Year ended 31.3.X5						4,015.67	4,908.04			
Year ended 31.3.X6						2,208.62	2,699.42			
Year ended 31.3.X7						1,214.74	1,484.68			
M104 PTY	Yard	15/3/X5	8,643.00		8,643.00			Cash		
Year ended 31.3.X5						3,889.35	4,753.65			
Year ended 31.3.X6						2,139.14	2,614.51			
Year ended 31.3.X7						1,176.53	1,437.98			
N33 FGY	Yard	18/9/X6	10,065.34		10,065.34			Cash plus trade in		
Year ended 31.3.X6						4,529.40	5,535.94			
Year ended 31.3.X7						2,491.17	3,044.77			
P321 HDR	Yard	13/12/X6	9,460.26		9,460.26			Cash		
Year ended 31.3.X7						4,257.12	5,203.14			

ANSWERS (Tasks 1, 2, 4, 6, 7)

NOMINAL (GENERAL) LEDGER

Account Administration overheads					
Debit			Credit		
Date 20X8	Details	Amount £	Date 20X8	Details	Amount £
1 Mar	Balance b/f	15,071.23			

Account Brandreth capital account					
Debit			Credit		
Date 20X8	Details	Amount £	Date 20X8	Details	Amount £
			1 Mar	Balance b/f	17,063.24

Account Brandreth capital account					
Debit			Credit		
Date 20X8	Details	Amount £	Date 20X8	Details	Amount £
1 Mar	Balance b/f	11,056.73			

ANSWERS (Tasks 1, 2, 4, 6, 7 continued)

NOMINAL (GENERAL) LEDGER

Account Company cars: cost

Debit / Credit

Date 20X8	Details	Amount £	Date 20X8	Details	Amount £
1 Mar	Balance b/f	37,092.31			

Account Company cars: depreciation charge

Debit / Credit

Date 20X8	Details	Amount £	Date 20X8	Details	Amount £

Account Company cars: accumulated depreciation

Debit / Credit

Date 20X7	Details	Amount £	Date 20X7	Details	Amount £
			1 Apr	Balance b/f	25,921.74

BPP PUBLISHING

ANSWERS (Tasks 1, 2, 4, 6, 7 continued)

NOMINAL (GENERAL) LEDGER

Account Company cars: disposals

Date 20X8	Details	Amount £	Date 20X8	Details	Amount £

Debit — Credit

Account Direct labour costs

Date 20X8	Details	Amount £	Date 20X8	Details	Amount £
1 Mar	Balance b/f	60,012.64			

Debit — Credit

Account Factory overheads

Date 20X8	Details	Amount £	Date 20X8	Details	Amount £
1 Mar	Balance b/f	27,109.67			

Debit — Credit

ANSWERS (Tasks 1, 2, 4, 6, 7 continued)

NOMINAL (GENERAL) LEDGER

Account Other fixed assets: cost

Debit			Credit		
Date 20X8	Details	Amount £	Date 20X8	Details	Amount £
1 Mar	Balance b/f	18,923.50			

Account Other fixed assets: depreciation charge

Debit			Credit		
Date 20X8	Details	Amount £	Date 20X8	Details	Amount £

Account Other fixed assets: accumulated depreciation

Debit			Credit		
Date 20X7	Details	Amount £	Date 20X7	Details	Amount £
			1 Apr	Balance b/f	6,224.12

BPP
PUBLISHING

ANSWERS (Tasks 1, 2, 4, 6, 7 continued)

NOMINAL (GENERAL) LEDGER

Account Other fixed assets: disposals

Debit			Credit		
Date 20X8	Details	Amount £	Date 20X8	Details	Amount £

Account Plant and equipment: cost

Debit			Credit		
Date 20X8	Details	Amount £	Date 20X8	Details	Amount £
1 Mar	Balance b/f	14,993.27			

Account Plant and equipment: depreciation charge

Debit			Credit		
Date 20X8	Details	Amount £	Date 20X8	Details	Amount £

ANSWERS (Tasks 1, 2, 4, 6, 7 continued)

NOMINAL (GENERAL) LEDGER

Account Plant and equipment: accumulated depreciation
Debit · Credit

Date 20X7	Details	Amount £	Date 20X7	Details	Amount £
			1 Apr	Balance b/f	7,239.68

Account Plant and equipment: disposals
Debit · Credit

Date 20X8	Details	Amount £	Date 20X8	Details	Amount £

Account Purchases
Debit · Credit

Date 20X8	Details	Amount £	Date 20X8	Details	Amount £
1 Mar	Balance b/f	54,231.89			

NOMINAL (GENERAL) LEDGER

Account Purchases ledger control

Date 20X8	Details	Amount £	Date 20X8	Details	Amount £
			1 Mar	Balance b/f	18,457.20

Debit — Credit

Account Sales

Date 20X8	Details	Amount £	Date 20X8	Details	Amount £
			1 Mar	Balance b/f	225,091.42

Debit — Credit

Account Sales ledger control

Date 20X8	Details	Amount £	Date 20X8	Details	Amount £
1 Mar	Balance b/f	24,617.03			

Debit — Credit

ANSWERS (Tasks 1, 2, 4, 6, 7 continued)

NOMINAL (GENERAL) LEDGER

Account Selling and distribution overheads

Debit			Credit		
Date 20X8	Details	Amount £	Date 20X8	Details	Amount £
1 Mar	Balance b/f	14,303.12			

Account Sondin capital account

Debit			Credit		
Date 20X8	Details	Amount £	Date 20X8	Details	Amount £
			1 Mar	Balance b/f	8,703.28

Account Sondin current account

Debit			Credit		
Date 20X8	Details	Amount £	Date 20X8	Details	Amount £
1 Mar	Balance b/f	12,912.29			

NOMINAL (GENERAL) LEDGER

Account Stock: raw materials

Debit				Credit	
Date 20X7	Details	Amount £	Date 20X8	Details	Amount £
1 Apr	Balance b/f	6,294.33			

Account Stock: finished goods

Debit				Credit	
Date 20X7	Details	Amount £	Date 20X7	Details	Amount £
1 Apr	Balance b/f	12,513.77			

Account Suspense

Debit				Credit	
Date 20X8	Details	Amount £	Date 20X8	Details	Amount £
26 Jan	Bank	750.00	24 Feb	Bank	1,124.55

ANSWERS (Tasks 1, 2, 4, 6, 7 continued)

NOMINAL (GENERAL) LEDGER

Account VAT					
Debit			Credit		
Date 20X8	Details	Amount £	Date 20X8	Details	Amount £
			1 Mar	Balance b/f	5,091.27

MEMO

To:

From:

Subject:

Date:

ANSWERS (Task 5)

AAT Sample simulation

ANSWERS (Tasks 7, 11, 12)

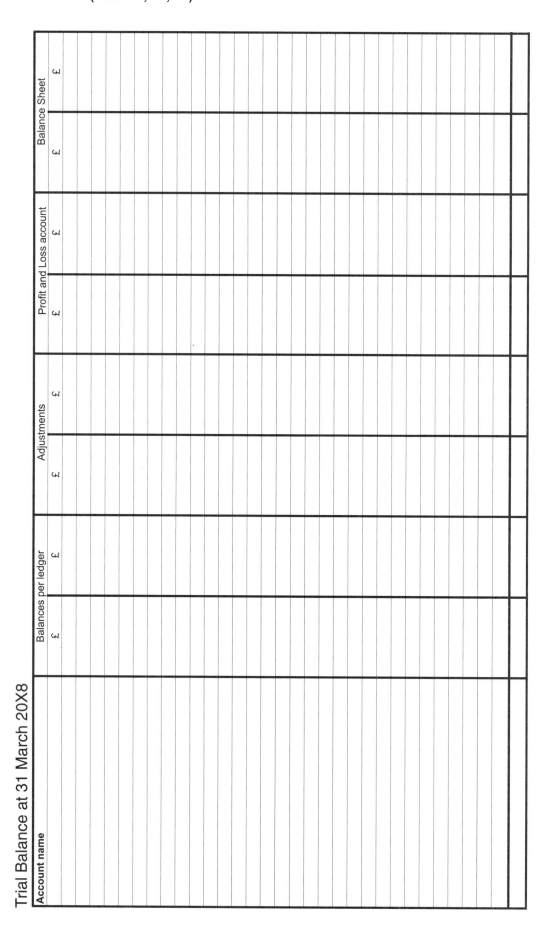

Trial Balance at 31 March 20X8

Account name	Balances per ledger £	£	Adjustments £	£	Profit and Loss account £	£	Balance Sheet £	£

BPP PUBLISHING

238

ANSWERS (Tasks 8)

ANSWERS (Tasks 8)

JOURNAL

Date 20X8	Account names and narrative	Debit £	Credit £

ANSWERS (Task 10)

Practice central assessments

PRACTICE CENTRAL ASSESSMENT 1: INFORTEC (December 1999)

This central assessment is in TWO sections. Section 1 contains two parts, part A and part B. Part A is made up of longer questions whilst part B consists of short answer questions. You are reminded that competence must be achieved in each section. You should therefore attempt and aim to complete EVERY task in EACH section.

All essential workings should be included within your answer where appropriate.

SECTION 1

PART A

The suggested time allocation for this extended trial balance exercise is 60 minutes.

Phil Townsend is the proprietor of Infortec Computers, a wholesale business which buys and sells computer hardware and software.

- You are employed by Phil Townsend to assist with the bookkeeping.
- The business currently operates a manual system consisting of a general ledger, a sales ledger and a purchases ledger.
- Double entry takes place in the general ledger and the individual accounts of debtors and creditors are therefore regarded as memoranda accounts.
- Day books consisting of a purchases day book, a sales day book, a purchases returns day book and a sales returns day book are used. Totals from the various columns of the day books are transferred into the general ledger.

At the end of the financial year, on 30 November 20X9, the following balances were extracted from the general ledger.

	£
Capital	134,230
Purchases	695,640
Sales	836,320
Stock at 1 December 20X8	84,300
Rent paid	36,000
Salaries	37,860
Motor Vehicles (MV) at cost	32,400
Provision for depreciation (MV)	8,730
Fixtures and fittings (F&F) at cost	50,610
Provision for depreciation (F&F)	12,340
Purchases returns	10,780
Sales returns	5,270
Drawings	55,910
Insurance	4,760
Debtors control account	73,450
Creditors control account	56,590
Bad debts	3,670
Provision for doubtful debts	3,060
Bank overdraft	10,800
Cash	1,980
VAT (credit balance)	5,410
Discounts allowed	6,770
Discounts received	4,380

Task 1

Enter the balances into the columns of the trial balance provided below. Total the two columns and enter an appropriate suspense account balance to ensure that the two totals agree.

Trial Balance at 30th November 20X9

DESCRIPTION	Debit £	Credit £
Capital		
Purchases		
Sales		
Stock at 1 December 20X8		
Rent paid		
Salaries		
Motor vehicles (MV) at cost		
Provision for depreciation (MV)		
Fixtures and fittings (F&F) at cost		
Provision for depreciation (F&F)		
Purchase returns		
Sales returns		
Drawings		
Insurance		
Debtors control account		
Creditors control account		
Bad debts		
Provision for doubtful debts		
Bank overdraft		
Cash		
VAT (credit balance)		
Discounts allowed		
Discounts received		
Suspense account		
Totals		

Subsequent to the preparation of the trial balance a number of errors were discovered which are detailed below.

(a) Drawings of £400 had been debited to the salaries account.

(b) The net column of the sales day book had been undercast by £100.

(c) The VAT column of the sales returns day book had been overcast by £60.

(d) A cheque for £120 paid to a credit supplier had been entered in the cash book but not in the relevant control account.

(e) A £3,000 cheque paid for rent had been debited to both the bank account and the rent paid account.

 246

(f)   The total column of the purchases day book had been overcast by £10.

(g)   The discounts received column of the cash book had been overcast by £40.

(h)   A £65 cheque paid for insurance, although correctly entered in the cash book, had been entered in the insurance account as £55.

Task 2

Prepare journal entries to record the correction of these errors. Dates and narratives are not required. Use the blank journal on page 248.

Task 2

JOURNAL	Debit £	Credit £

The individual balances of the accounts in the sales ledger were listed, totalled and compared with the £73,450 balance of the debtors control account. The total of the list came to £76,780 and after investigation the following errors were found.

(a) A customer account with a balance of £400 was omitted from the list.

(b) A £50 discount allowed had been debited to a customer's account.

(c) A customer's account with a balance of £2,410 was included twice in the list.

(d) A customer's balance of £320 was entered in the list as £230.

(e) A customer with a balance of £540 had been written off as a bad debt in October but the balance was still included in the list.

(f) Sales returns totalling £770 (including VAT) had been omitted from the relevant customer accounts.

Task 3

Make appropriate adjustments to the total of the list using the table below. For each adjustment show clearly the amount involved and whether the amount is to be added or subtracted.

	£
Total from list of balances	76,780
Adjustment for (a) add / subtract★	
Adjustment for (b) add / subtract★	
Adjustment for (c) add / subtract★	
Adjustment for (d) add / subtract★	
Adjustment for (e) add / subtract★	
Adjustment for (f) add / subtract★	
Revised total to agree with debtors control account	

★Circle your answer to show add or subtract.

PART B

The suggested time allocation for this set of short answer questions is 50 minutes.

Task 4

On 1 December 20X8 Infortec Computers owned motor vehicles costing £28,400. During the year ended 30 November 20X9 the following changes to the motor vehicles took place:

		£
1 March 20X9	Sold vehicle – original cost	18,000
1 June 20X9	Purchased new vehicle – cost	10,000
1 September 20X9	Purchased new vehicle – cost	12,000

Depreciation on motor vehicles is calculated on a monthly basis at 20% per annum on cost.

Complete the table below to calculate the total depreciation charge to profits for the year ended 30 November 20X9.

	£
Depreciation for vehicle sold 1 March 20X9	
Depreciation for vehicle purchased 1 June 20X9	
Depreciation for vehicle purchased 1 September 20X9	
Depreciation for other vehicles owned during the year	
Total depreciation for the year ended 30 November 20X9	

Task 5

At the end of the previous financial year, on 30 November 20X8, Phil Townsend had produced an extended trial balance. Prior to the calculation of the profit the balance sheet columns showed a total of £247,000 for the debit balances and £231,000 for the credit balances. The balances included capital of £164,230 and drawings of £46,000.

(a) **Calculate the profit or loss for the year ended 30 November 20X8.**

(b) **Calculate the final capital balance representing the investment by Phil Townsend in the business on 30 November 20X8.**

Task 6

Infortec Computers needs to have use of a powerful computer for 3 months to carry out some development work. Phil Townsend has two choices. He can lease the computer for £500 a month or he can purchase it for £8,000, in which case he calculates that it could be sold 3 months later for £7,000. The payment of £8,000 would increase the business overdraft by that sum for the 3 months. Interest is payable on the overdraft at 12% per annum.

Calculate the total charge to the profits of the business over the 3-month period.

(a) If the computer was leased over the 3 months (Ignore the effect of the lease payments on the overdraft).

(b) If the computer was purchased and then sold at the end of the 3 months.

Task 7

Phil Townsend is the treasurer of a computer club. During the year ended 31 December 20X9 the club will have received £230,000 in cash and cheques from members which includes £10,000 prepaid for the following year. £240,000 is to be entered into the income and expenditure account for 20X9. No members are in arrears with their subscriptions at either the beginning or end of 20X9.

If the subscription payable per member is £200 per annum.

(a) **Calculate the number of members in the club for 20X9.**

(b) **Calculate the number of members who prepaid their 20X9 subscription during the year ended 31 December 20X8.**

Task 8

You receive the following note from Phil Townsend:

"I have been looking at the stock valuation for the year end and I have some concerns about the Mica 40z PCs.

We have ten of these in stock each of which cost £500 and are priced to sell to customers at £580. Unfortunately they all have faulty hard drives which will need to be replaced before they can be sold. The cost is £100 for each machine.

However, as you know, the Mica40z is now out of date and having spoken to some computer retailers I am fairly certain that we are going to have to scrap them or give them away for spares. Perhaps for now we should include them in the closing stock figure at cost. Can you please let me have your views."

Using the headed paper on page 252, write a memo in reply to Phil Townsend's note. Your memo should refer to alternative stock valuations and to appropriate statements of standard accounting practice.

Task 8

MEMORANDUM

To: Phil Townsend
From:
Ref: Valuation of stock
Date: 29 November 20X9

SECTION 2

The suggested time allocation for this exercise is 60 minutes.

Phil Townsend is planning to manufacture computers with effect from 1 January 20X0. If he decides to go ahead then he would open a new business called Infortec Manufacturing. He has produced the following estimated figures for the year ended 31 December 20X0 and has asked you to help in preparing some information.

		£
•	Raw materials to be purchased	180,000
•	Production wages	41,750
•	Production supervisory wages	22,000
•	Other production overheads	15,170
•	Selling and distribution expenses	38,800

In order to set up the business Phil Townsend would need to do the following with effect from 1 January 20X0.

- Open a new business bank account.

- Take out a business bank loan of £40,000. (Interest at 8% per annum to be paid out of the new business bank account).

- Place £50,000, which includes the £40,000 from the bank loan, into the new business bank account to cover future expenditure.

- Purchase, out of his own personal money, new production machinery and equipment costing £72,500. (Depreciation on this is to be calculated at 10% per annum at cost.)

On 31 December 20X0:

		£
•	Closing stock of raw materials	15,600
•	Closing stock of work in progress	10,170
•	Closing stock of finished goods	20,400
•	Closing debtors estimated to be $^{1}/_{12}$ of sales for the year	
•	Closing creditors estimated to be $^{1}/_{12}$ of raw materials purchased for the year	

NOTE:

- The profit mark up is to be 20% on factory cost of sales.

- All payments and receipts to pass through the new business bank account.

Task 1

Calculate the capital which would be invested by Phil Townsend in the business on 1 January 20X0.

Task 2

Calculate the prime cost of production of Infortec Manufacturing for the year ending 31 December 20X0.

Task 3

Calculate the total production cost of the finished goods to be made by Infortec Manufacturing during the year ending 31 December 20X0.

Task 4

Produce a statement showing the planned sales, factory cost of sales, gross profit and net profit of Infortec Manufacturing for the year ending 31 December 20X0.

Task 5

Produce a summary of the business bank account for the year ending 31 December 20X0 showing clearly the payments, the receipts and the closing balance.

PRACTICE CENTRAL ASSESSMENT 2: SIMPLE STATION (June 2000)

This central assessment is in TWO sections. You are reminded that competence must be achieved in both sections. You should therefore attempt and aim to complete EVERY task in BOTH sections.

Essential calculations should be included within your answers where appropriate.

You are advised to spend 110 minutes on section 1 and 70 minutes on Section 2.

SECTION 1

You are advised to spend approximately 110 minutes on this section.

NOTE: Clearly show your workings for all tasks.

Data

Heather Simpson is the proprietor of Simple Station, a wholesale business which buys and sells tinned food.

- The year end is 31 May 20X1.

- You are employed by Heather Simpson to assist with the bookkeeping.

- The business currently operates a manual system consisting of a general ledger, a sales ledger and a purchase ledger

- Double entry takes place in the general ledger. The individual accounts of debtors and creditors are therefore regarded as memoranda accounts.

- Day books consisting of a purchases day book, a sales day book, a purchase returns day book and a sales returns day book are used. Totals from the various columns of the day books are transferred into the general ledger.

At the end of the financial year, on 31 May 20X1, the following balances were extracted from the general ledger.

	£
Capital	36,000
Sales	313,740
Sales returns	2,704
Purchases	208,906
Purchases returns	980
Stock at 1 June 20X0	21,750
Rent	22,000
Wages	24,700
General expenses	10,957
Motor expenses	4,134
Motor vehicles (MV) at cost	18,900
Provision for depreciation (MV))	9,450
Office equipment (OE) at cost	27,410
Provision for depreciation (OE)	8,152
Drawings	18,000
Debtors control	30,450
Creditors control	19,341
Bank (debit balance)	811
Cash	1,005
VAT (credit balance)	3,664

After the preparation of the trial balance, you discovered that the year end bank reconciliation had not been carried out. During the reconciliation, you discovered:

(a)   The bank statement showed a direct debit of £350 for electricity which had not been accounted for by Simple Station. Payments for electricity are shown in the general expenses account. Any VAT implications are to be ignored.

(b)   The bank statement showed a deduction of £78 for bank charges and interest. This had not been accounted for by Simple Station. Payments for bank charges and interest are shown in the general expenses account.

(c)   The bank account in the general ledger showed two cheques, paid to suppliers, totalling £70 which were not shown on the bank statement.

(d)   The bank account in the general ledger showed a receipt from a debtor of £690 which was not shown on the bank statement.

Task 1.1

Showing clearly the individual debits and credits, update the closing balance of the bank account in Simple Station's general ledger.

BANK ACCOUNT

	£		£
Balance b/f	811		

Task 1.2

Calculate the closing bank balance as shown on the bank statement, clearly showing whether the closing balance is a debit or a credit on the bank statement.

Task 1.3

Enter the updated account balances into the first two columns of the extended trial balance provided on Page 258. Total the two columns, entering an appropriate suspense account balance.

(Note. It is the updated balances that should be entered, ie after taking into account the effects of the actions taken in Task 1.1.)

Task 1.4

Make appropriate entries in the adjustments columns of the extended trial balance on Page 258 to take account of the following.

(a)   Depreciation is to be provided as follows:

Motor vehicles :   25% per annum straight line method
Office equipment :   10% per annum straight line method

(b)   Closing stock was valued at cost at £25,890 on 31 May 20X1. However, this valuation included goods which had been damaged. The goods could be sold for £110 after repackaging, with an estimated cost of £40, had been carried out. The goods had originally cost £200.

(c)   Heather Simpson reviews the debtors and decides that a provision for doubtful debts should be made. This provision is to be 2% of the outstanding debtors.

(d)   In April 20X1, motor insurance of £240 was paid for the year ended 31 March 20X2.

Tasks 1.3 and 1.4

Extended Trial Balance at 31 May 20X1

DESCRIPTION	Ledger balances		Adjustments	
	DR £	CR £	Dr £	Cr £
Capital				
Sales				
Sales returns				
Purchases				
Purchases returns				
Stock at 1 June 20X0				
Rent				
Wages				
General expenses				
Motor expenses				
Motor vehicles (MV) at cost				
Provision for depreciation (MV)				
Office equipment (OE) at cost				
Provision for deprecation (OE)				
Drawings				
Debtors control				
Creditors control				
Bank				
Cash				
VAT				
Suspense				
Deprecation				
Closing stock – P&L				
Closing stock – balance sheet				
Prepayment				
Provision for doubtful debts – P&L				
Provision for doubtful debts – balance sheet				
TOTALS				

Task 1.5

Data

- You review the accounts, and find that the error which led to the opening of the suspense account was caused by the incorrect posting of an invoice.

- An invoice for purchases of stationery, for £200 net of VAT, was correctly entered into the general expenses account, but wrongly debited to the creditors control account.

- The VAT element of the invoice had not been posted at all.

Show the journal entries which would be required to correct the above errors.

(Note. State clearly for each entry, the name of the account, the amount and whether it is a debit or a credit. Dates and narratives are not required.)

Task 1.6

Included in the motor expenses of £4,134 is £2,000 paid by Simple Station for a motor vehicle which is being purchased under a hire purchase agreement.

When should Simple Station record the motor vehicle as a fixed asset in the books of the business?

(Note: you should circle the most appropriate answer)

When the first instalment is paid

When the final instalment is paid

The motor vehicle is never shown as a fixed asset

Task 1.7

Heather Simpson has been looking at the trial balance and noticed that you have made an adjustment for depreciation. She has heard of depreciation, but is unsure what it is for.

Briefly outline the purpose of providing depreciation.

Task 1.8

Heather Simpson also notices an amount of £36,000 on the trial balance in an account called 'Capital'. She does not understand what this account represents.

Briefly explain what a capital account represents.

SECTION 2

You are advised to spend approximately 70 minutes on this section.

NOTE: Clearly show your workings for all tasks.

Data

Edward Dyer has recently been appointed the treasurer of his golf club. He discovers that the previous treasurer has not prepared any figures for the year ended 31 March 20X1. Edward Dyer knows that you are training to be an accountant, and has asked you to help him prepare the 31 May 20X1 accounts. He tells you that:

- The main source of income for the club is from subscriptions, but the club also has a bar which members use to buy general refreshments.

- The golf club has a total of 80 members. Each member pays £200 subscription per year for use of the club's facilities.

- The bank account summary shows:

	£		£
Opening balance	2,150	Bar purchases	5,870
Bar sales	12,010	Bar staff wages	3,600
Subscriptions	15,600	Maintenance of golf course	1,690
		General expenses	8,250
		Club wages	9,750
		Closing balance	600
	29,760		29,760

- The year end balances for the bar are:

	31 March 20X0	31 March 20X1
	£	£
Stock of purchases	345	680
Debtors	580	900
Creditors	700	370

- Other year end balances are:

	31 March 20X1	31 March 20X1
	£	£
Golf course land	15,000	15,000
General expenses accrued	180	240
Subscriptions in arrears	200	unknown

Task 2.1

Calculate the sales made from the bar during the year ended 31 March 20X1.

Task 2.2

Calculate the purchases made for the bar during the year ended 31 March 20X1.

Task 2.3

Calculate the net profit made from the bar during the year ended 31 March 20X1.

Task 2.4

Calculate the total subscriptions figure to be used in the calculation of the surplus or deficit for the year ended 31 March 20X1.

Task 2.5

Calculate the figure for subscriptions outstanding on 31 March 20X1.

Task 2.6

Calculate the surplus or deficit made by the golf club for the year ended 31 March 20X1.

Task 2.7

Edward Dyer has looked at the calculation you have made for the answer to task 2.6. He does not understand why you have used a different figure for the subscriptions to the receipt shown in the bank account of £15,600.

(a)   **What is the concept applied when determining which subscriptions figure to use in task 2.6?**

(b)   **Briefly explain how this concept is applied.**

Task 2.8

Data

Edward Dyer informs you that:

•   The golf club is trying to expand.

•   To expand, it is going to need new premises and costs will increase.

•   He understands that not all the payments associated with the expansion will be shown in the income and expenditure statement.

•   He does not know how it will be decided which payments associated with the expansion are shown o the statement, and which ones are not.

Using the headed paper on Page 262, write a memo to Edward Dyer stating how the distinction between capital and revenue expenditure is made. Your memo should explain how each type of expenditure affects the income and expenditure statement.

(Note: two pages have been included for this memo. However, it is anticipated that the majority of candidates will find one page sufficient.)

Task 2.8

MEMO

To: Edward Dyer   **Ref:** Expansion payments

From: **Date:** 19 June 20X1

Task 2.8, continued

This page is for the continuation of the memo. It will not be needed by all candidates.

BPP
PUBLISHING

PRACTICE CENTRAL ASSESSMENT 3: FINE TIME (December 2000)

This central assessment is in TWO sections. You are reminded that competence must be achieved in both sections. You should therefore attempt and aim to complete EVERY task in BOTH sections.

Essential calculations should be included within your answers where appropriate.

You are advised to spend 100 minutes on Section 1 and 80 minutes on Section 2.

SECTION 1

You are advised to spend approximately 100 minutes on this section.

Data

Martin and Helen Fine are the proprietors of Fine Time, a business which buys and sells clocks and watches.

- The year end is 31 October 20X1.

- You are employed by Martin and Helen Fine to assist with the bookkeeping.

- The business currently operates a manual system consisting of a general ledger, a sales ledger and purchase ledger.

- Double entry takes place in the general ledger. The individual account of debtors and creditors are therefore regarded as memoranda accounts.

- Day books consisting of a purchases day book and a sales day book are used. Totals from the various columns of the day books are transferred into the general ledger.

    At the end of the financial year on 31 October 20X1, the following balances were extracted.

	£
Capital – Martin Fine	56,000
Capital – Helen Fine	42,000
Sales	296,857
Purchases	189,545
Stock at 1 November 20X0	25,850
Rent and rates	31,850
General expenses	60,320
Motor expenses	8,900
Motor vehicles (MV) at cost	25,200
Provision for depreciation (MV)	8,500
Office equipment (OE) at cost	42,800
Provision for depreciation (OE)	12,760
Drawings – Martin Fine	12,000
Drawings – Helen Fine	12,000
Debtors control	55,890
Provision for doubtful debts	1,560
Creditors control	42,230
Bank (debit balance)	2,450
Cash	212
VAT (credit balance)	8,370

Task 1.1

Enter the balances into the columns of the trial balance below. Total the two columns and enter an appropriate suspense account balance to ensure the two totals agree.

Trial Balance as at 31 October 20X1

DESCRIPTION	Dr £	Cr £
Capital – Martin Fine		56000
Capital - Helen Fine		42000
Sales		296,857
Purchases	189,545	
Stock at 1 November 20X0	25,850	
Rent and rates	31,850	
General expenses	60,320	
Motor expenses	8,900	
Motor vehicles (MV) at cost	25,200	
Provision for depreciation (MV)		8500
Office equipment (OE) at cost	42,800	
Provision for depreciation (OE)		12,760
Drawings – Martin Fine	12,000	
Drawings – Helen Fine	12,000	
Debtors control	55,890	
Provision for doubtful debts		1560
Creditors control		42,230
Bank (debit balance)	2450	
Cash	212	
VAT (credit balance)		8370
Suspense	1260	
	468,277	468,277

1638

265

Data

After extracting the trial balance, you discover:

- A number of errors that need correcting; and
- A number of year end adjustments that need to be made

Task 1.2

Prepare the journal entries to record the following adjustments and errors. Dates and narratives are not required. Use the blank journal on page 364.

(a)   Stock had been valued at cost on 31 October 20X1 at £19,750.

(b)   Depreciation is to be provided for as follows:

Motor vehicles   - 20% per annum straight line method   5040

Office equipment   - 15% per annum reducing balance method   4506

(c)   A bad debt of £1,290 should be written off.

(d)   The provision for doubtful debts should be adjusted to 3% of the remaining debtors.

(e)   A payment of £270 had been made for telephone costs. The entry into the general expenses account was correctly made, but the corresponding entry into the bank account was made on the wrong side. Any VAT implications are to be ignored.

(f)   Credit purchases of £2,412 had been correctly debited in the purchases account, but had been credited to the creditors control account as £4,212. Any VAT implications are to be ignored.

(g)   The purchase day book totals for the month of September 20X1 were:

	£
Goods for resale	15,780
Other items	5,100
Net	20,880
VAT	3,654
Total	24,534

You find that

- 'Other items' of £5,100 represent general expenses.
- The total of £24,534 had been debited to the purchases account and credited to the creditors control account.

JOURNAL

		Dr £	Cr £
a)	STOCK – Balance sheet STOCK – P + L	19,750	19,750

b)	D'PN charge – MV 5040
	         OE 4506
	 PROVISION FOR D'PN – MV 5040
	         OE 4506
		9546	9546

c)	Bad debt A/c DEBTORS CONTROL	1290	1290
d)	Bad debts Expense A/c PROVISION FOR DOUBTFUL DEBTS	78	78
e)	Suspense Bank A/c	540	540
f)	CREDITORS A/C Suspense A/c	1800	1800
g)	General Exp's A/c Purchases A/c VAT	5100 3654	8754

Data

- Included in the stock valuation as at 31 October 20X1 were 20 identical clocks each costing £150.

- Stock movements during the month of November 20X1 were as follows:

Purchases	3.11.X1	15 at £160 each
Sales	12.11.X1	10 at £300 each
Purchases	15.11.X1	5 at £155 each
Sales	25.11.X1	15 at £310 each

(handwritten annotations in right margin):

```
Stock        20   150
                         20  150     3000
             20  150  + 35< 15 160   2400
                         10 @ 150 ──────
                      -           5400
                                 (1500)
                                 ──────
                                  3900
                      + 5 @ 155    775
                                 ──────
                   10 @150        4675
              - 15< 5 @160       (1500)
                                  (800)
                                 ──────
                                  2375
```

- Stock is valued on a FIFO basis.

Task 1.3

Calculate the value of the following:

(a) Sales of clocks for November 20X1

```
10 × 300  =  3000
15 × 310  =  4650
             ────
             7650
```

(b) Closing stock of clocks on 30 November 20X1

```
c/s £2375
```

Task 1.4

The trial balance shows a figure of £296,857 for the sales.

(a) Does this figure include or exclude VAT?

```
EXCLUDE VAT
```

(b) Briefly explain the reason for your answer, referring to relevant accounting standards.

```
No profit out of vat only collects it
for customs & excise
for this reason SSAP 5 states that VAT
is excluded from sales in the Profit &
Loss A/c
```

Data

- The £1,290 bad debt, referred to in Task 1.2, is for a debtor who has been made bankrupt.

- Martin and Helen Fine feel that there is some chance of getting the money from the debtor next year.

- Because of this, they ask whether it is necessary to write off the debt.

Task 1.5

Using the headed paper on Pages 270 and 271, write a memo to Martin and Helen Fine stating whether or not the debt should be written off. Your answer should refer to appropriate accounting standards.

(NOTE. Two pages have been included for this memo. However, most candidates should find one page sufficient.)

Task 1.5

MEMO

To: **Martin and Helen Fine**   **Ref:** BAD DEBT

From: **Accounting Technician**   **Date:** 20X1

IF YOU ARE NOT SURE WHETHER A DEBT WILL BE PAID

THERE ARE TWO THINGS YOU COULD DO.

1. WRITE IT OFF & PUT INTO BAD DEBTS A/c OR

2. PUT £1290 INTO A PROVISION FOR DOUBTFUL DEBTS

THE ACCOUNTING STANDARD FRS18 HAS A CONCEPT

OF PRUDENCE WHICH MEANS IF YOU HAVE DOUBTS

WHETHER AN AMOUNT IS GOING TO BE PAID OR NOT

THEN YOU MUST ASSUME THAT THE DEBT MIGHT NOT

BE.

AS THE DEBTOR HAS BECOME BANKRUPT IT IS UNLIKELY

THAT THE DEBT WILL BE PAID BACK SO THE AMOUNT

SHOULD BE WRITTEN OFF AS A BAD DEBT UNDER THE

CONCEPT OF PRUDENCE

IF THE DEBT IS IN FACT RECOVERED NEXT YEAR THE

BAD DEBT EXPENSE CAN BE REVERSED IN NEXT YEARS

P+L A/c

Task 1.5, continued

This page is for the continuation of the memo. It will not be needed by all candidates.

BPP PUBLISHING

SECTION 2

You are advised to spend approximately 80 minutes on this section.

NOTE. Clearly show your workings for all tasks.

Data

Scott George is the proprietor of Tiny Tots, a business which manufactures children's clothing. The year end for Tiny Tots is 30 November.

Scott George asks you to produce some information from the following figures for the year ended 30 November 20X1.

- Bank account summary:

	£		£
Opening balance	390	Payment to creditors	97,400
Receipts from debtors	201,010	Production wages	24,000
		Supervisory wages	28,000
		Office wages	15,000
		Factory overheads	10,710
		Office overheads	7,780
		Drawings	18,000
		Closing balance	510
	201,400		201,400

All receipts and payments for the business pass through the bank account.

- Year end balances were:

	30 November 20X0	30 November 20X1
	£	£
Stocks of raw materials	9,800	7,650
Stocks of finished goods	12,540	11,380
Debtors	18,700	21,310
Creditors	14,210	14,890
Factory premises at cost	100,000	100,000
Factory equipment at cost	48,000	48,000

Work-in-progress is to be ignored.

- The depreciation policy for Tiny Tots is:

    - factory premises   2% per annum straight line method
    - factory equipment   10% per annum straight line method

Task 2.1

Calculate the cost of raw materials purchased during the year ended 30 November 20X1.

Creditors

BK	97,400	B/F	14,210
		Purchases	98,080
C/F	14,890		
	112,290		112,290

Task 2.2

Calculate the prime cost of production for the year ended 30 November 20X1.

```
O/s R M              9800
Purchases        98,080
                107,880
c/s               7,650
                100,230
+ prod wages    24,000
                124,230  prime cost
```

Task 2.3

Calculate the total production cost of the finished goods for the year ended 30 November 20X1.

£   £

```
        Prime Cost                        124,230
+   Sup wages            28000
    Factory o/hd's       10,710
    D'PN - F premises     2000
          F Equip         4800
                                           45510
    Total prod cost                       169,740
```

Task 2.4

Calculate the total sales for the year ended 30 November 20X1.

```
                        DEBTORS
    B/f         18700     Banked    201,010

    Sales   203,620      C/F        21310
            222,320                 222,320
```

Task 2.5

Calculate the gross profit for the year ended 30 November 20X1.

	£	£
Sales		203,620
Cost of sales :- O/S F.Goods 12,540		
Total prod cost 169,740		
182,280		
− C/S F.Goods 11,380		
		170,900
GROSS PROFIT		32,720

Task 2.6

Calculate the net profit for the year ended 30 November 20X1.

	£	£
GROSS PROFIT		32,720
LESS Office wages 15,000		
Office o/hds 7,780		
		22,780
NET PROFIT		9940

Task 2.7

Scott George is researching new types of material for the children's clothing. He want to know how this expenditure should be treated in the accounts.

Using the headed paper on Page 275, write a memo to Scott George stating how this expenditure would be shown in the account. Your answer should refer to the appropriate accounting standards.

(NOTE. Two pages have been included for this memo. However, most candidates should find one page sufficient.)

Task 2.7

MEMO

To: Scott George

From: Accounting Technician

Ref:

Date:

SSAP 13 ACCOUNTING FOR RESEARCH & DEVELOPMENT

SSAP 13 RECOGNISING TWO CATEGORIES OF RESEARCH

KNOWN AS PURE & APPLIED RESEARCH. BOTH SHOULD

BE WRITTEN OFF AS AN EXPENSE ON THE P+L A/C IN

THE YEAR THAT IT INCURRED

HOWEVER DEVELOPEMENT EXPENDITURE IS DIFFERANT.

DEVELOPMENT EXPENDITURE IS DUE TO PROVIDE THE BUSINESS

WITH FUTURE BENEFITS IE NEW PRODUCT, PROCESS. SO INITIALLY

SHOULD BE TREATED AS FIXED ASSET ON BAL SHEET &

THEN WRITTEN OFF TO THE P+L A/C WHEN NEW PRODUCT IS

SOLD OR PROCESS COMES INTO OPERATION

AN ACCOUNTING CONCEPT OF PRUDENCE, SSAP 13

STATES FIVE CRITERIA THAT MUST BE MET IF IT IS GOING TO
BE A FIXED ASSET

1) CLEARING DEFINED PROJECT   5) TECHNICALLY FEASIBLE
                                                        & COMMERCIALLY
2) ADEQUATE RESOURCES TO COMPLETE   VIABLE

    EXPENDITURE IS
3) SEPERATELY INDENTIFITABLE

4) REVENUE EXCEEDS THE COSTS

Task 2.7, continued

This page is for the continuation of the memo. It will not be needed by all candidates.

Task 2.8

Scott George tells you that capital expenditure costing less than £50 per item is charged to the overheads account.

(a) **Is this treatment regarded as acceptable accounting practice?**

  (NOTE.) You should circle the most appropriate answer.)

  (Yes) / No

(b) **Briefly explain the reason for your answer, referring to the relevant accounting concept.**

AS THE CAPITAL EXPENDITURE IS SO SMALL THE CONCEPT OF MATERIALITY WOULD ALLOW IT TO BE WRITTEN OFF TO THE P+L A/s AS AN EXPENSE INSTEAD OF BEING SHOWN ON BAL SHEET AS FIX ASSET & DEPRECIATED

PRACTICE CENTRAL ASSESSMENT 4: SLEEP EASY (June 2001)

This central assessment is in TWO sections. You are reminded that competence must be achieved in both sections. You should therefore attempt and aim to complete EVERY task in BOTH sections.

Essential calculations should be included within your answers where appropriate.

You are advised to spend 100 minutes on Section 1 and 80 minutes on Section 2.

SECTION 1

You are advised to spend approximately 100 minutes on this section.

Data

Daniel James is the proprietor of Sleep Easy, a business which buys and sells bedroom furniture.

- The year end is May 20X1.

- You are employed to assist with the bookkeeping.

- The business currently operates a manual system, consisting of a general ledger, a sales ledger and a purchase ledger.

- Double entry takes place in the general ledger. Individual accounts of debtors and creditors are kept in memorandum accounts.

- You use a purchases day book, a sales day book, a purchases returns day book and a sales returns day book. Totals from the day books are transferred into the general ledger.

At the end of the financial year on 31 May 20X1, the balances were extracted from the general ledger and entered into an extended trial balance as shown on Page 279

It was found that the total of the debit column of the trial balance did not agree with the total of the credit column. The difference was posted to a suspense account.

Task 1.1

Make appropriate entries in the adjustment columns of the extended trial balance on Page X to take account of the following.

(a) Depreciation needs to be provided as follows.

    (i)   Motor vehicles: 15% per annum reducing balance method.

    (ii)   Fixtures and fittings: 20% per annum straight line method.

(b) The bank loan was taken out on 1 June 20X0. Interest is charged at 7.5% per annum.

(c) Rent payable is £6,500 per month

(d) The provision for doubtful debts should be adjusted to 5% of the debtors.

(e) Stock was valued at cost on 31 May 20X1 at £98,400.

278

SLEEP EASY
EXTENDED TRIAL BALANCE AS AT 31 MAY 20X1

DESCRIPTION	LEDGER BALANCE		ADJUSTMENTS	
	Debit £	Credit £	Debit £	Credit £
Capital		150,750		
Sales		757,210		
Sales returns	2,850			
Purchases	439,400			
Purchases returns		5,090		
Stock at 1 June 20X0	112,410			
Rent	71,500		6500	
Wages	185,400			
Insurance	6,900			
Motor expenses	10,790			
Motor vehicles (MV) at cost	101,850			
Provision for depreciation (MV)		38,150		9555
Fixtures and fittings (F&F) at cost	31,300			
Provision for depreciation (F&F)		6,330		6260
Drawings	31,000			
Bad debts	2,500			
Provision for doubtful debts		6,050	2111	
Debtors control account	78,780			
Creditors control account		38,220		
Bank	5,680			
VAT		8,800		
Bank loan		60,000		
Bank interest	3,750		750	
Suspense		13,510		
Depreciation			9555 6260 15815	
Closing stock: P&L				98,400
Closing stock: balance sheet			98,400	
Provision for doubtful debts: adjustment				2111
Loan interest owing				750
Other accruals				6500
TOTALS	**1,084,110**	**1,084,110**	123,576	123,576

BPP PUBLISHING

Data

After the preparation of the extended trial balance the following errors were found.

(a) Motor expenses of £150 were debited to the Motor Vehicles at Cost account. Ignore depreciation.

(b) The VAT column in the purchases returns book was undercast by £400.

(c) On 31 May 20X1 some of the fixtures and fittings were sold. The original cost of the assets was £11,000 and they were bought two years ago on 1 June 20W9. Depreciation provision to the date of disposal was made in the accounts. The disposal proceeds were £7,000. This money was correctly entered in the bank account, but no other entry was made.

(d) Sales of £9,500 were entered into the sales account as £5,900. All other entries were correct.

(e) A wages payment of £1,255 was debited to both the wages account and the bank account.

Task 1.2

Prepare the journal entries to record the correction of the errors using the blank journal on Page 281. Dates and narratives are not required.

Task 1.3

Showing clearly the individual debits and credits, update the suspense account using the journals shown in Task 1.2.

SUSPENSE ACCOUNT			
	£		£
	400	Balance b/d	13,510
	7000		
	3600		
	2510		
	13510		13510

JOURNAL		
	Dr £	Cr £
a) MOTOR EXP's	150	
MV @ COST A/C or suspense		150
b) SUSPENSE A/C	400	
VAT A/c		400
DEBIT c) DISPOSAL A/c	11000	
CREDIT FIXTURES & FITTINGS A/c		11000
DEBIT PROVISION FOR D'PN	4400	
CREDIT DISPOSAL A/c		4400
DEBIT SUSPENSE A/c	7000	
CREDIT DISPOSAL A/c		7000
DEBIT DISPOSAL A/c	400	
P+L A/c		400
d) SUSPENSE A/c	3600	
SALES A/c		3600
e) SUSPENSE A/C	2510	
BANK A/c		2510

BPP PUBLISHING

Data

The closing stock figure of £98,400 as at 31 May 20X1 was valued on a FIFO basis. This has always been the policy of Sleep Easy. It was suggested that this stock figure should now be recalculated on a LIFO basis.

Task 1.4

(a) **The prices paid by Sleep Easy for goods have been gradually rising throughout the year. What impact would the suggested change in stock valuation have had on the profit for the year ended 31 May 20X1.**

(Circle the correct answer)

Increase / Decrease / No impact

(b) **Which accounting concept states that a business should not normally change its policy for stock valuation?**

....

Data

Daniel James is considering expanding the business to manufacture bedroom furniture. The following are the estimated figures for the next financial periods.

	£
Direct materials	35,760
Production wages	22,410
Supervisory wages	15,000
Factory overheads	18,080
Office overheads	5,150
Closing stocks of raw materials	3,060
Closing stocks of finished goods	6,900

Ignore work in progress.

Task 1.5

(a) **Calculate the prime cost of production.**

....

....

....

....

....

(b) **Calculate the total cost of production.**

....

....

....

....

SECTION 2

You are advised to spend approximately 80 minutes on this section.

Note. **Clearly show your workings for all tasks.**

Data

Sarah Glass is considering buying a small wholesale business from Hassan Abdul.

Hassan Abdul has provided some financial information for his business, which is set out below and on Page 284.

Assets and liabilities as at 30 April 20X0

	£
Freehold premises at cost	104,000
Less depreciation to date	20,800
	83,200
Fixtures and fittings at cost	22,750
Less depreciation to date	13,650
	9,100
Stock	43,160
Debtors	52,300
Prepaid general expenses	700
Cash	1,000
	97,160
Creditors	46,750
Bank overdraft	22,600
	69,350

SUMMARY OF THE BUSINESS BANK ACCOUNT
FOR THE YEAR ENDED 30 APRIL 20X1

	£		£
Bankings from cash sales	292,180	Opening balance	22,600
Receipts from debtors	722,800	Payments to creditors	789,950
		General expenses	8,110
		Salaries	92,420
		Drawings	36,800
		Closing balance	65,100
	1,014,980		1,014,980

Other information

(a) The profit margin achieved on all sales was 20%.

(b) The value of the closing stock held on 30 April 20X1 is unknown.

(c) Depreciation is calculated as follows.

   •   Premises: 2% per annum on cost

   •   Fixtures and fittings: 10% per annum on cost

(d) All cash is banked at the end of each day, apart from a cash float. During the year, the cash float was decreased from £1,000 to £800.

(e)   On 30 April 20X1 the outstanding balances were:

	£
Creditors	64,100
Debtors	59,020
Accrual for general expenses	210

Sarah Glass has asked you to calculate some key figures for the year ended 30 April 20X1.

Task 2.1

Calculate the total value of the credit sales for the year ended 30 April 20X1.

....

....

....

....

....

Task 2.2

Calculate the total sales for the year ended 30 April 20X1.

....

....

....

....

....

....

....

Task 2.3

Calculate the total value of the purchases for the year ended 30 April 20X1.

....

....

....

....

....

....

....

Task 2.4

Calculate the value of the closing stock held on 30 April 20X1.

....

....

....

....

....

....

Task 2.5

Calculate the net profit made for the year ended 30 April 20X1.

....

....

....

....

....

....

....

....

....

Task 2.6

Show the net book value of the fixed assets held on 30 April 20X1.

....

....

....

....

....

....

Task 2.7

When Sarah Glass looks at your figures, she does not understand why the closing balance in the bank account is different to the net profit shown in Task 2.5

(a) **Give two examples of transactions that affect the profit figure, but do not affect the bank account.**

....

....

....

....

(b) **Give one example of a transaction that affects the bank account, but does not affect the profit figure.**

....

....

....

....

Data

Sarah Glass is considering forming a partnership with her brother who could provide some of the money needed to fund the purchase of the business from Hassan Abdul.

Sarah Glass does not understand how partnerships are shown in accounts. She is worried that the money each partner puts into, and takes out of, the business, will not be shown separately.

Task 2.8

Using the headed paper on Pages 287-288 write a memo to Sarah Glass explaining:

- How partner interests are shown in the financial statements of a partnership

- The difference between the types of accounts that exist

- What types of transactions the different accounts would show

MEMO

To:	Sarah Glass	**Date:**	18 June 20X1
From:	Accounting Technician		
Subject:	Partnership accounts		

BPP PUBLISHING

Task 2.8, continued

This page is for the continuation of the memo. It will not be needed by all candidates.

Trial run central assessment

TRIAL RUN CENTRAL ASSESSMENT

INTERMEDIATE STAGE - NVQ/SVQ3

Unit 5

Maintaining Financial Records

and Preparing Accounts

(December 2001)

The suggested time allowance for this Trial Run Central Assessment is three hours, plus fifteen minutes reading time. You are advised to spend approximately 100 minutes on Section 1 and 80 minutes on Section 2.

Calculators may be used but no reference material is permitted.

**DO NOT OPEN THIS PAPER UNTIL YOU ARE READY TO START
UNDER TIMED CONDITIONS**

TRIAL RUN CENTRAL ASSESSMENT (December 2001)

This central assessment is in TWO sections. You are reminded that competence must be achieved in both sections. You should therefore attempt and aim to complete EVERY TASK in BOTH sections.

Essential calculations should be included within your answers where appropriate.

You are advised to spend 100 minutes on Section 1 and 80 minutes on Section 2.

SECTION 1

You are advised to spend approximately 100 minutes on this section.

Data

Kelly Wainwright is the proprietor of KW Enterprise, a business that buys and sells carpets and other floor coverings.

- The financial year end is 31 October 20X1.

- You are employed by Kelly Wainwright to assist with the bookkeeping.

- The business currently operates a manual system consisting of a general ledger, a sales ledger and a purchase ledger.

- Double entry takes place in the general ledger. Individual accounts of debtors and creditors are kept in memorandum accounts.

- You use a purchases day book, a sales day book, a purchases returns day book and a sales returns day book. Totals from various columns of the day books are transferred into the general ledger.

At the end of the financial year on 31 October 20X1, the balances were extracted from the general ledger and entered in an extended trial balance as shown on Page 294.

It was found that the total of the debit column of the trial balance did not agree with the total of the credit column. The difference was posted to a suspense account.

Task 1.1

Make appropriate entries in the adjustment columns of the extended trial balance on Page 294 to take account of the following.

(a) Depreciation needs to be provided as follows.

    (i)   Motor vehicles: 25% per annum reducing balance method
    (ii)   Fixtures and fittings: 15% per annum straight line method

(b) Rent payable is £3,000 per month

(c) An invoice relating to goods received by KW Enterprise on 29 October 20X1 had not been entered in the accounts. The invoice totalled £2,350, including VAT at 17.5%. The goods have been included in the stock valuation on 31 October 20X1.

(d) Stock was valued at cost on 31 October 20X1 at £30,040. This includes £625 which is the cost of a carpet that is dirty and needs cleaning. The cost of cleaning it will be £50, and the carpet can then be sold for £300.

(e) On reviewing the debtors, Kelly Wainwright decides that £300 should be written off. The provision for doubtful debts should be 4% of the outstanding debtors.

KW ENTERPRISE
TRIAL BALANCE AS AT 31 OCTOBER 20X1

DESCRIPTION	LEDGER BALANCE		ADJUSTMENTS	
	Debit £	*Credit* £	*Debit* £	*Credit* £
Capital		61,280		
Sales		487,360		
Sales returns	8,900			
Purchases	286,330			
Purchases returns		650		
Stock at 1 November 20X0	25,870			
Rent	33,000			
General expenses	87,700			
Motor expenses	28,540			
Bad debts	1,220			
Provision for doubtful debts		3,200		
Motor vehicles (MV) at cost	36,000			
Provision for depreciation (MV)		19,560		
Fixtures and fittings (F&F) at cost	57,020			
Provision for depreciation (F&F)		34,580		
Drawings	30,000			
Debtors control account	56,550			
Creditors control account		31,500		
Bank		2,700		
VAT		10,070		
Suspense		230		
Depreciation				
Provision for doubtful debts: adjustment				
Closing stock: P&L				
Closing stock: balance sheet				
Accruals				
TOTALS	**651,130**	**651,130**		

Data

You have found the following errors.

(a) The VAT column of the sales day book had been undercast by £380.

(b) The Net column of the sales day book had been overcast by £870.

(c) Sales of £5,080 had been transferred from the Total column of the sales day book into the debtors control account as £5,800.

Task 1.2

Prepare journal entries to correct the errors using the blank journal on Page 296. Dates and narratives are not required.

Note. **Do** *not* **adjust your answer to Task 1.1(e).**

Data

On 31 October 20X1 the balances of the accounts in the purchase ledger were listed, totalled and compared with the updated balance in the creditors control account.

The list of balances totalled £33,770. After an investigation, the following errors were found in the list taken from the purchase ledger.

(a) A creditor account with a balance of £290 had been omitted from the list.

(b) A credit purchase of £960 (inclusive of VAT) had been omitted from a creditor's account.

(c) Purchase returns of £80 (inclusive of VAT) had been omitted from a creditor's account.

(d) A payment to a creditor of £500 had been credited to the creditor's account.

(e) A creditor's balance of £780 had been entered in the list as £870.   90

Task 1.3

Enter the appropriate adjustments in the table below. For each adjustment show clearly the amount involved and whether the amount is to be added or subtracted.

£

Total from purchase ledger

Adjustment for (a)   add / subtract

Adjustment for (b)   add / subtract

Adjustment for (c)   add / subtract

Adjustment for (d)   add / subtract

Adjustment for (e)   add / subtract

Revised total to agree with creditors control account

JOURNAL		
	Dr £	Cr £

Task 1.4

Some of the fixtures and fittings used by KW Enterprise were originally purchased on 1 May 20X0 for £8,400. Assume these fixtures and fittings were sold on 1 December 20X1 for £6,000.

(a) What would be the net book value of these fixtures and fittings on the date of disposal if the depreciation is calculated on a monthly basis?

£...

....

(b) What would be the amount of profit or loss on the disposal of the fixtures and fittings?

(Circle the correct answer)

Profit / Loss

£...

....

Task 1.5

The list of balances on Page 294 includes an amount of £10,070 as VAT.

(a) Who will KW Enterprise pay this amount to?

....

(b) Explain how the VAT balance has been arrived at.

....
....
....
....
....
....

Data

- Kelly Wainwright has looked at the work you have done so far on the accounts.

- She is interested in the reconciliation you did between the purchases ledger and the creditors control account.

- She does not understand why you did the reconciliation.

Task 1.6

Using the headed paper on Page 298, write a brief memo to Kelly Wainwright. You memo should include:

- **The purpose of the purchase ledger**

- **Whether the purchase ledger is part of the double entry accounting system**

- **The purpose of the creditors control account**

- Whether the creditors control account is part of the double entry accounting system

- The reasons for doing the reconciliation.

MEMO

To:	Kelly Wainwright	Ref:	Reconciliations
From:	Accounting Technician	Date:	3 December 20X1

Task 1.6, continued

This page is for the continuation of the memo. It will not be needed by all candidates.

SECTION 2

You are advised to spend approximately 80 minutes on this section.

Note. Clearly show your workings for all tasks.

Data

Amit Mall is the treasurer of the local tennis club. He needs to prepare some financial statements and has asked you to help.

The following information is available for the year ended 30 November 20X1.

- The bank account summary shows:

	£		£
Opening balance	850	Bar purchases	6,400
Subscriptions	33,000	Wages	25,500
Bar sales	8,700	General expenses	4,850
Bank loan	5,400	Purchase of land	12,000
Closing balance	800		
	48,750		48,750

- The year end balances are:

	30 November 20X0	31 November 20X1
	£	£
Stock of bar purchases	680	890
Creditors for bar purchases	1,000	540
Subscriptions in arrears	1,000	4,000
Accrual for general expenses	150	250

- 20% of the wages relate to the bar, 80% to other activities.

- 30% of expenses relate to the bar, 70% to other activities.

- The loan was taken out on 1 January 20X1 at the rate of interest of 8% per annum.

- The subscription is £100 per member per year.

Task 2.1

Calculate the purchases made for the bar for the year ended 30 November 20X1.

....

....

....

....

....

....

Task 2.2

Calculate the net profit or loss made from the bar for the year ended 30 November 20X1.

....
....
....
....
....
....
....
....
....
....

Task 2.3

Calculate the total number of members who should have paid a subscription to the tennis club for the year ended 30 November 20X1.

....
....
....
....
....
....
....
....
....
....

Task 2.4

Calculate the surplus or deficit made by the tennis club for the year ended 30 November 20X1.

....
....
....
....
....
....
....
....
....
....

Task 2.5

List the assets and liabilities held by the tennis club on 30 November 20X1.

Assets   £

....
....
....
....
....
....
....

Liabilities   £

....
....
....
....
....
....
....

Task 2.6

The tennis club does not provide depreciation on land. Briefly explain why.

....

....

....

....

....

Data

The Chairperson of the tennis club is reviewing the figures you have prepared. He makes the following points.

- He sees that the income and expenditure account only shows the interest on the loan.

- He cannot understand why the income and expenditure account does not show the loan as income.

- He asks you where the amount of the loan would be shown in the tennis club's accounts.

Task 2.7

On the headed paper on Page 304, write a memo to the Chairperson responding to each of his points.

BPP PUBLISHING

MEMO

To: Chairperson   Date: Loans

From: Accounting Technician   Date: 3 December
20X1

Task 2.8, continued

This page is for the continuation of the memo. It will not be needed by all candidates.

BPP PUBLISHING

Answers to practice activities

CHAPTERS 1-4 ACCOUNTING PRINCIPLES

1   PICTURE THIS CASH BOOK

Task 1, 3 and 5

CASH BOOK: RECEIPTS

Date	Details	Cash	Discount allowed	Sales Ledger Control	Cash sales	VAT	Capital	Interest
		£	£	£	£	£	£	£
20X6								
5 October	Cash/cheques	7,309.83	245.02	6,959.41	305.00	45.42		
9 October	BACS receipt	1,293.94		1,293.94				
12 October	Cash/cheques	2,738.64	67.00	1,212.86	1,298.54	227.24		
17 October	Cash/cheques	800.00		800.00				
24 October	Cash/cheques	5,309.30	278.27	3,663.72	1,400.50	245.08		
31 October	Cheques paid in	6,293.66		6,088.66	174.47	30.53		
		23,745.37	590.29	20,018.59	3,178.51	548.27		
27 October	BACS receipt	5,000.00					5,000.00	
27 October	Interest	459.35						459.35
		29,204.72	590.29	20,018.59	3,178.51	548.27	5,000.00	459.35

CASH BOOK: PAYMENTS

Date	Details	Cheque No	Cash	Discount received	Purchase Ledger Control	Other
20X6			£	£	£	£
1 October	Jedburgh County Council	DD	1,092.87			1,092.87
1 October	Society of Picture Framers	DD	250.00			250.00
2 October	Timbmet Wood Ltd	1397	3,298.93	45.00	3,298.93	
3 October	Glass Products Ltd	1398	5,209.36		5,209.36	
7 October	Lamination Ltd	1399	1,376.84	24.50	1,376.84	
10 October	The Contract Cleaning Co	1400	563.37		563.37	
11 October	Just a Minute Courier Company	1401	357.00		357.00	
12 October	Lynn's Caterers	1402	175.00		175.00	
15 October	Thor Stationery	1403	736.83	13.00	736.83	
16 October	Kinetic Electricity Ltd	DD	200.00			200.00
20 October	High Stick Adhesives	1404	245.09		245.09	
21 October	Big Gas Company Ltd	BACS	150.00			150.00
22 October	Quality Paper Company	1405	1,983.09		1,983.09	
24 October	Glass Ceramics Ltd	1406	3,736.94	51.00	3,736.94	
27 October	Chrome Sheeting Ltd	1407	398.65		398.65	
28 October	Salaries	BACS	3,378.24			3,378.24
			23,152.21	133.50	18,081.10	5,071.11
25 October	ATM withdrawal	Debit card	100.00			100.00
25 October	Debit card payment	Debit card	248.97			248.97
			23,501.18	133.50	18,081.10	5,420.08
	Analysis:					
	Direct labour					3,378.24
	Administration					1,692.87
	Drawings					348.97
						5,420.08

	£
Cash book balance at 1/10/X6	(2,190.87)
Receipts in October	29,204.72
Payments in October	(23,501.18)
	3,512.67

Task 2

Bank reconciliation at 31 October 20X6

	£	£
Balance per bank statement at 31/10/X6		5,010.53
Add outstanding lodgement		6,293.66
Less unpresented cheques:		
1397	3,298.93	
1401	357.00	
1406	3,736.94	
1407	398.65	
		(7,791.52)
Balance per cash book at 31/10/X6		3,512.67
Cash book balance at 1/10/X6		(2,190.87)
Receipts		23,745.37
Payments		(23,152.21)
Cash book balance at 31/10/X6		(1,597.71)
Adjustments to cash book:		
Personal payments by debit card, not recorded in cash book		(248.97)
Cash withdrawal, not recorded in cash book		(100.00)
Receipt from proprietor by BACS, not recorded in cash book		5,000.00
Interest received 31 October		459.35
Amended cash book balance at 31/10/X6		3,512.67

Task 4

MEMO

To: Harry Gold

From: A Student

Date: 1 November 20X6

Re: Items appearing on the bank statement at 31 October 20X6

There are three items appearing on the bank statement that have no supporting documentation, so I hoped you may be able to shed some light on them.

First, there is a BACS receipt on 27 October for £5,000.00 which is stated to be from 'Harry Gold Personal Account'. Please could you confirm the exact nature of this receipt?

Secondly, there is an ATM withdrawal of £100.00 on 25 October, and finally a debit card payment to Siren.com on the same date. Again, could you please confirm the exact nature of these payments?

Thank you.

---

2   TOUCHSTONE CASH BOOK

Task 1, 3 and 4

CASH BOOK: RECEIPTS

Date	Details	Bank	Discount allowed	Sales Ledger Control	Cash sales	VAT	Other
		£	£	£	£	£	£
20X3							
2 Feb	Cheques etc paid in	2,244.27	25.00	1,928.20	269.00	47.07	
6 Feb	Interest paid	54.00					54.00
7 Feb	Cheques etc paid in	3,160.47	19.00	2,298.02	734.00	128.45	
10 Feb	BACS – StraightCall Insurance	200.00					200.00
12 Feb	Cheques etc paid in	1,584.02	14.50	1,290.27	250.00	43.75	
14 Feb	Cheques etc paid in	896.28		896.28			
17 Feb	Cheques etc paid in	3,746.95	65.00	3,291.29	387.80	67.86	
21 Feb	Cheques etc paid in	4,887.27	32.00	4,182.27	600.00	105.00	
23 Feb	Cheques etc paid in	582.33		582.33			
28 Feb	Cheques etc paid in	8,539.54	15.00	8,209.54	280.86	49.14	
		25,895.13	170.50	22,678.20	2,521.66	441.27	254.00
25 Feb	BACS receipt – Assignia plc	6,283.02		6,283.02			
		32,178.15	170.50	28,961.22	2,521.66	441.27	254.00
Analysis	Disposals						200.00
	Interest						54.00
							254.00

BPP PUBLISHING

CASH BOOK: PAYMENTS

Date	Details	Cheque No	Bank	Discount received	Purchase Ledger Control	Other
20X3			£	£	£	£
1 Feb	South Oxon Council (rates)	DD	231.50			231.50
1 Feb	Thanet Pension Fund (rent)	DD	500.00			500.00
2 Feb	Drake Bicycles	6295	2,638.39	20.00	2,638.39	
3 Feb	David Lett Shopfitting	6296	4,029.38	55.00	4,029.38	
7 Feb	Sama Newsagents	6297	176.93		176.93	
10 Feb	Mike Cuthbertson - drawings	S/O	3,000.00			3,000.00
11 Feb	Essex Cycles	6298	2,378.49	35.00	2,378.49	
12 Feb	Firebrand Tyres	6299	1,287.35	10.00	1,287.35	
15 Feb	Patrick's Pumps	6300	1,243.66		1,243.66	
16 Feb	South Oxon Council (waste collection)	DD	35.00			35.00
20 Feb	Crutchleys Accountants (fees)	6301	235.00		235.00	
21 Feb	Lurrells & Co (fees)	6302	293.75		293.75	
22 Feb	Heartlands Electric	DD	150.00			150.00
24 Feb	Midland Gas	DD	90.00			90.00
27 Feb	Salaries	BACS	4,622.12			4,622.12
			20,911.57	120.00	12,282.95	8,628.62
25 Feb	Handley & Co – cheque returned unpaid		352.50			352.50
25 Feb	ATM withdrawal		200.00			200.00
			21,464.07	120.00	12,282.95	9,181.12
	Analysis:					
	Sales ledger control					352.50
	Staff costs					4,622.12
	Administration/ overheads					1,006.50
	Drawings					3,200.00
						9,181.12

Task 2

Bank reconciliation at 28 February 20X3

	£	£
Balance per bank statement at 28/2/X3		15,810.22
Add outstanding lodgement		8,539.54
Less unpresented cheques:		
6297	176.93	
6298	2,378.49	
6301	235.00	
6302	293.75	
		(3,084.17)
Balance per cash book at 28/2/X3		21,256.39
Cash book balance at 1/2/X3		10,542.51
Receipts		25,895.13
Payments		(20,911.57)
Cash book balance at 28/2/X3		15,526.07
Adjustments to cash book:		
Cheque returned unpaid – Handley & Co		(352.50)
ATM withdrawal		(200.00)
BACS receipt – Assignia plc		6,283.02
Amended cash book balance at 31/10/X3		21,256.59

BPP PUBLISHING

Task 5

ADMINISTRATION/OVERHEADS					
Date	**Details**	**Amount £**	**Date**	**Details**	**Amount £**
20X3			20X3		
28/2	Cash book	1,006.50			

BANK					
Date	**Details**	**Amount £**	**Date**	**Details**	**Amount £**
20X3			20X3		
1/2	Balance b/d	10,542.51	28/2	February payments	21,464.07
28/2	February receipts	32,178.15	28/2	Balance c/d	21,256.59
		42,720.66			42,720.66

DISCOUNT ALLOWED AND RECEIVED					
Date	**Details**	**Amount £**	**Date**	**Details**	**Amount £**
20X3			20X3		
28/2	Discount allowed	170.50	28/2	Discount received	120.00

DISPOSALS					
Date	**Details**	**Amount £**	**Date**	**Details**	**Amount £**
20X3			20X3		
			28/2	Insurance receipt	200.00

DRAWINGS					
Date	**Details**	**Amount £**	**Date**	**Details**	**Amount £**
20X3			20X3		
28/2	February drawings	3,200.00			

INTEREST RECEIVED					
Date	Details	Amount £	Date	Details	Amount £
20X3			20X3		
			28/2	Interest received	54.00

PURCHASE LEDGER CONTROL					
Date	Details	Amount £	Date	Details	Amount £
20X3			20X3		
28/2	Cash paid	12,282.95			
28/2	Discount received	120.00			

SALES					
Date	Details	Amount £	Date	Details	Amount £
20X3			20X3		
			28/2	Cash sales	2,521.66

SALES LEDGER CONTROL					
Date	Details	Amount £	Date	Details	Amount £
20X3			20X3		
28/2	Cheque returned unpaid	352.50	28/2	Cash received	28,961.22
			28/2	Discount allowed	170.50

STAFF COSTS					
Date	Details	Amount £	Date	Details	Amount £
20X3			20X3		
28/2	February salaries	4,622.12			

VAT					
Date	Details	Amount £	Date	Details	Amount £
20X3			20X3		
			28/2	Cash sales	441.27

3   **TRURO LEDGER**

Task 1

CASH BOOK: RECEIPTS

Date	Details	Cash £	Discount allowed £	Sales Ledger Control £	Interest £
20X5					
1 Jan	Cheques received	3,109.26	45.00	3,109.26	
3 Jan	Cheques received	4,289.20	60.00	4,289.20	
7 Jan	Cheques received	1,901.82		1,901.82	
11 Jan	Cheques received	5,298.20	15.00	5,298.20	
13 Jan	BACS receipt	4,265.26		4,265.26	
17 Jan	Cheques received	2,198.02	11.00	2,198.02	
21 Jan	Cheques received	3,294.11		3,294.11	
25 Jan	BACS receipt	1,278.34	7.00	1,278.34	
30 Jan	Cheques received	7,289.52	65.00	7,289.52	
31 Jan	Interest credited	103.00			103.00
		33,026.73	203.00	32,923.73	103.00

CASH BOOK: PAYMENTS

Date	Details	Cheque No	Cash	Discount received	Purchase Ledger Control	Other
20X5			£	£	£	£
1 Jan	Mr G Formwell	7421	1,910.26	12.00	1,910.26	
4 Jan	Ms S Parker	7422	2,877.46		2,877.46	
8 Jan	Jensen Ltd	7423	7,209.45	52.50	7,209.45	
12 Jan	Norton Motors Ltd (new car)	7425	15,000.00	100.00		15,000.00
12 Jan	Mr J Jones drawings	DD	2,000.00			2,000.00
18 Jan	Tremayne Holdings plc	7426	263.29		263.29	
20 Jan	Kerrier District Council (rates)	DD	350.00		350.00	
24 Jan	Westworld Computers Ltd	7427	638.23		638.23	
29 Jan	Quest plc	7428	2,190.63	32.00	2,190.63	
31 Jan	Salaries	BACS	7,092.87			7,092.87
			39,532.19	196.50	15,439.32	24,092.87

MONTH ENDED 31 JANUARY 20X5

Purchases Day Book	£
Administration	1,298.02
Warehouse overheads	2,892.19
Despatch	2,817.29
Marketing	3,198.29
VAT	1,786.01
Total value of invoices	11,991.80

Sales Day Book	£
Sales invoices	20,189.73
VAT	3,533.20
Total value of invoices	23,722.93

Purchases Returns Day Book	£
Administration	0.00
Warehouse overheads	0.00
Despatch	192.64
Marketing	32.00
VAT	39.31
Total value of credit notes	263.95

MONTH ENDED 31 JANUARY 20X5

Sales Returns Day Book	£
Sales credit notes	200.00
VAT	35.00
Total value of credit notes	235.00

Task 2 and 5

ADMINISTRATION					
Date	Details	Amount £	Date	Details	Amount £
20X5			20X5		
31/1	PDB	1,298.02			

CASH					
Date	Details	Amount £	Date	Details	Amount £
20X5			20X5		
31/1	CB	33,026.73	31/1	CB	39,532.19

DESPATCH					
Date	Details	Amount £	Date	Details	Amount £
20X5			20X5		
31/1	PDB	2,817.29	31/1	PRDB	192.64

DISCOUNTS ALLOWED AND RECEIVED					
Date	Details	Amount £	Date	Details	Amount £
20X5			20X5		
31/1	CB	203.00	31/1	CB	196.50
31/1		270.00			

DRAWINGS					
Date	Details	Amount £	Date	Details	Amount £
20X5			20X5		
31/1	CB	2,000.00			

INTEREST RECEIVED

Date	Details	Amount £	Date	Details	Amount £
20X5			20X5		
			31/1	CB	103.00

MARKETING

Date	Details	Amount £	Date	Details	Amount £
20X5			20X5		
31/1	PDB	3,198.29	31/1	PRDB	32.00
31/1	Journal	742.13			

MOTOR VEHICLES

Date	Details	Amount £	Date	Details	Amount £
20X5			20X5		
31/1	CB	15,000.00			

PURCHASE LEDGER CONTROL

Date	Details	Amount £	Date	Details	Amount £
20X5			20X5		
31/1	PRDB	263.95	31/1	Balance b/d	19,190.62
31/1	CB	196.50	31/1	PDB	11,991.80
31/1	CB	15,439.32			
31/1	Balance c/d	15,282.65			
		31,182.42			31,182.42
31/1	Journal	582.45	31/1	Balance b/d	15,282.65
31/1	Balance c/d	15,842.20	31/1	Journal	872.00
			31/1	Journal	270.00
		16,424.65			16,424.65

SALARIES					
Date	**Details**	**Amount £**	**Date**	**Details**	**Amount £**
20X5			**20X5**		
31/1	CB	7,092.87			

SALES					
Date	**Details**	**Amount £**	**Date**	**Details**	**Amount £**
20X5			**20X5**		
31/1	SRDB	200.00	31/1	SDB	20,189.73
31/1	Journal	1,225.54			
31/1	Journal	900.00			

SALES LEDGER CONTROL					
Date	**Details**	**Amount £**	**Date**	**Details**	**Amount £**
20X5			**20X5**		
31/1	Balance b/d	40,563.29	31/1	SRDB	235.00
31/1	SDB	23,722.93	31/1	CB	203.00
			31/1	CB	32,923.73
			31/1	Balance c/d	30,924.49
		64,286.22			64,286.22
31/1	Balance b/d	30,924.49	31/1	Journal	1,440.00
			31/1	Journal	582.45
			31/1	Journal	900.00
			31/1	Balance c/d	28,002.04
		30,924.49			30,924.49

VAT					
Date	**Details**	**Amount £**	**Date**	**Details**	**Amount £**
20X5			**20X5**		
31/1	PDB	1,786.01	31/1	SDB	3,533.20
31/1	SRDB	35.00	31/1	PRDB	39.31
31/1	Journal	214.46			
31/1	Journal	129.87			

WAREHOUSE OVERHEADS					
Date	Details	Amount £	Date	Details	Amount £
20X5			**20X5**		
31/1	PDB	2,892.19			

Task 3

Debtors' reconciliation

	£
Balance per sales ledger control account	30,924.49
Less overcast of January SDB invoice totals	(900.00)
Invoice total duplicated in SDB	(1,440.00)
Contra on account of Tremayne Holdings plc with Purchase Ledger	(582.45)
	28,002.04
Total sales ledger balances brought down	28,242.04
Less posting of cash received £120.00 to wrong side (DR) of Nelson Ltd account	(240.00)
	28,002.04

Creditors' reconciliation

	£
Balance per purchase ledger control account	15,282.65
Add undercast of January PDB invoice totals	270.00
Invoice total missing in PDB	872.00
Contra on account of Tremayne Holdings plc with Sales Ledger	(582.45)
	15,842.20
Total purchase ledger balances brought down	16,934.55
Less duplicated invoice posted to Harrier Ltd purchase ledger account	(1,092.35)
	15,842.20

Task 4

Journal

Date 20X5	Account names and narrative	Debit £	Credit £
31/1	Sales (1,440.00 × 40/47)	1,225.54	
	VAT (1,440.00 × 7/47)	214.46	
	Sales ledger control		1,440.00
	Purchase ledger control	582.45	
	Sales ledger control		582.45
	Sales ledger control		900.00
	Sales	900.00	
	Being correction of errors in sales ledger control account		
	Marketing (872.00 × 40/47)	742.13	
	VAT (872.00 × 7/47)	129.87	
	Purchase ledger control		872.00
	Purchase ledger control		270.00
	Despatch	270.00	
	Being correction of errors in purchase ledger control account		

4   GREEN LEDGER

Task 1 and 4

ADMINISTRATION AND MARKETING					
Date	Details	Amount £	Date	Details	Amount £
20X1			20X1		
1/4	Balance b/d	32,290.29	30/4	Balance c/d	40,381.95
30/4	Cash book	5,982.38			
30/4	PDB	2,109.28			
		40,381.95			40,381.95
30/4	Balance b/d	40,381.95			

CAPITAL					
Date	**Details**	**Amount** **£**	**Date**	**Details**	**Amount** **£**
20X1			**20X1**		
30/4	Balance c/d	50,000.00	1/4	Balance b/d	50,000.00
		50,000.00			50,000.00
			30/4	Balance b/d	50,000.00

CASH					
Date	**Details**	**Amount** **£**	**Date**	**Details**	**Amount** **£**
20X1			**20X1**		
30/4	Cash book	61,947.68	¼	Balance b/d	2,398.20
			30/4	Cash book	45,461.99
			30/4	Balance c/d	14,087.49
		61,947.68			61,947.68
30/4	Balance b/d	14,087.49			

DISCOUNTS ALLOWED AND RECEIVED					
Date	**Details**	**Amount** **£**	**Date**	**Details**	**Amount** **£**
20X1			**20X1**		
¼	Balance b/d	375.29	30/4	Cash book	636.00
30/4	Cash book	653.00	30/4	Balance c/d	392.29
		1,028.29			1,028.29
30/4	Balance c/d	392.29			

DRAWINGS					
Date	**Details**	**Amount** **£**	**Date**	**Details**	**Amount** **£**
20X1			**20X1**		
¼	Balance b/d	15,000.00			
30/4	Cash book	3,000.00	30/4	Balance c/d	18,000.00
		18,000.00			18,000.00
30/4	Balance b/d	18,000.00			

FACTORY LABOUR					
Date	Details	Amount £	Date	Details	Amount £
20X1			**20X1**		
1/4	Balance b/d	43,529.18			
30/4	Cash book	7,209.86	30/4	Balance c/d	50,739.04
		50,739.04			50,739.04
30/4	Balance b/d	50,739.04	30/4	Journal	270.00
			30/4	Balance c/d	50,469.04
		50,739.04			50,739.04
30/4	Balance c/d	50,469.04			

FACTORY OVERHEADS					
Date	Details	Amount £	Date	Details	Amount £
20X1			**20X1**		
1/4	Balance b/d	28,254.38	30/4	Cash book	123.95
30/4	PDB	1,290.38	30/4	PRDB	139.25
			30/4	Balance c/d	29,281.56
		29,544.76			29,544.76
30/4	Balance b/d	29,281.56			

FIXED ASSETS (NBV)					
Date	Details	Amount £	Date	Details	Amount £
20X1			**20X1**		
1/4	Balance b/d	32,100.10	30/4	Balance c/d	32,100.10
		32,100.10			32,100.10
30/4	Balance b/d	32,100.10			

INTEREST PAID					
Date	**Details**	**Amount £**	**Date**	**Details**	**Amount £**
20X1			**20X1**		
1/4	Balance b/d	1,920.27	30/4	Balance c/d	2,150.27
30/4	Cash book	230.00			
		2,150.27			2,150.27
30/4	Balance b/d	2,150.27			

LOAN					
Date	**Details**	**Amount £**	**Date**	**Details**	**Amount £**
20X1			**20X1**		
30/4	Balance c/d	15,000.00	1/4	Balance b/d	15,000.00
		15,000.00			15,000.00
			30/4	Balance b/d	15,000.00

PURCHASE LEDGER CONTROL					
Date	**Details**	**Amount £**	**Date**	**Details**	**Amount £**
20X1			**20X1**		
30/4	Cash book	636.00	1/4	Balance b/d	25,131.14
30/4	Cash book	29,039.75	30/4	PDB	14,948.21
30/4	PRDB	1,320.07			
30/4	Balance c/d	9,083.53			
		40,079.35			40,079.35
			30/4	Balance b/d	9,083.53
30/4	Balance c/d	9,263.53	30/4	Journal	180.00
		9,263.53			9,263.53
			30/4	Balance b/d	9,263.53

RAW MATERIALS

Date	Details	Amount £	Date	Details	Amount £
20X1			20X1		
1/4	Balance b/d	80,265.35	30/4	PRDB	984.22
30/4	PDB	9,365.47			
			30/4	Balance c/d	88,646.60
		89,630.82			89,630.82
30/4	Balance b/d	88,646.60			

SALES

Date	Details	Amount £	Date	Details	Amount £
20X1			20X1		
30/4	SRDB	2,673.36	1/4	Balance b/d	215,189.19
			30/4	SDB	35,864.86
30/4	Balance c/d	248,380.69			
		251,054.05			251,054.05
			30/4	Balance b/d	248,380.69

SALES LEDGER CONTROL

Date	Details	Amount £	Date	Details	Amount £
20X1			20X1		
1/4	Balance b/d	67,585.12	30/4	Cash book	653.00
30/4	SDB	42,141.21	30/4	Cash book	61,823.73
			30/4	SRDB	3,141.19
			30/4	Balance c/d	44,108.41
		109,726.33			109,726.33
30/4	Balance b/d	44,108.41	30/4	Journal	1,191.38
			30/4	Balance c/d	42,917.03
		44,108.41			44,108.41
30/4	Balance b/d	42,917.03			

STOCK					
Date	**Details**	**Amount £**	**Date**	**Details**	**Amount £**
20X1			**20X1**		
1/4	Balance b/d	10,198.19			
			30/4	Balance c/d	10,198.19
		10,198.19			10,198.19
30/4	Balance b/d	10,198.19			

SUSPENSE					
Date	**Details**	**Amount £**	**Date**	**Details**	**Amount £**
20X1			**20X1**		
30/4	Journal	1,641.38	30/4	Balance	1,641.38

VAT					
Date	**Details**	**Amount £**	**Date**	**Details**	**Amount £**
20X1			**20X1**		
30/4	PDB	2,183.08	1/4	Balance b/d	2,158.26
30/4	SRDB	467.83	30/4	SDB	6,276.35
			30/4	PRDB	196.60
30/4	Balance c/d	5,980.30			
		8,631.21			8,631.21
			30/4	Balance b/d	5,980.30

Task 2

	Trial Balance	
	£	£
Administration and marketing	40,381.95	
Capital		50,000.00
Cash	14,087.49	
Discount allowed and received	392.29	
Drawings	18,000.00	
Factory labour	50,739.04	
Factory overheads	29,281.56	
Fixed assets (NBV)	32,100.10	
Interest paid	2,150.27	
Loan		15,000.00
Purchase ledger control		9,083.53
Raw materials	88,646.60	
Sales		248,380.69
Sales ledger control	44,108.41	
Stock	10,198.19	
Suspense		1,641.38
VAT		5,980.30
	330,085.90	**330,085.90**

Task 3

Journal

Date 20X1	Account names and narrative	Debit £	Credit £
30/4	Suspense	1,641.38	
	Factory labour		270.00
	Purchase ledger control		180.00
	Sales ledger control		1,191.38
	Being correction of errors in brought forward balances		

Task 5

	Trial Balance	
	£	£
Administration and marketing	40,381.95	
Capital		50,000.00
Cash	14,087.49	
Discount allowed and received	392.29	
Drawings	18,000.00	
Factory labour	50,469.04	
Factory overheads	29,281.56	
Fixed assets (NBV)	32,100.10	
Interest paid	2,150.27	
Loan		15,000.00
Purchase ledger control		9,263.53
Raw materials	88,646.60	
Sales		248,380.69
Sales ledger control	42,917.03	
Stock	10,198.19	
Suspense		
VAT		5,980.30
	328,624.52	**328,624.52**

BPP PUBLISHING

CHAPTER 5 CAPITAL ACQUISITION AND DISPOSAL

5   FINBAR'S FIXED ASSETS

Task 1

FIXED ASSET REGISTER

Description/serial no	Date acquired	Original cost £	Depreciation £	NBV £	Funding method	Disposal proceeds £	Disposal date
Office and shop equipment							
Depreciation: 20% p.a. on cost (straight line basis)							
Computer	1/9/X1	3,000.00			Cash		
Year ended 31/8/X2			600.00	2,400.00			
Year ended 31/8/X3			600.00	1,800.00			
Year ended 31/8/X4			600.00	1,200.00			
Printer and photocopier	1/9/X1	2,000.00			Cash		
Year ended 31/8/X2			400.00	1,600.00			
Year ended 31/8/X3			400.00	1,200.00			
Year ended 31/8/X4			400.00	800.00			
Fax machine	30/9/X1	800.00			Cash		
Year ended 31/8/X2			160.00	640.00			
Year ended 31/8/X3			160.00	480.00			
Year ended 31/8/X4			160.00	320.00			
Chiller cabinets	1/4/X2	7,000.00			Cash		
Year ended 31/8/X2			1,400.00	5,600.00			
Year ended 31/8/X3			1,400.00	4,200.00			
Year ended 31/8/X4			1,400.00	2,800.00			
Till	1/9/X2	5,000.00			Cash	200.00	31/8/X4
Year ended 31/8/X3			1,000.00	4,000.00			
NBV at 31/8/X4 c/f				**5,120.00**			

FIXED ASSET REGISTER

Description/serial no	Date acquired	Original cost £	Depreciation £	NBV £	Funding method	Disposal proceeds £	Disposal date
Office and shop equipment							
Depreciation: 20% p.a. on cost (straight line basis)							
Security shutters	30/9/X1	6,000.00			Cash		
Year ended 31/8/X2			1,200.00	4,800.00			
Year ended 31/8/X3			1,200.00	3,600.00			
Year ended 31/8/X4			1,200.00	2,400.00			
Desk	31/8/X4	800.00			Cash		
Year ended 31/8/X4			160.00	640.00			
Computerised till	31/8/X4	3,500.00			Cash		
Year ended 31/8/X4			700.00	2,800.00			
NBV at 31/8/X4				5,840.00			
NBV at 31/8/X4 b/f				5,120.00			
NBV at 31/8/X4				10,960.00			

FIXED ASSET REGISTER

Description/serial no	Date acquired	Original cost £	Depreciation £	NBV £	Funding method	Disposal proceeds £	Disposal date
Butchery equipment							
20% p.a. on net book value (reducing balance basis)							
Workbenches (6)	1/9/X1	6,000.00			Cash		
Year ended 31/8/X2			1,200.00	4,800.00			
Year ended 31/8/X3			960.00	3,840.00			
Year ended 31/8/X4			768.00	3,072.00			
Grinding machine	1/9/X1	3,600.00			Cash		
Year ended 31/8/X2			720.00	2,880.00			
Year ended 31/8/X3			576.00	2,304.00			
Year ended 31/8/X4			460.80	1,843.20			
Slicer	1/9/X1	2,350.00			Cash		
Year ended 31/8/X2			470.00	1,880.00			
Year ended 31/8/X3			376.00	1,504.00			
Year ended 31/8/X4			300.80	1,203.20			
Freezer (600 cu ft)	1/9/X2	9,000.00			Cash		
Year ended 31/8/X3			1,800.00	7,200.00			
Year ended 31/8/X4			1,440.00	5,760.00			
Freezer (1,200 cu ft)	31/8/X4	15,500.00			Cash		
Year ended 31/8/X4			3,100.00	12,400.00			
NBV at 31/8/X4				**24,278.40**			

FIXED ASSET REGISTER

Description/serial no	Date acquired	Original cost £	Depreciation £	NBV £	Funding method	Disposal proceeds £	Disposal date
Delivery vehicles							
25% p.a. on cost (straight line basis)							
Van TY61 CVB	1/4/X2	15,000.00			Cash		
Year ended 31/8/X2			3,750.00	11,250.00			
Year ended 31/8/X3			3,750.00	7,500.00			
Year ended 31/8/X4			3,750.00	3,750.00			
Van GH62 UYT	1/5/X3	12,000.00			Cash		
Year ended 31/8/X3			3,000.00	9,000.00			
Year ended 31/8/X4			3,000.00	6,000.00			
Van TY72 BNM	1/1/X4	11,500.00			Cash		
Year ended 31/8/X4			2,875.00	8,625.00			
NBV at 31/8/X4				18,375.00			

Answers to practice activities

Journal 1

Date 20X4	Account names and narrative	Debit £	Credit £
31/8	Butchery equipment (cost)	15,500.00	
	Office and shop equipment (cost)	4,300.00	
	VAT	3,410.75	
	Sundry creditors		23,210.75
	Being new fixed assets acquired at 31 August		

Task 2

Journal 2

Date 20X4	Account names and narrative	Debit £	Credit £
31/8	Suspense	200.00	
	Disposals		200.00
	Office and shop equipment (accumulated depreciation)	1,000.00	
	Disposals		1,000.00
	Disposals	5,000.00	
	Office and shop equipment (cost)		5,000.00
	Being disposal of the old till		

Task 3

Journal 3

Date 20X4	Account names and narrative	Debit £	Credit £
31/8	Depreciation charge	20,314.60	
	Office and shop equipment: Accumulated depreciation (600.00 + 400.00 + 160.00 + 1,400.00 + 1,200.00 + 160.00 + 700.00))		4,620.00
	Butchery equipment: Accumulated depreciation (768.00 + 460.80 + 300.80 + 1,440.00 + 3,100.00)		6,069.60
	Delivery vehicles: Accumulated depreciation (3,750.00 + 3,000.00 + 2,875.00)		9,625.00
	Being depreciation for the year		

Task 4

BUTCHERY EQUIPMENT (ACCUMULATED DEPRECIATION)					
Date	Details	Amount £	Date	Details	Amount £
20X4			20X4		
			31/8	Balance b/d	6,102.00
31/8	Balance c/d	12,171.60	31/8	Journal 3	6,069.60
		12,171.60			12,171.00

BUTCHERY EQUIPMENT (COST)					
Date	Details	Amount £	Date	Details	Amount £
20X4			20X4		
31/8	Balance b/d	20,950.00			
31/8	Journal 1	15,500.00	31/8	Balance c/d	36,450.00
		36,450.00			36,450.00

DELIVERY VEHICLES (ACCUMULATED DEPRECIATION)					
Date	Details	Amount £	Date	Details	Amount £
20X4			20X4		
			31/8	Balance b/d	10,500.00
31/8	Balance c/d	20,125.00	31/8	Journal 3	9,625.00
		20,125.00			20,125.00

DELIVERY VEHICLES (COST)					
Date	Details	Amount £	Date	Details	Amount £
20X4			20X4		
31/8	Balance b/d	38,500.00	31/8	Balance c/d	38,500.00

DEPRECIATION CHARGE					
Date	Details	Amount £	Date	Details	Amount £
20X4			20X4		
31/8	Journal 3	20,314.60			

DISPOSALS					
Date	Details	Amount £	Date	Details	Amount £
20X4			20X4		
31/8	Journal 2	5,000.00	31/8	Journal 2	200.00
			31/8	Journal 2	1,000.00

OFFICE AND SHOP EQUIPMENT (ACCUMULATED DEPRECIATION)					
Date	Details	Amount £	Date	Details	Amount £
20X4			20X4		
31/8	Journal 2	1,000.00	31/8	Balance b/d	8,520.00
31/8	Balance c/d	12,140.00	31/8	Journal 3	4,620.00
		13,140.00			13,140.00

OFFICE AND SHOP EQUIPMENT (COST)					
Date	Details	Amount £	Date	Details	Amount £
20X4			20X4		
31/8	Balance b/d	23,800.00	31/8	Journal 2	5,000.00
31/8	Journal 1	4,300.00	31/8	Balance c/d	23,100.00
		28,100.00			28,100.00

SUNDRY CREDITORS					
Date	Details	Amount £	Date	Details	Amount £
20X4			20X4		
			31/8	Journal 1	23,210.75

SUSPENSE					
Date	Details	Amount £	Date	Details	Amount £
20X4			20X4		
31/8	Journal 2	200.00	31/8	Balance b/d	200.00

VAT					
Date	Details	Amount £	Date	Details	Amount £
20X4			20X4		
31/8	Journal 1	3,410.75			

Task 5

Balances per general ledger accounts:

	Cost £	Accumulated depreciation £	Net book value per fixed asset register £
Butchery equipment	36,450.00	12,171.60	24,278.40
Office and shop equipment	23,100.00	12,140.00	10,960.00
Delivery vehicles	38,500.00	20,125.00	18,375.00

6 NORTHMOOR'S FIXED ASSETS

FIXED ASSET REGISTER

Description/serial no	Date acquired	Original cost £	Depreciation £	NBV £	Funding method	Disposal proceeds £	Disposal date
Showroom and office equipment							
Depreciation: 25% p.a. on cost (straight line basis)							
Display pedestals (5 in total)	1/4/X5	3,000.00			Cash		
Year ended 31/3/X6			750.00	2,250.00			
Year ended 31/3/X7			750.00	1,500.00			
Year ended 31/3/X8			750.00	750.00			
Reception sofas	30/9/X6	2,500.00			Cash		
Year ended 31/3/X7			625.00	1,875.00			
Year ended 31/3/X8			625.00	1,250.00			
Coffee vending machine	30/9/X6	1,800.00			Cash		
Year ended 31/3/X7			450.00	1,350.00			
Year ended 31/3/X8			450.00	900.00			
Team PC	1/4/X5	3,500.00			Cash	1,000.00	31/3/X8
Year ended 31/3/X6			875.00	2,625.00			
Year ended 31/3/X7			875.00	1,750.00			
Dingly PC	30/9/X6	4,000.00			Cash		
Year ended 31/3/X7			1,000.00	3,000.00			
Year ended 31/3/X8			1,000.00	2,000.00			

FIXED ASSET REGISTER

Description/serial no	Date acquired	Original cost £	Depreciation £	NBV £	Funding method	Disposal proceeds £	Disposal date
Showroom and office equipment							
Depreciation: 25% p.a. on cost (straight line basis)							
Laser printer	30/9/X6	1,500.00			Cash		
Year ended 31/3/X7			375.00	1,125.00			
Year ended 31/3/X8			375.00	750.00			
Photocopier	30/9/X5	2,100.00			Cash		
Year ended 31/3/X6			525.00	1,575.00			
Year ended 31/3/X7			525.00	1,050.00			
Year ended 31/3/X8			525.00	525.00			
Dingly laptop	31/3/X8	1,400.00			Cash		
Year ended 31/3/X8			350.00	1,050.00			

FIXED ASSET REGISTER

Description/serial no	Date acquired	Original cost £	Depreciation £	NBV £	Funding method	Disposal proceeds £	Disposal date
Workshop equipment							
20% p.a. on net book value (reducing balance basis)							
Ramp (3 metre)	1/4/X5	500.00			Cash		
Year ended 31/3/X6			100.00	400.00			
Year ended 31/3/X7			80.00	320.00			
Year ended 31/3/X8			64.00	256.00			
Diagnostic machine	1/4/X5	15,000.00			Cash		
Year ended 31/3/X6			3,000.00	12,000.00			
Year ended 31/3/X7			2,400.00	9,600.00			
Year ended 31/3/X8			1,920.00	7,680.00			
Service equipment	1/4/X5	21,000.00			Cash		
Year ended 31/3/X6			4,200.00	16,800.00			
Year ended 31/3/X7			3,360.00	13,440.00			
Year ended 31/3/X8			2,688.00	10,752.00			
Ramp (4 metre)	31/3/X8	1,100.00			Cash		
Year ended 31/3/X8			220.00	880.00			

FIXED ASSET REGISTER

Description/serial no	Date acquired	Original cost £	Depreciation £	NBV £	Funding method	Disposal proceeds £	Disposal date
Breakdown vehicles							
15% p.a. on cost (reducing balance basis)							
Tow truck RT21 GHJ	1/4/X5	32,000.00			Cash		
Year ended 31/3/X6			4,800.00	27,200.00			
Year ended 31/3/X7			4,080.00	23,120.00			
Year ended 31/3/X8			3,468.00	19,652.00			
Tow truck RT22 DFG	1/5/X5	35,000.00			Cash		
Year ended 31/3/X6			5,250.00	29,750.00			
Year ended 31/3/X7			4,462.50	25,287.50			
Year ended 31/3/X8			3,793.12	21,494.38			

Journal 1

Date 20X8	Account names and narrative	Debit £	Credit £
31/3	DEBIT Fixed assets: showroom and office equipment	1,400.00	
	DEBIT Fixed assets: workshop equipment	1,100.00	
	DEBIT VAT (245.00 + 192.50)	437.50	
	CREDIT Sundry creditors		2,937.50
	Being recording of fixed assets acquired in March 20X8		

Task 2

Journal 2

Date 20X8	Account names and narrative	Debit £	Credit £
31/3	DEBIT Accumulated depreciation: showroom and office equipment	1,750.00	
	CREDIT Disposals		1,750.00
	DEBIT Disposals	3,500.00	
	CREDIT Fixed assets: showroom and office equipment		3,500.00
	DEBIT Sundry debtors	1,000.00	
	CREDIT Disposals		1,000.00
	Being recording of disposal of Team computer in general ledger		

Task 3

Journal 3

Date 20X8	Account names and narrative	Debit £	Credit £
31/3	DEBIT Depreciation charge (showroom and office equipment) (750.00 + 625.00 + 450.00 + 1,000.00 + 375.00 + 525.00 + 350.00)	4,075.00	
	DEBIT Depreciation charge (workshop equipment) (64.00 + 1,920.00 + 2,688.00 + 220.00)	4,892.00	
	DEBIT Depreciation charge (breakdown vehicles) (3,468.00 + 3,793.12)	7,261.12	
	CREDIT Factory equipment: accumulated depreciation		4,075.00
	CREDIT Office equipment: accumulated depreciation		4,892.00
	CREDIT Motor vehicles: accumulated depreciation		7,261.12
	Being depreciation for the year		

Chapters 6-11 Final accounts

7   MELANIE LANCTON

Task 1

DEBTORS CONTROL A/C				
	£			£
1 June 20X5 Balance b/f	39,470	Cash from debtors		863,740
Credit sales (balance)	872,010	Bad debts written off		2,340
		31 May 20X6 Balance c/f		45,400
	911,480			911,480

Task 2

	£
Credit sales (see above)	872,010
Cash sales	147,890
Adjustment to float	100
	1,020,000

Task 3

CREDITORS CONTROL A/C				
	£			£
Cash to creditors	607,650	1 June 20X5 Balance b/f		35,960
31 May 20X6 Balance c/f	49,310	Purchases (balance)		621,000
	656,960			656,960

Task 4

	£	£
Sales		1,020,000
Cost of sales		
Opening stock	33,200	
Purchases	621,000	
	654,200	
Closing stock (balance)	42,200	
		612,000
Gross profit (£1,020,000 × 40%)		408,000

Stolen stock = £42,200 – £38,700 = £3,500.

Task 5

	£	£
Sales proceeds		1,360
Net book value		
Cost	4,000	
Depreciation		
10% for 66 months	2,200	
		1,800
Loss on disposal		440

Task 6

	£
Prepaid general expenses at 31 May 20X5	550
General expenses paid	6,240
Owed at year end	170
Profit and loss account	6,960

8   ANDREW HALLGROVE

Task 1

	£	£
1 September balance paid in		50,000
Payments		
Fixtures and fittings	22,500	
Stock	47,300	
Rent	9,000	
Insurance	480	
General	220	
		(79,500)
		(29,500)
Balance c/f		
Bank	10,000	
Cash	500	
		(10,500)
Loan from bank		40,000

Task 2

Business assets at 30 September 20X6

	£
Fixtures and fittings	22,500
Stock	47,300
Prepayments	
Rent (£9,000 × 5/6)	7,500
Insurance (£480 × 11/12)	440
Bank	10,000
Cash	500

Task 3

TRADE CREDITORS

	£		£
Discount received	1,250	Balance b/f	-
Cash paid	20,250	Purchases on credit (bal fig)	24,900
Balance c/f	3,400		
	24,900		24,900

Task 4

Statement of net profit for October 20X6

	£	£
Sales (£20,000 + £2,400)		22,400
Cost of sales		
Opening stock	47,300	
Purchases	24,900	
	72,200	
Closing stock (£55,000 + (£2,000 × 70%))	(56,400)	
		15,800
Gross profit		6,600
Discount received		1,250
		7,850
Expenses		
Wages	2,400	
Depreciation: fixtures and fittings (20% × £22,500 × 1/12)	375	
Bank interest (£40,000 × 12% × 1/12)	400	
Stationery	320	
General expenses	500	
Rent (£9,000 × 1/6)	1,500	
Insurance (£480 × 1/12)	40	
		(5,535)
Net profit		2,315

9 HIGHBURY STOCKS

Stock sheets	Value £
Total b/f from previous pages	18,000
Bambino choir of Prague	3,500
The Joyful Singers sing Wesley	1,200
Bach at St Thomas's	5,000
VALUE OF STOCK as at 31 May 20X5	27,700

10 JASON BROWN

(a) *Book value of van at sale*

   (i)   *Cost*

	£
	6,000
Accumulated depreciation	
1.11.X3 - 31.10.X4 = £6,000 × 20%	1,200
	4,800
1.11.X4 - 31.10.X5 = £4,800 × 20%	960
	3,840
1.11.X5 - 30.4.X5 = £3,840 × 20% × $^6/_{12}$	384
Book value at date of sale	3,456

BPP PUBLISHING

(ii) *Disposals account*

MOTOR VANS DISPOSAL ACCOUNT			
	£		£
Vans: cost	6,000	Motor vans: provision for depreciation £(6,000 – 3,456)	2,544
		Cash	3,200
		Profit and loss a/c	256
	6,000		6,000

(b) The argument in favour of including the advertising costs in the calculation of profit for the year ended 31 October 20X7 is based on the *accruals concept*. The costs of advertising will be 'matched' with the associated revenues of the service. (However, the prudence concept might dictate that the costs should be written off against current profits if there is no guarantee that the consultancy will be profitable.)

(c) (i)   Decreased by £250
     (ii) Decreased by £360

(d) (i)   Sales for October

     (2 + 4 + 6) × £50 = £600

     (ii) *Cost of goods sold for October*

		£
Sale 13.10.X5: Cost =	2 × £30	60
Sale 18.10.X5: Cost =	4 × £30	120
Sale 30.10.X5: Cost =	4 × £30	120
	2 × £32	64
	12	364

     (iii) *Closing stock*

	£
10 at £32	320
10 at £31	310
	630

(e) This statement is not true because fixed assets must be depreciated over their useful economic lives. The periodic depreciation charge passes through the profit and loss account as an expense, thus reducing profit. The benefit obtained from use of the asset is thus matched against its cost.

(f) (i)   It excludes VAT.

     (ii) SSAP 5 *Accounting for VAT* requires all figures in the accounts, in particular sales and purchases, to be shown net of VAT, where VAT is recoverable.

(g)

MEMORANDUM

To:	Jason Brown	Ref:	
From:	Accounting Technician 20X5	Date: 8 December	
Subject:	Profit and accounting rules		

There are various problems with the changes you propose to make next year to improve profitability.

(i) At the year end the cost of sales is matched with sales to calculate profit. Where stocks are held at the year end, these must be matched against future sales (under the accruals, or matching concept), and so they are deducted from the current cost of sales. You can see then that running down stocks at the year end would therefore have no impact, for example:

	Higher year end stocks	*Lower year end stocks*
	£	£
Purchases (and opening stock)	120,000	100,000
Closing stock	30,000	10,000
	90,000	90,000

There is no effect on profit, just a lower closing stock figure in the balance sheet, and a higher cash balance (fewer purchases made).

(ii) The prudence concept states that all losses must be recognised as soon as they are foreseen. It is therefore not acceptable to 'put off' writing off a debt until the following year (when in any case it would have just as bad an effect on profit).

(iii) It is not acceptable to change the method of depreciation of assets from year to year because of the consistency concept. This requires items to be treated in the same way over time in order to allow comparison between accounts from year to year.

I am afraid that the only real ways to increase profitability are to increase sales and cut costs!

(h)

MEMORANDUM

To: Jason Brown   Ref:
From: Accounting Technician   Date: 8 December 20X5
Subject: *Sales ledger errors*

The error discovered, that £96.20 had not been posted to the account of John Pearce Furniture Ltd, will not be discovered by a trial balance because the account in question is not part of the system of double entry. It is, rather, a 'personal' account kept as a memorandum of how much an individual owes your business, along with all other such accounts in the sales ledger.

The account within the system which relates to debtors, the debtors control account, is an impersonal, summary account which shows only the *total* owed to your business by debtors.

These accounts are both posted from the same sources (such as the sales day book and the cash book), but the debtors control account postings are in total, whereas the personal accounts in the sales ledger are posted with individual transactions.

The control account balance should therefore, in theory, be equal to the total of all the balances in the personal accounts in the sales ledger. In practice, discrepancies arise, and by comparing the two totals and investigating these discrepancies, errors can be found in both types of account and thereby corrected.

This is a good way of making sure that the figure from the control account, which appears under debtors in the balance sheet, is correct, as well as ensuring that you receive the correct amounts from the individual debtors of the business.

11 SUNDRY QUERIES

(a) (i)   Understated

(ii)   Understated

			£	£
(b) (i)	DEBIT	Debtors control account	705	
	CREDIT	Sales		600
	CREDIT	VAT		105
(ii)	DEBIT	Bank	705	
	CREDIT	Debtors control account		705

(c) (i)   Disagree

(ii)   SSAP 13 *Accounting for research and development expenditure* states that both pure and applied research should be written off as incurred. Only development costs relating to new products which are technically and financially feasible may be capitalised.

(d) The prudence concept suggests that Julie Owens' debt of £5,000 should be provided for as it is likely that Explosives will lose the entire amount.

(e) Stay the same.

			£	£
(f)	DEBIT	Suspense account	200	
	CREDIT	Cash		200

(The original credit entry should have been to cash.)

(g)

MEMORANDUM

To: Melanie Lancton   Ref:

From: Accounting technician   Date: 8 July 20X6

Subject: *Stock valuation*

Statement of Standard Accounting Practice 9 (SSAP 9) *Stocks and long-term contracts* requires stock to be valued at the lower of cost and net realisable value (where NRV is the selling price less any further costs to be incurred to bring the stocks to a saleable condition).

The prudence concept requires losses to be provided for as soon as they are foreseen. Here, the 'loss' is the difference between the cost and the NRV of the stock and it must therefore be written off immediately.

I hope this answers your query satisfactorily.

Chapter 10 Incomplete records

12 BRIAN HOPE

Tutorial note. The three most difficult accounts to complete are trade debtors, cash and drawings. It is best to put in all the figures you know and complete the 'easier' accounts first. You should then be able to calculate, as a balancing figure, the amount for debtors who pay in cash. This will slot into the 'cash account', enabling you to calculate cash drawings as a balancing figure. The suggested time allocation for this incomplete records exercise is 1 hour.

TRADE DEBTORS

Balance b/f	1,420	Bank	21,120
		Allowance	300
Sales	26,720	Bad debt	90
		Balance c/f	1,030
		£(1120-90)	
		Cash	5,600
	28,140		28,140

VEHICLE RUNNING EXPENSES

		Balance b/f	80
Cash	500		
Bank	1,040	Profit & loss	1,520
Balance c/f	60		
	1,600		1,600

TRADE CREDITORS

Balance c/f	2,460	Balance b/f	2,220
Cash discount	200	Purchases	4,510
Bank *	4,070		
	6,730		6,730

* Payments to creditors: £(3,930 - 70 + 210) = £4,070

INSURANCE

Balance b/f	340		
		Profit & loss	920
Bank	960		
		Balance c/f	380
	1,300		1,300

RENT

Balance b/f	400		
		Balance c/f	480
Bank	2,640	Profit & loss	2,560
	3,040		3,040

CASH

Balance b/f	10	Bank	510
		Vehicle running costs	500
Debtors	5,600	Other expenses	500
		Drawings (bal)	4,100
	5,610		5,610

VEHICLES			
Balance b/f	6,000	Acc. dep'n	1,200
Bank	3,600	Profit & loss*	400
		Balance c/f	8,000
	9,600		9,600

* £(6,000 - 1,200 - 4,400) = £400 loss

DRAWINGS			
Bank	8,000	Capital	12,100
Cash	4,100		
	12,100		12,100

353

13 KULDIPA POTIWAL

Task 1

CALCULATION OF NET PROFIT
FOR THE YEAR ENDED 31 OCTOBER 20X3

	£	£
Sales (W1)		133,590
Opening stock	12,200	
Purchases (W2)	78,080	
Closing stock	(13,750)	
Cost of sales		76,530
Gross profit		57,060
Rent received (W3)		2,750
		59,810
Expenses		
Rent and rates (W3)	6,700	
Postage and packing	2,200	
Motor expenses	5,050	
Admin expenses (W3)	5,390	
Wages	18,200	
Stock loss (£6,000 × 100/150 × 50%)	2,000	
Depreciation £(17,500 – 12,500)	5,000	
		44,540
Net profit		15,270

Task 2

CALCULATION OF CAPITAL AS AT 31 OCTOBER 20X3

	£
Opening capital (W4)	23,775
Profit	15,270
	39,045
Additional capital (investment income)	1,500
	40,545
Drawings (W5)	11,760
Closing capital	28,785

This figure can be confirmed by producing a balance sheet as at 31 October 20X3, although this is not required by the question.

BALANCE SHEET AS AT 31 OCTOBER 20X3

	£	£
Fixed assets		
Van		12,500
Current assets		
Stock	13,750	
Debtors	7,200	
Prepayments	200	
Insurance claim (50%)	2,000	
Rent receivable	250	
Bank	6,500	
	29,900	
Current liabilities		
Creditors	13,400	
Accruals	215	
	13,615	
		16,285
Net current assets		28,785
Closing capital		28,785

Workings

1   *Sales*

CASH BOOK

	Cash £		Bank £		Cash £			Bank £
Sales	86,390	Bankings	56,000	Bankings	56,000	Bal	b/f	3,250
						1.11.X2		
		Debtors	46,000	Wages		Creditors		78,000
		Investment		(350 × 52)	18,200	Postage &		
		income	1,500	Drawings		packing		2,200
		Rent	2,500	(220 × 52)	11,440	Rent & rates		6,400
				Admin exps	750	Motor exps		5,050
						Admin exps		4,600
						Bal c/f		
						31.10 X3		6,500
	86,390		106,000		86,390			106,000

Note. As cash is banked daily, there will be no cash in hand b/fwd or c/fwd.

DEBTORS CONTROL A/C

		£			£
1.11.X2	Balance b/fwd	6,000	31.10.X2	Bank	46,000
	Sales (bal fig)	47,200		Balance c/fwd	7,200
		53,200			53,200

Total sales = £(86,390 + 47,200) = £133,590

Answers to practice activities

2 Purchases

CREDITORS CONTROL A/C

	£			£
Bank	78,000	1.11 X2	Bal b/fwd	9,000
31.10.X3 Bal c/fwd	13,400		Purchases (bal fig)	82,400
	91,400			91,400

	£
Purchases per CC a/c	82,400
Less stolen games £6,000 × 100/150	(4,000)
Less Christmas presents £480 × 100/150	(320)
	78,080

3 Expenses

Rent and rates: £(6,400 + 500 − 200) = £6,700
Admin expenses: £(750 + 4,600 − 175 + 215) = £5,390
Rent received: £(2,500 + 250) = £2,750

4 Opening capital

	£	£
Assets		
Van	17,500	
Stock	12,200	
Debtors	6,000	
Prepayments	500	
		36,200
Liabilities		
Creditors	9,000	
Accruals	175	
Bank overdraft	3,250	
		12,425
Net assets = capital		23,775

5 Drawings

	£
Cash (W1)	11,440
Christmas presents* 480 × 100/150	320
	11,760

*Note. Drawings from stock are at cost price. Selling price inclusive of VAT may also be used.

14 LYNDA BOOTH

Tutorial notes

(1) Be careful when calculating the discounts received figure. The £30,060 paid to creditors is 90% of the normal price, so the discount is $£30,060 \times \dfrac{10\%}{90\%}$, ie £3,340.

(2) The van owned at the beginning of the year is shown at net book value. It has been depreciated for one year, so the original cost was £7,500 × 4/3 = £10,000.

BANK

	£		£
Balance b/f	323	Trade creditors	30,060
Cash	2,770	Drawings	12,000
Trade debtors	43,210	Motor van	4,800
Capital	10,000	Rent	5,330
		Motor expenses	3,400
		Balance c/d	713
	56,303		56,303
Balance b/d	713		

CASH

	£		£
Balance b/f	25	Bank	2,770
Trade debtors	8,340	Motor expenses	600
		Drawings (bal fig)	4,961
		Balance c/d	34
	8,365		8,365
Balance b/d	34		

MOTOR EXPENSES

	£		£
Bank	3,400	Balance b/f	174
Cash	600	Profit and loss	4,035
Balance c/d	209		
	4,209		4,209
		Balance b/d	209

MOTOR VAN(S)

	£		£
Balance b/f	7,500	Depreciation charge (P&L) £(10,000 ÷ 4) + $(4,800 \div 4 \times {}^4/_{12})$	2,900
Bank	4,800	Balance c/d	9,400
	12,300		12,300
Balance b/d	9,400		

RENT AND INSURANCE

	£		£
Balance (insurance) b/f	180	Balance (rent) b/f	250
Bank	5,330	Profit and loss	5,060
		Balance (insurance) c/d	200
	5,510		5,510
Balance (insurance) b/d	200		

MATERIALS USED

	£		£
Balance b/f	1,530	Profit and loss	33,910
Purchases	33,980	Balance c/d	1,600
	35,510		35,510
Balance b/d	1,600		

TRADE CREDITORS

	£		£
Bank	30,060	Balance b/f	3,650
Discounts received		Purchases (bal fig)	33,980
(£30,060 × 10%/90%)	3,340		
Balance c/d	4,230		
	37,630		37,630
		Balance b/d	4,230

TRADE DEBTORS

	£		£
Balance b/f	1,550	Bank	43,210
Work done	52,000	Bad debts	480
		Cash (bal fig)	8,340
		Balance c/d £(2,000 – 480)	1,520
	53,550		53,550
Balance b/d	1,520		

DRAWINGS

	£		£
Bank	12,000	Capital	16,961
Cash	4,961		
	16,961		16,961

15 NATASHA

Task 1

	£
Premises	74,400
Fixtures and fittings	28,800
Stocks £(15,613 – 10,000)	5,613
	108,813
Less bank loan	48,000
	60,813
Surplus funds	1,220
Original capital invested	62,033

Task 2

CARLTON OFFICE SUPPLIES			
	£		£
Oct X5		*Oct X5*	
		Credit purchases	10,000
Nov X5		*Nov X5*	
Bank	9,800	Credit purchases	12,500
Discount received	200	Credit purchases	8,600
Bank	12,250		
Discount received	250		
Creditor c/f	8,600		
	31,100		31,100

Task 3

	£
Carlton Office Supplies	
October	10,000
November £(12,500 + 8,600)	21,100
Cash purchases £(187 + 5,613)	5,800
	36,900

Task 4

Profit for November 20X5

	£	£
Sales (balancing figure)		32,125
Cost of sales		
Purchases	36,900	
Closing stock	11,200	
		25,700
Gross profit (£25,700 × 25/100)		6,425
Discounts received		450
		6,875
Expenses		
Insurance (384 × 1/12)	32	
Depreciation		
Premises (2% × £74,400 × 1/12)	124	
Fixtures (10% × £28,800 × 1/12)	240	
Computer (1/3 × £(1,402 – 250) × 1/12)	32	
Interest (£48,000 × 10% × 1/12)	400	
Postages	43	
Sundry £(52 + 61)	113	
		984
Net profit		5,891

Task 5

CASH ACCOUNT			
	£		£
Sales	32,125	Postages	43
		Cash purchases	187
		Sundry expenses	52
		Cash banked	30,408
		Drawings (bal)	1,435
	32,125		32,125

16 RICHARD FAIRLEY

Task 1

	£
Bank receipts	126,790
Debtors at 31/12/X7	290
Debtors at 31/12/X6	(630)
Sales	126,450

Task 2

	£
Bank payments	83,410
Creditors at 31/12/×7	7,400
Creditors at 31/12/×6	(4,750)
Purchases	86,060

Task 3

	£
Sales (from Task 1)	126,450
Gross profit (30%)	(37,935)
Cost of sales	88,515

Task 4

	£
Opening stock	15,750
Purchases (from Task 2)	86,060
Goods for own use	(270)
	101,540
Cost of sales (from Task 3)	(88,515)
Closing stock	13,025

Task 5

	£
General expenses - from bank	16,060
Accrual – electricity	260
Accrual – insurance ($1/12 \times £600$)	50
Prepayment for insurance	495
	16,865

Task 6

	£	£
Gross profit (from Task 3)		37,935
General expenses (from Task 5)	16,865	
Salaries	5,110	
Dep'n - F&F	1,750	
MV	3,125	
		(26,850)
Net profit		11,085

17   SHEENA GORDON

Task 1

	£
Opening stock	1,800
Payments : bank	18,450
: cash	3,800
Creditors	1,400
Total purchases	25,450

Task 2

	£
Purchases (from Task 1)	25,450
Closing stock	(2,200)
Total cost of sales	23,250

Task 3

	£
Cost of sales (from Task 2)	23,250
Total sales (× 2)	46,500

Task 4

	£	£
Sales (from Task 3)		46,500
Payments: materials	3,800	
general expenses	490	
bank account	27,000	
drawings (bal fig)	15,110	
		(46,400)
Float		100

Task 5

	£
Bank account	6,200
Cash account (From Task 4)	15,110
Total drawings	21,310

Task 6

	£	£
Sales (From Task 3)		46,500
Cost of sales (From Task 2)		(23,250)
Gross profit		23,250
General expenses (870 + 490)	1,360	
Depreciation (4,000 × 20%)	800	
		(2,160)
Net profit		21,090

CHAPTER 11 CLUB ACCOUNTS AND MANUFACTURING ACCOUNTS

18   PAT HALL

Task 1

	£
Opening stock : raw materials	4,300
Purchases : raw materials	95,600
	99,900
Closing stock: raw materials	(9,400)
Raw materials used	90,500
Wages: furniture production	38,000
Prime cost	128,500

Task 2

	£
Prime cost (from Task 1)	128,500
Wages: factory supervisory	28,000
Factory overheads	12,500
Depreciation: factory premises	1,600
Depreciation: factory machinery	2,000
Production cost	172,600

Task 3

	£
Receipts from debtors	294,700
Less debtors at 1 December 20X7	(22,200)
	272,500
Add debtors at 30 November 20X8	24,500
Total sales	297,000

Task 4

	£	£
Sales (from Task 3)		297,000
Less cost of goods sold:		
Opening stock finished goods	10,360	
Add production cost of finished goods (from Task 3)	172,600	
	182,960	
Closing stock of finished goods	(12,510)	
		(170,450)
Gross profit		126,550

Task 5

	£
Purchases	95,600
Add creditors at 1 December 20X7	12,100
	107,700
Less creditors at 30 November 20X8	(13,300)
Payments to creditors	94,400

BANK

	£		£
Debtors	294,700	Balance b/d	3,600
		Creditors	94,400
		Production wages	38,000
		Supervisory wages	28,000
		Office wages	16,000
		Factory overheads	12,500
		Office expenses	8,300
		Balance c/d	93,900
	294,700		294,700

19 ANANDA CARVER

Task 1

		£
Assets		
NBV of clubhouse (24,000 – 7,200)		16,800
Stocks		120
Cash at bank		1,200
		18,120
Liabilities		
Creditors	860	
Subscriptions in advance	400	
		(1,260)
Accumulated fund @1 January 20X8		16,860

Task 2

	£
Subscriptions in advance @1 January 20X8	400
Subscriptions	30,000
Subscriptions in advance @31 December 20X8	(550)
Subscriptions for the year	29,850

Task 3

	£
Amount paid for refurbishments	10,600
Opening creditors	(860)
Closing creditors	780
Purchases	10,520

Task 4

	£	£
Sales of refreshments		15,260
Opening stocks	120	
Purchases (from Task 3)	10,520	
	10,640	
Closing stocks	(230)	
		(10,410)
Gross profit		4,850
Expenses		
Wages (15% of 28,000)	4,200	
Electricity (2% of 1,780)	356	
		(4,556)
Net profit		294

Task 5

Income		£
Subscriptions (from **Task 2**)		29,850
Donations		500
Profit on refreshments		294
		30,644
Expenditure		
Wages (85% of 28,000)	23,800	
Electricity (80% of 1,780)	1,424	
Sundry expenses	1,820	
Repairs to tennis court	800	
Rent of land	3,400	
Depreciation of clubhouse ([24,000+6,400]@5%)	1,520	
Loan interest ([6,000@10%]$\times^6/_{12}$)	300	
		33,064
Deficit for the year		2,420

Chapter 12 Extended trial balance

20 CLEGG AND CO

	Trial balance		Adjustments		Profit and loss account		Balance sheet	
	£	£	£	£	£	£	£	£
Administration costs	72,019.27		480.00	320.00	72,179.27			
Bank overdraft		8,290.12						8,290.12
Capital		50,000.00		10,000.00				60,000.00
Loan		100,000.00						100,000.00
Depreciation charge	12,000.00		15,000.00		28,000.00			
			1,000.00					
Drawings	36,000.00						36,000.00	
Fixed assets: Cost	120,287.00		4,000.00				124,287.00	
Fixed assets: Depreciation		36,209.28		1,000.00				37,209.28
Interest payable	12,182.26		650.00		12,832.26			
Interest receivable		21.00				21.00		
Labour	167,302.39		14,248.40		181,550.79			
Raw materials	104,293.38				104,293.38			
Stock as at 1/6/X8	25,298.30				25,298.30			
Purchase ledger control		42,190.85						42,190.85
Sales		481,182.20				481,182.20		
Sales ledger control	156,293.00			6,092.35			150,200.65	
Suspense	17,156.05		6,092.35	15,000.00				
			10,000.00	14,248.40				
				4,000.00				
VAT		4,938.20						4,938.20
Accruals				480.00				1,130.00
				650.00				
Prepayments			320.00				320.00	
Closing stock			32,125.28	32,125.28		32,125.28	32,125.28	
Profit					89,174.48			89,174.48
	722,831.65	722,831.65	83,916.03	83,916.03	513,328.48	513,328.48	342,932.93	342,932.93

21 SADIE PET PRODUCTS

Tasks 1 and 2

ADMINISTRATION					
Date	**Details**	**Amount £**	**Date**	**Details**	**Amount £**
20X3			**20X3**		
1/11	Balance b/d	4,209.38			
30/11	PDB	456.87	30/11	Balance c/d	4,666.25
		4,666.25			4,666.25
30/11	Balance b/d	4,666.25			

CAPITAL					
Date	**Details**	**Amount £**	**Date**	**Details**	**Amount £**
20X3			**20X3**		
30/11	Balance c/d	5,000.00	1/11	Balance b/d	5,000.00
		5,000.00			5,000.00
			30/11	Balance b/d	5,000.00

CASH					
Date	**Details**	**Amount £**	**Date**	**Details**	**Amount £**
20X3			**20X3**		
30/11	Cash book	5,209.38	1/11	Balance b/d	1,278.39
30/11	Balance c/d	221.38	30/11	Cash book	4,152.37
		5,430.73			5,430.73
			30/11	Balance b/d	221.38

DEPRECIATION ON WORKSHOP EQUIPMENT					
Date	**Details**	**Amount £**	**Date**	**Details**	**Amount £**
20X3			**20X3**		
30/11	Charge for the year	1,500.00	30/11	Balance c/d	1,500.00
		1,500.00			1,500.00
30/11	Balance b/d	1,500.00			

DRAWINGS					
Date	**Details**	**Amount £**	**Date**	**Details**	**Amount £**
20X3			**20X3**		
1/11	Balance b/d	11,000.00			
30/11	Cash book	1,000.00	30/11	Balance c/d	12,000.00
		12,000.00			12,000.00
30/11	Balance b/d	12,000.00			

FIXED ASSETS (COST)					
Date	**Details**	**Amount £**	**Date**	**Details**	**Amount £**
20X3			**20X3**		
1/11	Balance b/d	15,000.00	30/11	Balance c/d	15,000.00
		15,000.00			15,000.00
30/11	Balance b/d	15,000.00			

FIXED ASSETS (ACCUMULATED DEPRECIATION)					
Date	**Details**	**Amount £**	**Date**	**Details**	**Amount £**
20X3			**20X3**		
			1/11	Balance b/d	9,000.00
30/11	Balance c/d		30/11	Charge for the year	1,500.00
		10,500.00			
		10,500.00			10,500.00
			1/11	Balance b/d	10,500.00

INTEREST PAID					
Date	**Details**	**Amount £**	**Date**	**Details**	**Amount £**
20X3			**20X3**		
1/11	Balance b/d	1,100.00			
30/11	Cash book	100.00	30/11	Balance c/d	1,200.00
		1,200.00			1,200.00
30/11	Balance b/d	1,200.00			

LABOUR

Date	Details	Amount £	Date	Details	Amount £
20X3			20X3		
1/11	Balance b/d	16,683.33			
30/11	Cash book	1,516.67	30/11	Balance c/d	18,200.00
		18,200.00			18,200.00
30/11	Balance b/d	18,200.00			

LOAN

Date	Details	Amount £	Date	Details	Amount £
20X3			20X3		
30/11	Balance c/d	15,000.00	1/11	Balance b/d	15,000.00
		15,000.00			15,000.00
			30/11	Balance b/d	15,000.00

PURCHASE LEDGER CONTROL

Date	Details	Amount £	Date	Details	Amount £
20X3			20X3		
30/11	Cash book	1,535.70	1/11	Balance b/d	2,954.06
30/11	Balance c/d	6,040.03	30/11	PDB	4,621.67
		7,575.73			7,575.73
			30/11	Balance b/d	6,040.03

RAW MATERIALS

Date	Details	Amount £	Date	Details	Amount £
20X3			20X3		
1/11	Balance b/d	19,972.05			
30/11	PDB	2,821.07	30/11	Balance c/d	22,793.12
		22,793.12			22,793.12
30/11	Balance b/d	22,793.12			

SALES					
Date	**Details**	**Amount £**	**Date**	**Details**	**Amount £**
20X3			**20X3**		
			1/11	Balance b/d	49,306.52
30/11	Balance c/d	54,511.71	30/11	SDB	5,205.19
		54,511.71			54,511.71
			30/11	Balance b/d	54,511.71

SALES LEDGER CONTROL					
Date	**Details**	**Amount £**	**Date**	**Details**	**Amount £**
20X3			**20X3**		
1/11	Balance b/d	5,251.29	30/11	Cash book	5,209.38
30/11	SDB	6,116.09	30/11	Balance c/d	6,158.00
		11,367.38			11,367.38
30/11	Balance b/d	6,158.00			

STOCK (RAW MATERIALS)					
Date	**Details**	**Amount £**	**Date**	**Details**	**Amount £**
20X2			**20X2**		
1/12	Balance b/d	3,093.84			
20X3			**20X3**		
			30/11	Balance c/d	3,093.84
		3,093.84			3,093.84
30/11	Balance b/d	3,093.84			

VAT					
Date	**Details**	**Amount £**	**Date**	**Details**	**Amount £**
20X3			**20X3**		
30/11	PDB	688.33	1/11	Balance b/d	980.29
30/11	Balance c/d	1,202.86	30/11	SDB	910.90
		1,891.19			1,891.19
			30/11	Balance b/d	1,202.86

WORKSHOP OVERHEADS					
Date	Details	Amount £	Date	Details	Amount £
20X3			20X3		
1/11	Balance b/d	7,209.37			
30/11	PDB	655.40	30/11	Balance c/d	7,864.77
		7,864.77			7,864.77
30/11	Balance b/d	7,864.77			

Tasks 1, 2 , 4 and 5

	Trial balance		Adjustments		Profit and loss account		Balance sheet	
	£	£	£	£	£	£	£	£
Administration	4,666.25		140.00	1,500.00 564.00	2,742.25			
Capital		5,000.00						5,000.00
Cash		221.38						221.38
Depreciation on workshop equipment	1,500.00				1,500.00			
Drawings	12,000.00						12,000.00	
Fixed assets (cost)	15,000.00						15,000.00	
Fixed assets (accumulated depreciation)		10,500.00						10,500.00
Interest paid	1,200.00				1,200.00			
Labour	18,200.00				18,200.00			
Loan		15,000.00						15,000.00
Purchase ledger control		6,040.03						6,040.03
Raw materials	22,793.12				22,793.12			
Sales		54,511.71				54,511.71		
Sales ledger control	6,158.00			600.00			5,558.00	
Stock: finished goods			1,797.30	1,797.30		1,797.30	1,797.30	
Stock: raw materials	3,093.84		3,527.27	3,527.27	3,093.84	3,527.27	3,527.27	
VAT		1,202.86						1,202.86
Workshop overheads	7,864.77				7,864.77			
Bad debts expense			600.00		600.00			
Accruals				140.00				140.00
Prepayments			1,506.00 564.00				2,064.00	
Profit					1,842.30			1,862.30
	92,475.98	**92,475.98**	**8,128.57**	**8,728.57**	**59,836.28**	**59,836.28**	**39,946.57**	**39,946.57**

Task 3

STOCK VALUATION AT 30 November 20X3

Raw materials

	£
Pine wood $(170 \times 4.80) + (210 \times 5.40)$	1,950.00
Miscellaneous items $(250.00 + 927.27 + 400.00)$	1,577.27
Raw materials stock at year end	3,527.27

Finished goods
Manufacturing account for the year ended 30 November 20X3

	£	£
Raw material stock at 1 December 20X2		3,093.84
Purchases: raw materials		22,793.12
		25,886.96
Raw material stock at 30 November 20X3		
Pine wood	1,950.00	
Miscellaneous items	1,577.27	
		(3,527.27)
		22,359.69
Direct labour		18,200.00
Prime cost		40,559.69
Workshop overheads	7,864.77	
Depreciation of workshop equipment	1,500.00	
		9,364.77
Factory cost of finished goods produced		49,924.46

Cost per hutch: £49,924.46/250 = £199.70 per hutch.

Finished goods stock at the year end: $9 \times £199.70 = £1,797.30$.

22   PINE WAREHOUSE

Task 1

Extended trial balance

DESCRIPTION	LEDGER BALANCES		ADJUSTMENTS	
	Dr	Cr	Dr	Cr
	£	£	£	£
Sales		1,240,600		
Purchases	826,400		1,800	
Debtors' control account	93,340			
Creditors' control account		70,870		2,115
Bad debts	8,750			
Provision for bad debts		4,010		657
Motor vehicles (MV) at cost	80,500			
Provision for depreciation (MV)		15,760		16,100
Machinery (Mach) at cost	24,000			
Provision for depreciation (Mach)		2,000		1,900
Equipment (Equip) at cost	27,400			
Provision for depreciation (Equip)		5,850		2,155
Drawings	33,000		3,000	
Cash	3,000			
Bank		12,500		3,000
Lighting and heating	3,250			
Insurance	1,020			
Advertising	10,620			2,400
VAT (credit balance)		13,600	315	
Stock at 1 December 20X7	125,560			
Motor expenses	8,670			
Discounts allowed	4,200			
Discounts received		1,200		
Salaries and wages	120,650			
Rent	24,600		4,920	
Capital		32,030		
Suspense	3,460			
Prepayments			2,400	
Depreciation			20,155	
Closing stock : P&L				132,800
Closing stock : balance sheet			132,800	
Provision for bad debts - adjustment			657	
Accrued expenses				4,920
	1,398,420	1,398,420	166,047	166,047

Task 2

JOURNAL		
Details	DR £	CR £
Debtors' control account	630	
Suspense		630
Suspense	500	
VAT		500
Sales	4,450	
Suspense		4,450
Suspense	1,200	
Debtors' control account		1,200
Discounts allowed	40	
Discounts received	40	
Suspense		80

Proof

Suspense account balance	3,460
Add (500+1200)	1,700
Less (630+4450+ 80)	5,160
Balance	NIL

23   CREATIVE CATERING

Task 1

Extended Trial Balance at 30 April 20X8

CREATIVE CATERING	Trial balance		Adjustments	
Account	Debit	Credit	Debit	Credit
	£	£	£	£
Sales		620,700		860
Purchases	410,650			
Purchases returns		390		
Salaries and wages	90,820			
Rent	16,300			1,300
Debtors control account	51,640			
Creditors control account		33,180		
Bad debts	6,650			
Provision for bad debts		3,100	518	
Motor vehicles (cost)	60,700			
Motor vehicles (prov for depreciation)		12,600		12,140
Equipment (cost)	24,200			
Equipment (prov for depreciation)		6,300		1,790
Drawings	28,500		5,000	
Cash	7,000			5,000
Bank	6,250			
Lighting and heating	2,100			
Insurance	760			
Advertising	3,470		2,750	
VAT (credit balance)		8,400		
Stock at 1 May 20X7	5,660			
Motor expenses	4,680			
Bank deposit amount	20,000			
Bank interest received		700		700
Capital		54,010		
Polar Insurance Company			860	
Depreciation			13,930	
Closing stock (P&L)				5,340
Closing stock (B/S)			5,340	
Provision for bad debts (adjustment)				518
Deposit account interest owing			700	
Prepayments / Accruals			1,300	2,750
Subtotal	739,380	739,380	30,398	30,398
Profit for the year				
TOTAL	739,380	739,380	30,398	30,398

Task 2

	£	£
Balance at bank as per cash book (15 May)		5,800
Add unpresented cheques		
606842	120	
606843	440	
606844	260	
		820
		6,620
Less Credit already in cash book		320
Balance at bank as per bank statement		6,300

Task 3

CREATIVE CATERING
BANK RECONCILIATION AS AT 29 MAY 20X8

	£	£
Balance at bank as per cash book		7,365
Add unpresented cheques		
606845	620	
606847	490	
606850	260	
606851	320	
606852	1,400	
		3,090
		10,455
Less Tennis Club credit not yet banked		1,810
Balance as per bank statement		8,645

24   ELECTRONICS WORLD

Task 1

	Debit £	Credit £
Entries from purchases day book		
Purchases	20,400	
VAT	3,570	
Creditors control account		23,970
Entries from sales day book		
Debtors control account	35,955	
VAT		5,355
Sales		30,600
Entries from sales returns day book		
Sales returns	1,200	
VAT	210	
Debtors control account		1,410
Cheques issued		
Creditors control account	5,000	
Bank		5,000

Task 2

See extended trial balance on Page 377.

Task 3

For entries on the extended trial balance: see Page 377.

(a) *Depreciation*

Motor vehicles: £22,400 × 20% = £4,480

Fixtures and fittings: £(140,000 – £6,000 – £65,000) × 10% = £6,900

Total deprecation = £11,380

(b) *Interest*

Interest due = £150,000 × 6% × 6/12 = £4,500

Bank interest owing = £4,500 – £3,750 = £750

(c) *General expenses*

Prepaid £2,400 × 4/6 = £1,600

(d) *Stock*

Valued at cost = £198,650

Insurance proceeds:

DEBIT	Regis Insurance	£420	
CREDIT	Purchases		£420

(e) *Insurance*

DEBIT	Insurance	£60	
CREDIT	Bank		£60

(f) *Provision for bad debts*

	£
Existing provision	6,000
Provision required (£272,400 × 5%)	13,620
Additional provision	7,620

ELECTRONICS WORLD	Trial balance		Adjustments	
Account	Debit	Credit	Debit	Credit
	£	£	£	£
Share capital		600,000		
Premises	360,000			
Fixtures & fittings at cost	140,000			
Fixtures & fittings (prov for depreciation)		65,000		6,900
Purchases (972,140 + 20,400)	992,540			420
Sales (1,530,630 + 30,600)		1,561,230		
Salaries	206,420			
Sales returns (23,200 + 1,200)	24,400			
Purchases returns		17,350		
General expenses	74,322			1,600
Insurance	16,390		60	
Bad debts	7,506			
Provision for bad debts		6,000		7,620
Debtors control account (£237,855 + £35,955 - £1,410)	272,400			
Creditors control account (£121,433 + £23,970 - £5,000)		140,403		
Stock at 1 June 20X6	188,960			
Bank (65,200 + 5,000)	60,200			60
Bank deposit account	150,000			
Bank interest received		3,750		750
Motor vehicles (cost)	22,400			
Motor vehicles (prov for depreciation)		3,800		4,480
VAT: Credit balance (24,720 - 3,570 + 5,355 - 210)		26,295		
Profit and loss		91,710		
Depreciation			11,380	
Regis Insurance			420	
Closing stock (P&L)				198,650
Closing stock (B/S)			198,650	
Provision for bad debts (adjustment)			7,620	
Bank interest owing			750	
Prepayments			1,600	
Subtotal	2,515,538	2,515,538	220,480	220,480
Profit for the year				
TOTAL	2,515,538	2,515,538	220,480	220,480

25 DREW INSTALLATIONS

Task 1

DREW INSTALLATIONS	Trial balance		Adjustments	
Account	Debit	Credit	Debit	Credit
	£	£	£	£
Purchases	339,500			
Sales		693,000		
Purchases returns		6,320		
Sales returns	1,780			
Carriage inwards	8,250			
Salaries and wages	106,200			
Bad debts	4,890			
Provision for bad debts		4,500	756	
Debtors control account	46,800			
Creditors control account		28,760		
Stock at 1 November 20X6	113,450			
Motor vehicles expenses	5,780			260
Motor vehicles (cost)	86,000			
Motor vehicles (prov for depreciation)		12,800		16,000
Equipment (cost)	24,500			
Equipment (prov for depreciation)		6,700		1,780
Rent	58,000		2,000	
Drawings	32,900		260	
Insurance	5,720			1,800
Bank	8,580			
Bank loan account		50,000		
Bank interest paid	2,400		2,000	
VAT (credit balance)		12,400		
Capital		32,750		
Suspense account	2,480			
Depreciation			17,780	
Closing stock (P&L)				106,800
Closing stock (B/S)			106,800	
Provision for bad debts (adjustment)				756
Loan interest owing				2,000
Prepayments / Accruals			1,800	2,000
Subtotal	847,230	847,230	131,396	131,396
Profit for the year				
TOTAL	847,230	847,230	131,396	131,396

Task 2

	Debit £	Credit £
Suspense	200	
VAT		200
Motor Vehicle expenses	40	
Motor Vehicles		40
Sales returns	160	
Purchases returns	160	
Suspense		320
Suspense	90	
Purchases		90
Creditors control account	2,450	
Suspense		2,450

26 TULIPS

Task 1

<table>
<tr><td colspan="3" align="center">JOURNAL</td></tr>
<tr><td>Details</td><td>DR
£</td><td>CR
£</td></tr>
<tr><td>Drawings account</td><td>1,000</td><td></td></tr>
<tr><td>Wages</td><td></td><td>1,000</td></tr>
<tr><td>Creditors' control account</td><td>280</td><td></td></tr>
<tr><td>Debtors' control account</td><td></td><td>280</td></tr>
<tr><td>VAT account</td><td>98</td><td></td></tr>
<tr><td>Suspense account</td><td></td><td>98</td></tr>
<tr><td>Creditors' control account</td><td>1,128</td><td></td></tr>
<tr><td>Suspense account</td><td></td><td>1,128</td></tr>
<tr><td>Suspense account</td><td>1,500</td><td></td></tr>
<tr><td>Disposal account</td><td></td><td>1,500</td></tr>
<tr><td>Disposal account</td><td>2,500</td><td></td></tr>
<tr><td>Greenhouse cost account</td><td></td><td>2,500</td></tr>
<tr><td>Greenhouse depreciation account</td><td>750</td><td></td></tr>
<tr><td>Disposal account</td><td></td><td>750</td></tr>
<tr><td>Loss on disposal</td><td>250</td><td></td></tr>
<tr><td>Disposal account</td><td></td><td>250</td></tr>
</table>

Answers to practice activities

Tasks 2 and 3

DESCRIPTION	LEDGER BALANCES		ADJUSTMENTS	
	Dr	Cr	Dr	Cr
	£	£	£	£
Sales		313,746		
Sales returns	971			
Purchases	186,574			
Purchases returns		714		
Stock at 1 December 20X7	25,732			
Wages	39,000			
Rent and rates	18,608		3,000	
Light and heat	11,940			
Office expenses	9,530			
Greenhouse running expenses	11,290			
Motor expenses	4,782			
Sundry expenses	5,248			
Motor vehicle (MV) at cost	25,810			
Provision for depreciation MV		5,162		5,162
Greenhouses (GH) at cost	23,000			
Provision for depreciation GH		6,900		2,300
Cash	100			
Bank current account	3,020			
Bank loan		30,000		
Debtors' control account	6,580			
Creditors' control account		3,312		
Capital account		21,112		
Drawings account	12,000			
VAT account		3,489		
Suspense account	-	-		
Profit or loss on disposal of fixed asset	250			
Depreciation			7,462	
Provision for doubtful debts - P&L			329	
Provision for doubtful debts - balance sheet				329
Closing stock - P&L				24,895
Closing stock - balance sheet			24,895	
Accrual				3,000
	384,435	384,435	35,686	35,686

27   AUTOMANIA

EXTENDED TRIAL BALANCE AT 30TH APRIL 20X9

DESCRIPTION	Ledger balances		Adjustments	
	Dr	Cr	Dr	Cr
	£	£	£	£
Capital		135,000		
Drawings	42,150			
Rent	17,300		1,600	
Purchases	606,600			
Sales		857,300		
Sales returns	2,400			
Purchases returns		1,260		200
Salaries and wages	136,970			
Motor vehicles (M.V.)at cost	60,800			
Provision for depreciation (M.V)		16,740		12,160
Fixtures and fittings (F&F) at cost	40,380			
Provision for depreciation (F&F)		21,600		1,878
Bank		3,170		
Cash	2,100			
Lighting and heating	4,700			
VAT		9,200		35
Stock at 1 May 20X8	116,100			
Bad debts	1,410			
Provision for bad debts		1,050		87
Debtors control account	56,850			
Creditors control account		50,550	235	
Sundry expenses	6,810			
Insurance	1,300			100
Accruals				1,600
Prepayments			100	
Depreciation			14,038	
Provision for bad debts - Adjustment			87	
Closing stock - P&L				117,700
Closing stock - Balance sheet			117,700	
Totals	1,095,870	1,095,870	133,760	133,760

Workings

1   *Rent*

$(3 \times £1,500) + (9 \times £1,600)$ $= £18,900$

£18,900 less £17,300 $= £1,600$ accrual

2   *Insurance*

£100 prepayment

3   *Depreciation*

MV: £60,800 @20% $= £12,160$

FF: $(£40,380 – £21,600)$ @10% $= £1,878$

4   *Provision for bad debts*

	£
£56,850 @2% =	1,137
Existing provision	1,050
New provision	1,137
Adjustment	87

5   *Stock*

	£	£
Valued @	119,360	
Old stock cost	(3,660)	
NRV of old stock	2,060	
Car door cost	(60)	
	117,700	

6   *Credit note*

		£	£
DEBIT	Creditors control	235	
CREDIT	Purchase returns		200
CREDIT	VAT		35

28 FUTON ENTERPRISES

<table>
<tr><td colspan="3">JOURNAL</td><td>Page 20</td></tr>
<tr><td colspan="2">Details</td><td>DR
£</td><td>CR
£</td></tr>
<tr><td>(i)</td><td>Delivery vans: cost</td><td>10,000</td><td></td></tr>
<tr><td></td><td>Suspense account</td><td></td><td>10,000</td></tr>
<tr><td></td><td>Delivery vans: cost (£12,400 - £10,000)</td><td>2,400</td><td></td></tr>
<tr><td></td><td>Van disposal account</td><td></td><td>2,400</td></tr>
<tr><td></td><td>Being correct treatment of cost of
new van, clearing suspense account</td><td></td><td></td></tr>
<tr><td></td><td>Van disposal</td><td>12,000</td><td></td></tr>
<tr><td></td><td>Delivery van (cost)</td><td></td><td>12,000</td></tr>
<tr><td></td><td>Delivery van (provision for dep'n)</td><td>7,884</td><td></td></tr>
<tr><td></td><td>Van disposal</td><td></td><td>7,884</td></tr>
<tr><td></td><td>Loss on sale of van</td><td>1,716*</td><td></td></tr>
<tr><td></td><td>Van disposal</td><td></td><td>1,716</td></tr>
<tr><td></td><td>Being disposal of old van (in part exchange)</td><td></td><td></td></tr>
<tr><td>(ii)</td><td>Fixtures and fittings: cost</td><td>240</td><td></td></tr>
<tr><td></td><td>Production wages</td><td></td><td>240</td></tr>
<tr><td></td><td>Being cost of rebuilding reception area
in production wages (£12,480 ÷ 52 = £240)</td><td></td><td></td></tr>
<tr><td>(iii)</td><td>Sales</td><td>168</td><td></td></tr>
<tr><td></td><td>Sales ledger balances</td><td></td><td>168</td></tr>
<tr><td></td><td>Being reversal of treatment of two futons
given as presents (£48.00 × 2 × 175%)</td><td></td><td></td></tr>
<tr><td></td><td>Drawings</td><td>96</td><td></td></tr>
<tr><td></td><td>Materials</td><td></td><td>96</td></tr>
<tr><td></td><td>Being correct treatment of two futons
given as presents (£48.00 × 2)</td><td></td><td></td></tr>
</table>

Note. The credit entry to materials should be made to cost of sales. The alternative would be to post entries to materials, wages and overheads. However, overheads are split over several captions so this would be impractical.

	£
*Cost of van	12,000
Acc dep'n	7,884
NBV	4,116
Proceeds £(12,400	
−10,000)	2,400
Loss on disposal	1,716

BPP PUBLISHING

FUTON ENTERPRISES

Account	Trial balance Debit £	Trial balance Credit £	Adjustments Debit £	Adjustments Credit £	Profit and loss account Debit £	Profit and loss account Credit £	Balance sheet Debit £	Balance sheet Credit £
Delivery vans (cost)	12,400						12,400	
Assembling machine (costs)	3,650						3,650	
Furniture and fittings (cost)	11,030						11,030	
Delivery vans (prov for depreciation)		1,095		3,720				3,720
Assembling machine (prov for depreciation)				365				1,460
Furniture and fittings (prov for depreciation)		5,730		2,206				7,936
Stock : raw materials	1,320				1,320			
Stock : finished goods	1,440				1,440			
Sales : ledger total (1,860 - 168)	1,692			168			1,524	
Bank		320						320
Cash	50						50	
Purchase ledger total		4,265						4,265
Sales (120,240 - 168)		120,072				120,072		
Materials (35,465 - 96)	35,369				35,369			
Production wages (12,480-£240)	12,240				12,240			
Driver's wages	11,785				11,785			
Salaries	22,460				22,460			
Employer's NI	4,365				4,365			
Motor expenses	2,160			114	2,046			
Rent	3,930			786	3,144			
Sundry expenses	3,480		60		3,540			
VAT		1,220						1,220
Inland Revenue		1,365						1,365
Drawings (12,400 + 96)	12,496						12,496	
Capital		7,516						7,516
Depreciation: Delivery vans			3,720		3,720			
Depreciation: assembling machine			365		365			
Depreciation: furniture and fittings			2,206		2,206			
Loss on sale of van	1,716				1,716			
Closing stock (B/S): raw materials			1,526				1,526	
Closing stock (B/s): finished goods (£48 × 23)			1,104				1,104	
Closing stock (P&L): raw materials				1,526		1,526		
Closing stock (P&L): finished goods (£48 × 23)				1,104		1,104		
Insurance claim debtor			114				114	
Bad debts (48 × 1.75 × 2)			168		168			
Prepayments/accruals			786	60			786	60
Subtotal	141,583	141,583	10,049	10,049	105,884	122,702	44,680	27,862
Profit for the year					16,818			16,818
TOTAL	141,583	141,583	10,049	10,049	122,702	122,702	44,680	44,680

29   KIDDITOYS

JOURNAL		Page 20	
Details		DR £	CR £
(i)	DEBIT Suspense a/c CREDIT T. Ditton a/c (Purchase ledger) Being correction of misposting	1,908	1,908
(ii)	DEBIT Suspense a/c DEBIT Provision for depreciation a/c (shop fittings) (W1) DEBIT Loss on sale of fixed assets a/c CREDIT Shop fittings (cost a/c) Being disposal of shop fittings	50 1,944 1,246	3,240
	DEBIT Shop fittings (cost) a/c CREDIT Kingston Displays Ltd (Purchase ledger) Being purchase of new shop fittings	9,620	9,620
(iii)	DEBIT Drawings a/c (12 × £2,000) CREDIT Wages a/c Being correction of misposting	24,000	24,000
(iv)	DEBIT E. Molesey a/c (Purchase ledger) CREDIT Discount received a/c Being discount received from E. Molesey after accidental underpayment	3	3
(v)	DEBIT Drawings a/c CREDIT Sales a/c CREDIT VAT a/c Being stock withdrawn for own use	640	545 95
(vi)	DEBIT Bank current a/c CREDIT Interest received a/c Being posting of bank interest received credited on bank statement	9	9

BPP PUBLISHING

KIDDITOYS	Trial balance		Adjustments	
Account	Debit	Credit	Debit	Credit
	£	£	£	£
Sales		392,727		
Sales returns	1,214			
Purchases	208,217			
Purchase returns		643		
Stock	32,165			
Wages	26,000			
Rent	27,300			2,100
Rates	8,460			2,080
Light and heat	2,425		212	
Office expenses	3,162			
Selling expenses	14,112			
Motor expenses	14,728			
Sundry expenses	6,560			
Motor vans (cost)	12,640			
Shop fittings (cost)	9,620			
Office equipment (cost)	4,250			
Motor vans (prov for depreciation)		2,528		2,528
Shop fittings (prov for depreciation)				962
Office equipment (prov for depreciation)		2,550		850
Cash	100			
Bank current account	4,429			
Bank investment account	68,340			
Interest received		3,289		
Capital		22,145		
VAT		6,515		
Purchase ledger total		29,588		
Loss on sale of fixed assets	1,246			
Kingston Displays Limited		9,620		
Drawings	24,640			
Discount received		3		
Depreciation (motor vans)			2,528	
Depreciation (shop fittings)			962	
Depreciation (office equipment)			850	
Stock (closing): P&L				21,060
Stock (closing): B/S			21,060	
Prepayments / accruals			4,180	212
Subtotal	469,608	469,608	29,792	29,792
Profit for the year				
TOTAL	469,608	469,608	29,792	29,792

Workings

1   *Accumulated depreciation on shop fittings disposed of*

£324 × 6 years = £1,944

2   *Depreciation of fixed assets*

Motor van: annual depreciation charge $= \dfrac{£12,640}{5} = £2,528$

∴ Accumulated depreciation at 1.12.X3 = £2,528

Shop fittings: depreciation charge $= \dfrac{£9,620}{10} = £962$

Office equipment: annual depreciation charge $= \dfrac{£4,250}{5} = £850$

Accumulated depreciation as at $1.12.X3 = £850 \times 3 = £2,550$

3   *Business rates prepayment*

Prepayment $= £6,240 \times \dfrac{4 \text{ months}}{12 \text{ months}} = £2,080$

4   *Electricity accrual*

Accrual $= £318 \times \dfrac{2 \text{ months}}{3 \text{ months}} = £212$

Answers to practice devolved assessments

ANSWER TO PRACTICE DEVOLVED ASSESSMENT 1: REGGIE STIR

Tutorial note. When doing the journal entries you should not record the purchase of the potter's wheel. This is because the purchase was for *cash* and the journal only records *credit* purchases. The book of prime entry for cash purchases of fixed assets is the cash book.

(a)

Date	Details	Folio Ref	£	£
	JOURNAL			Page 50
3 August	Plant and equipment	P/E	1600	
	Plant and equipment disposals	P/D		500
	Cumere Oven Ltd	C/O		1100
	Being part exchange per agreement and invoice no 35X42			
3 August	Plant and equipment: disposals	NP/D	1200	
	Plant and equipment	P/E		1200
	Being transfer of plant (1/K) at cost to plant disposals a/c			
3 August	Plant and equipment: depreciation provision	PD/P	400	
	Plant and equipment: disposal	NP/D		400
	Being transfer of depreciation provision (1/K) to plant disposals a/c			
10 October	Motor vehicles	M/V	9000	
	Motor vehicles disposals	MV/D		1000
	Van Guard Ltd	V/G		8000
	Being part exchange per agreement and invoice no Z/2643			
10 October	Motor vehicles disposals	MV/D	4000	
	Motor vehicles	M/V		4000
	Being transfer of van 1/V at cost to disposals a/c			

	JOURNAL			Page 51
Date	Details	Folio Ref	£	£
10 October	Motor vehicles: depreciation provision	MV/DP	3051	
	Motor vehicles: disposals	MV/D		3051
	Being transfer of depreciation provision 1V to motor vehicles disposals a/c			
31 December	P & L a/c	P/L	300	
	Plant and equipment: disposals a/c	P/D		300
	Being loss on part exchange of kiln 1/K			
31 December	Motor vehicles: disposals	MV/D	51	
	P & L a/c	P/L		51
	Being profit on part exchange of van 1/V			
31 December	Plant and equipment: depreciation expense	P/DE	1147	
	Plant and equipment: depreciation provision	PD/P		1147
	Being year end provision for depreciation on plant			
31 December	Motor vehicles depreciation expense	MV/DE	4594	
	Motor vehicles depreciation provision	MV/DP		4594
	Being year end provision for depreciation on motor vehicles			

LEDGER ACCOUNTS

PLANT AND EQUIPMENT

Date		£	Date		£
20X5			*20X5*		
1 Jan	Balance b/f	4,970			
3 Aug	Creditors £(1,600 – 500)	1,100	3 Aug	Plant and equipment:	
3 Aug	Plant and equipment:			disposals	1,200
	disposals	500	31 Dec	Balance c/f	5,870
5 Sep	Bank	500			
		7,070			7,070

PLANT AND EQUIPMENT: PROVISION FOR DEPRECIATION

Date		£	Date		£
20X5			*20X5*		
3 Aug	Plant and equipment:		1 Jan	Balance b/f	2,330
	disposals	400	31 Dec	P & L a/c (W1)	1,147
31 Dec	Balance c/f	3,077			
		3,477			3,477

PLANT AND EQUIPMENT: DISPOSALS

Date		£	Date		£
20X5			*20X5*		
3 Aug	Plant and equipment	1,200	3 Aug	Depreciation	
				provision	400
			3 Aug	Plant and equipment	500
			31 Dec	P & L account	300
		1,200			1,200

MOTOR VEHICLES

Date		£	Date		£
20X5			*20X5*		
1 Jan	Balance b/f	18,000	10 Oct	Motor vehicles:	
10 Oct	Motor vehicles:			disposals	4,000
	disposals	1,000	31 Dec	Balance c/f	23,000
10 Oct	Creditors				
	£(9,000 – 1,000)	8,000			
		27,000			27,000

MOTOR VEHICLES: PROVISION FOR DEPRECIATION

Date		£	Date		£
20X5			*20X5*		
10 Oct	Motor vehicles:		1 Jan	Balance b/f	7,676
	disposals	3,051	31 Dec	P & L a/c (W2)	4,594
31 Dec	Balance c/f	9,219			
		12,270			12,270

MOTOR VEHICLES: DISPOSALS

Date		£	Date		£
20X5			*20X5*		
10 Oct	Motor vehicles	4,000	10 Oct	Depreciation	3,051
				provision	
31 Dec	P & L account	51	10 Oct	Motor vehicles	1,000
		4,051			4,051

					PLANT AND EQUIPMENT				
Ref	Description	Date of purchase	Cost £	Depreciation period	Accumulated depreciation 31 Dec 20X5 £	Date of disposal	Net book value 31 Dec 20X5 £	Sale/scrap proceeds £	(Loss)/ profit £
1/K	Kiln	1 Jan 20X3	1200	6 years	400	3 Aug 20X5	800	500	(300)
1/P	Pugmill	1 July 20X4	300	4 years	150		150		
2/K	Kiln	1 Mar 20X2	600	6 years	400		200		
3/K	Kiln	20 Aug 20X1	750	6 years	625		125		
1/W	Wheel	31 Mar 20X3	400	4 years	300		100		
2/W	Wheel	1 Feb 20X2	400	4 years	400		nil		
4/K	Kiln	1 Sep 20X2	900	6 years	600		300		
3/W	Wheel	1 Mar 20X4	420	4 years	210		210		
5/K	Kiln	3 Aug 20X5	1600	6 years	267		1333		
4/W	Wheel	5 Sept 20X5	500	4 years	125		375		
Totals			7070		3477		3593		
Disposals			1200		400		800	500	(300)
Totals c/f			5870		3077		2793		

				MOTOR VEHICLES					
Ref	Description	Date of purchase	Cost £	Depreciation type	Accumulated depreciation 31 Dec 20X5 £	Date of disposal	Net book value 31 Dec 20X5 £	Sale/scrap proceeds £	(Loss)/ profit £
1/V	Van reg D249 NPO	1 Feb 20X0	4000	Reducing balance 25%	3051	10 Oct 20X5	949	1000	51
2/V	Van reg K697 JKL	1 Jan 20X3	6000	Reducing balance 25%	3469		2531		
3/V	Van reg J894 TMG	30 Sept 20X4	8000	Reducing balance 25%	3500		4500		
4/V	Van reg N583 MNO	10 Oct 20X5	9000	Reducing balance 25%	2250		6750		
Totals			27000		12270		14730		
Disposals			4000		3051		949	1000	51
Totals c/f			23000		9219		13781		

Workings

1   *Depreciation charge: plant and equipment*

	£
Kilns £(600 + 750 + 900 + 1,600) ÷ 6	642
Other £(300 + 400 + 400 + 420 + 500) ÷ 4	505
	1,147

Note. It should be assumed from the question that all kilns are depreciated over 6 years and all wheels over 4 years.

2   *Depreciation charge: motor vehicles*

	£	£
Van 2/V: NBV 1 January 20X5	3,375	
Depreciation @ 25%		844
Van 3/V: NBV 1 January 20X5	6,000	
Depreciation @ 25%		1,500
Van 4/V: depreciation (25% × £9,000)		2,250
Total charge to P & L		4,594

(b) REGGIE STIR LIMITED
    BALANCE SHEET EXTRACT AS AT 31 DECEMBER 20X5

	Cost £	Accumulated depreciation £	NBV £
Fixed assets			
Plant and equipment	5,870	3,077	2,793
Motor vehicles	23,000	9,219	13,781
	28,870	12,296	16,574

ANSWER TO PRACTICE DEVOLVED ASSESSMENT 2: BOOTHS

Tutorial note. You will realise from your earlier studies that the sales and purchase invoices shown in the question would normally be posted to the sales day book and purchases day book respectively. We have bypassed the day books in the example, for the sake of simplicity and because the main emphasis of the assignment is the posting of transactions to the correct ledger accounts.

(a) and (b)

The ledger accounts will appear as follows after the postings for 30 June 20X7 and after being balanced off.

ADVERTISING					
20X7			20X7		
29 June Balance b/f	288	91			
30 June Bank	33	50	30 June P+L account	322	41
	322	41		322	41

ACCOUNTANCY FEES					
20X7			20X7		
29 June Balance b/f	1,500	00	30 June P+L account	1,500	00

BANK ACCOUNT					
20X7			20X7		
29 June Balance b/f	19,330	65			
			30 June Woodley Gazette	39	36
			Electricity	739	80
			M Able & Co	1,437	50
			Bank interest	67	48
			Motor expenses	372	97
				378	12
				2,312	50
				2,169	52
30 June Balance c/f	3,729	33		15,542	73
	23,059	98		23,059	98

DOUBTFUL DEBT PROVISION					
20X7			20X7		
30 June Balance c/f	1,242	94	29 June Balance b/f	1,242	94

ELECTRICITY					
20X7			20X7		
29 June Balance b/f	1,733	84			
30 June Bank	629	62	30 June P+L account	2,363	46
	2,363	46		2,363	46

FIXTURES AND FITTINGS					
20X7			20X7		
29 June Balance b/f	11,893	55	30 June Balance c/f	11,893	55

GAS					
20X7			20X7		
29 June Balance b/f	1,161	20	30 June P+L account	1,161	20

INSURANCE					
20X7			20X7		
29 June Balance b/f	658	38			
30 June Bank	1,437	50	30 June P+L account	2,095	88
	2,095	88		2,095	88

INTEREST					
20X7			20X7		
29 June Balance b/f	1,141	31			
30 June Bank	67	48	30 June P+L account	1,208	79
	1,208	79		1,208	79

MAINTENANCE

20X7			20X7		
29 June Balance b/f	3,807	43	30 June P+L account	3,807	43

MOTOR EXPENSES

20X7			20X7		
29 June Balance b/f	606	19			
30 June Bank	317	42			
Bank	100	00	30 June P+L account	1,023	61
	1,023	61		1,023	61

MOTOR VEHICLES

20X7			20X7		
29 June Balance b/f	43,675	07			
30 June Bank	15,442	73	30 June Balance c/f	59,117	80
	59,117	80		59,117	80

PROFIT AND LOSS ACCOUNT

20X7			20X7		
30 June Balance c/f	27,225	92	29 June Balance b/f	27,225	92

PURCHASES

20X7			20X7		
29 June Balance b/f	76,648	31			
30 June Larkin Lumber					
P/L Control a/c	3,295	00			
Plumbing supplies					
P/L Control a/c	1,536	05	30 June P+L account	81,479	36
	81,479	36		81,479	36

* A prepayment would not normally be required for such a small amount; in any case this would not be calculated until the ETB was prepared.

** This amount might have been posted to the insurance account, depending on company policy, but this is more appropriate.

Answers to practice devolved assessments

PURCHASE LEDGER CONTROL A/C					
20X7			20X7		
			29 June Balance b/f	9,554	93
			30 June Larkin Lumber	3,871	63
30 June Balance c/f	15,231	42	Plumbing supplies	1,804	86
	15,231	42		15,231	42

PRINT, POSTAGE & STATIONERY					
20X7			20X7		
29 June Balance b/f	117	29			
30 June Bank	378	12	30 June P+L account	495	41
	495	41		495	41

RENT					
20X7			20X7		
29 June Balance b/f	9,250	00			
30 June Bank	2,312	50	30 June P+L account	11,562	50
	11,562	50		11,562	50

Note. The rent invoice just paid is for rent to 30 September 20X7. This would be adjusted as a prepayment on the *extended* trial balance.

SHARE CAPITAL					
20X7			20X7		
30 June Balance c/f	10,000	00	29 June Balance b/f	10,000	00

ACCUMULATED DEPRECIATION					
20X7			20X7		
30 June Balance c/f	27,241	12	29 June Balance b/f	27,241	12

SALES

20X7			20X7		
			29 June Balance b/f	180,754	17
			30 June Sales Ledger		
			Control a/c		
			MP Price & Co	504	00
			H Contractors	90	45
			NP Plumbers	342	75
30 June Balance c/f	182,421	37	CR Harris & Co	730	00
	182,421	37		182,421	37

SALES LEDGER CONTROL A/C

20X7			20X7		
29 June Balance b/f	19,356	30			
30 June Sales					
MP Price & Co	592	20			
H Contractors	106	28			
NP PLumbers	402	73			
CR Harris & Co	857	75	30 June Balance c/f	21,315	26
	21,315	26		21,315	26

SUNDRY EXPENSES

20X7			20X7		
29 June Balance b/f	1,427	70	30 June P+L account	1,427	70

OPENING STOCK

20X7			20X7		
29 June Balance b/f	37,321	56	30 June Balance c/f	37,321	56

Answers to practice devolved assessments

TELEPHONE					
20X7			20X7		
29 June Balance b/f	3,879	09	30 June P & L account	3,879	09

UNIFORM BUSINESS RATE					
20X7			20X7		
29 June Balance b/f	4,917	94	30 June P & L account	4,917	94

VAT CONTROL A/C					
20X7			20X7		
30 June Bank	5	86	29 June Balance b/f	6,719	19
Bank	110	18	30 June Sales ledger	88	20
Bank	55	55	Sales ledger	15	83
Purchases ledger	576	63	Sales ledger	59	98
Purchases ledger	268	81	Sales ledger	127	75
Balance c/f	5,993	92			
	7,010	95		7,010	95

WAGES					
20X7			20X7		
29 June Balance b/f	21,575	63			
30 June Bank	2,169	52	30 June P & L account	23,745	15
	23,745	15		23,745	15

WATER RATES					
20X7			20X7		
29 June Balance b/f	2,447	92	30 June P & L account	2,447	92

(c) The balances on the ledger accounts, once extracted, will give the following trial balance.

FOLIO	DESCRIPTION	REF.	TRIAL BALANCE			
	Advertising		322	41		
	Accountancy fees		1,500	00		
	Bank				3,729	33
	Depreciation (accumulated)				27,241	12
	Doubtful debt provision				1,242	94
	Electricity		2,363	46		
	Fixtures and fittings		11,893	55		
	Gas		1,161	20		
	Insurance		658	38		
	Interest		1,208	79		
	Maintenance		3,807	43		
	Motor expenses		2,461	11		
	Motor vehicles		59,117	80		
	Profit and loss account				27,225	92
	Purchases		81,479	36		
	Purchase ledger control a/c				15,231	42
	Print, post and stationery		495	41		
	Rent		11,562	50		
	Share capital				10,000	00
	Sales				182,421	37
	Sales ledger control a/c		21,315	26		
	Sundry expenses		1,427	70		
	Stock 1.1 X4		37,321	56		
	Telephone		3,879	09		
	Unified Business Rate		4,917	94		
	VAT				5,993	92
	Wages		23,745	15		
	Water rates		2,447	92		
	TOTAL		273,086	02	273,086	02

BPP PUBLISHING

(d) The following accruals and prepayments should be identified.

Accruals

Franking services: £378.12 × 1/3 = £126.04

Prepayments

Rent: quarter to 30 September 20X7: £2,312.50

Motor insurance: £1,437.50 × 11/12 = £1,317.71

ANSWER TO PRACTICE DEVOLVED ASSESSMENT 3: LAKELAND CATERING

Shop and restaurant
Task (a)

STATEMENT OF AFFAIRS AS AT 1 JANUARY 20X6

	£	£
Assets		
Vehicle	5,800	
Restaurant fittings	3,900	
Stock	6,000	
Debtors	200	
Bank	350	
Prepayment	150	
		16,400
Less: liabilities		
Creditors	(1,100)	
Accruals: rent	(250)	
wages	(610)	
		(1,960)
Capital (as at 1 January 20X6)		14,440

Task (b)

CLOSING CASH POSITION AS AT 31 DECEMBER 20X6

	£	£
Receipts		
Opening balance	350	
Sales	31,970	
		32,320
Payments		(28,917)
Closing cash book balance		3,403

Task (c)

Control accounts

TRADE DEBTORS

	£		£
b/f 1 January 20X6	200	Cash/bank	4,910
P&L	5,325	c/f 31 December 20X6	615
	5,525		5,525
b/f 1 January 20X7	615		

TRADE CREDITORS

	£		£
Cash/bank	17,850	b/f 1 January 20X6	1,100
c/f 31 December 20X6	840	P&L	17,590
	18,690		18,690
		b/f 1 January 20X7	840

RENT

	£		£
Cash/bank	745	b/f 1 January 20X6	250
		P&L	435
		c/f 31 December 20X6	60
	745		745
b/f 1 January 20X7	60		

WAGES

	£		£
Cash/bank	8,090	b/f 1 January 20X6	610
		P&L	7,480
	8,090		8,090

ELECTRICITY

	£		£
b/f 1 January 20X6	150	P&L	1,040
Cash/bank	640		
c/f 31 December 20X6	250		
	1,040		1,040
		b/f 1 January 20X7	250

Task (d)

SHOP AND RESTAURANT
TRADING AND PROFIT AND LOSS ACCOUNT
FOR THE PERIOD ENDED 31 DECEMBER 20X6

		£	£
Sales			32,385
Opening stock		6,000	
Add: purchases		17,590	
		23,590	
Less: closing stock		(5,400)	
Cost of goods sold			(18,190)
Gross profit			14,195
Less: rent		435	
wages		7,480	
electricity		1,040	
depreciation	- fittings	780	
	- vehicle	1,740	
telephone		570	
restaurant maintenance		710	
insurance		312	
			(13,067)
Net profit			1,128

Task (e)

SHOP AND RESTAURANT
BALANCE SHEET AS AT 31 DECEMBER 20X6

	b/f £	*Depn* £	*NBV* £
Fixed assets			
Fittings	3,900	(780)	3,120
Van	5,800	(1,740)	4,060
	9,700	(2,520)	7,180
Current assets			
Stock	5,400		
Debtors	615		
Rent prepayment	60		
Cash	3,403		
		9,478	
Less current liabilities			
Creditors	840		
Accrual - electricity	250		
		(1,090)	
			8,388
			15,568
Financed by			
Capital as at 1 January 20X6			14,440
Net profit			1,128
			15,568

Task (f)

MEMORANDUM

To: David
From: Caroline
Date: 31 January 20X7

Depreciation methods

Straight line depreciation is obtained by calculating a fixed annual sum by which an asset will be depreciated. So, for example, if an asset was purchased for £10,000 and is to be depreciated over four years and have an expected selling price at the end of four years of £4,100 then the annual depreciation charge per annum will be £1,475.

The reducing balance method of depreciation means that the depreciation charged against profits reduces year on year. The main justification for using this method is that each year, as the machine wears out, more and more will be spent on repairing and maintaining it. The reducing balance method is expressed as a percentage of the book value so, for example, if we use a reducing balance percentage of 20% for the previous example the figures would be as follows.

Cost £10,000

		Calculation	*Depreciation*	*Book value*
End of year				
	1	£10,000 × 20%	£2,000	£8,000
	2	£8,000 × 20%	£1,600	£6,400

etc.

Task (g)

Van depreciation - straight line method

$$\text{Depreciation charge} = \frac{10,000 - 460}{6} = 1,590$$

		Depreciation charge for year £	*Book value* £
End of year	1	1,590	8,410
	2	1,590	6,820
	3	1,590	5,230
	4	1,590	3,640
	5	1,590	2,050
	6	1,590	460

Task (h)

Van depreciation - reducing balance method

Cost = £10,000

		Calculation of depreciation charge £	*Depreciation charge for year* £	*Book value* £
End of year	1	10,000 × 40%	4,000	6,000
	2	6,000 × 40%	2,400	3,600
	3	3,600 × 40%	1,440	2,160
	4	2,160 × 40%	864	1,296
	5	1,296 × 40%	518	778
	6	778 × 40%	311	467

LAKELAND CATERING - SPECIALIST CATERING DIVISION

Description	Trial balance Debit £	Trial balance Credit £	Adjustments Debit £	Adjustments Credit £	Profit and Loss a/c Debit £	Profit and Loss a/c Credit £	Balance Sheet Debit £	Balance Sheet Credit £
Sales		38,500				38,500		
Purchases	19,250				19,250			
Opening stock	4,000				4,000			
Wages	10,100				10,100			
Electricity	750		100		850			
P/L Depn								
- fittings			250		250			
- vehicles			1,590		1,590			
Telephone	600		50		650			
Insurance	450			50	400			
Rent	950			250	700			
Fixtures -								
cost	5,000						5,000	
depn		2,500		250				2,750
Vehicle -								
cost	10,000						10,000	
depn				1,590				1,590
Stock -								
bal sheet			3,000				3,000	
trading a/c				3,000		3,000		
Debtors	700						700	
Creditors		1,200						1,200
Cash in hand	100						100	
Bank overdraft		1,400						1,400
Capital		8,300						8,300
Prepayments			250				250	
Accruals				100				100
Net profit					3,710			3,710
TOTALS	51,900	51,900	5,240	5,240	41,500	41,500	19,050	19,050

ANSWER TO PRACTICE DEVOLVED ASSESSMENT 4: CUT PRICE ELECTRICALS

Task (a)

CUT PRICE ELECTRICALS RETAIL DIVISION
OPENING CAPITAL STATEMENT
AS AT 1 NOVEMBER 20X5

	Debit £'000	*Credit* £'000
Premises - cost	100	
Premises - depreciation		20
Fixtures - cost	85	
Fixtures - depreciation		15
Vans - cost	20	
Vans - depreciation		10
Stock	36	
Debtors	20	
Creditors		16
Wages - in advance	2	
Rent - in advance	7	
Rates - in arrears		6
Advertising - in arrears		5
Insurance - in advance	6	
Cash in hand		
Bank overdraft		3
Capital as at 1/11/X5 (balancing item)		199
	276	276

Task (b)

Control accounts - Retail Division

WAGES

	£'000		£'000
b/f 1/11/X5	2	P&L	76
Cash/bank	79	c/f 31/10/X6	5
	81		81
b/f 1/11/X6	5		

RENT

	£'000		£'000
b/f 1/11/X5	7	P&L	21
Cash/bank	17	c/f 31/10/X6	3
	24		24
b/f 1/11/X6	3		

RATES

	£'000		£'000
Cash/bank	14	b/f 1/11/X5	6
c/f 31/10/X6	2	P&L	10
	16		16
		b/f 1/11/X6	2

ADVERTISING

	£'000		£'000
Cash/bank	8	b/f 1/11/X5	5
c/f 31/10/X6	8	P&L	11
	16		16
		b/f 1/11/X6	8

INSURANCE

	£'000		£'000
b/f 1/11/X5	6	P&L	25
Cash/bank	16		
c/f 31/10/X6	3		
	25		25
		b/f 1/11/X6	3

TRADE DEBTORS

	£'000		£'000
b/f 1/11/X5	20	Cash/bank	212
P&L	206	c/f 31/10/X6	14
	226		226
b/f 1/11/X6	14		

TRADE CREDITORS

	£'000		£'000
Cash/bank	104	b/f 1/11/X5	16
c/f 31/10/X6	27	P&L	115
	131		131
		b/f 1/11/X6	27

Task (c)

CUT PRICE ELECTRICALS
BANK RECONCILIATION STATEMENT

	£
Balance as per bank statement (bal fig)	(44,350)
Unlodged credits	17,000
Uncleared cheques	(2,650)
Balance as per cash book	(30,000)

Tasks (d) and (e)

FIXED ASSET REGISTER AS AT 31 OCTOBER 20X6

Van number 2

Cost	Depreciation to 31/10/X5	Depreciation for year ended 31/10/X6	Net book value at 31/10/X6
£10,000	£4,000	£2,000	£4,000

Van number 1

VAN ACCOUNT

	£'000		£'000
b/f 1/11/X5	10	Asset disposal	10

VAN DEPRECIATION ACCOUNT

	£'000		£'000
Asset disposal	8	b/f 1/11/X5	6
	8	Charge for year	2
			8

ASSET DISPOSAL ACCOUNT

	£'000		£'000
Van	10.0	Depreciation account	8.0
Profit on disposal to P&L	1.5	Cash/bank	3.5
	11.5		11.5

Note. The cash/bank credit entry of £3,500 in the asset disposal account could also be shown as a debtor as the offer was accepted but cash not received.

CUT PRICE ELECTRICALS - INSTALLATION AND CONTRACTING DIVISION

Description	Trial balance Debit £'000	Trial balance Credit £'000	Adjustments Debit £'000	Adjustments Credit £'000	Profit and Loss a/c Debit £'000	Profit and Loss a/c Credit £'000	Balance Sheet Debit £'000	Balance Sheet Credit £'000
Sales		109				109		
Purchases	64				64			
Stock	11				11			
Wages	57				57			
Van expenses	14			3	11			
Travel expenses	3		3		6			
Garage rent	6			1	5			
Insurance	2				2			
Tools allowance	5				5			
Advertising	8		2		10			
Misc - expenses	4				4			
Vans - cost	20						20	
Vans - depn		12		6				18
Fixtures - cost	75						75	
Fixtures - depn		60		3				63
Capital		100						100
Debtors	36						36	
Creditors		21						21
Cash in hand	6						6	
Bank overdraft		9						9
Stock - B sheet			14				14	
- Trading a/c				14		14		
P/L Depn - Vans			6		6			
Fixtures			3		3			
Bad debt provsn				2				
- B sheet								2
- P/L a/c			2		2			
Prepayments / accruals			1	2			1	
Net loss						63	63	
	311	311	31	31	186	186	215	215

Answer to trial run devolved assessment

Task 1

CASH BOOK: RECEIPTS

Date	Details	Bank	Sales Ledger Control	Suspense
		£	£	£
20X3				
1 June	Balance bfwd	7,290.02		
7 June	Cheques banked	9,309.39	9,309.39	
14 June	Cheques banked	3,387.03	3,387.03	
15 June	BACS receipt	8,930.93	8,930.93	
24 June	Cheques banked	5,114.56	5,114.56	
28 June	Cheques banked	648.93	648.93	
		27,390.84	27,390.84	
30 June	BACS receipt	7,829.03		7,829.03
		35,219.87	27,390.84	7,829.03

CASH BOOK: PAYMENTS

Date	Details	Cheque No	Bank	Purchase Ledger Control	Other
20X3			£	£	£
7 June	Plastika Inc	8391	7,268.26	7,268.26	
8 June	Jensen Plastics	8392	2,004.87	2,004.87	
12 June	MetalFramer Ltd	8393	1,092.03	1,092.03	
13 June	Welsh Water Authority				
	– water usage	8394	736.99		736.99
20 June	Lentril Inks Ltd	8395	738.83	738.83	
27 June	Signmakers' Guild				
	– annual subscription	8396	93.00		93.00
27 June	Salaries	BACS	13,095.98		13,095.98
27 June	Orbitol Ltd	8397	373.49	373.49	
			25,403.45	11,477.48	13,925.97
30 June	FinLease Co Ltd	Debit card	5,000.00		5,000.00
30 June	Cash withdrawal	Debit card	3,000.00		3,000.00
			33,403.45	11,477.48	21,925.97
	Analysis:				
	Direct labour				13,095.98
	Administration				93.00
	Factory overheads				736.99
	Suspense				8,000.00
					21,925.97

Task 1, continued

Bank reconciliation at 30 June 20X3

	£	£
Cash book balance at 1/6/X3		7,290.02
Receipts		27,390.84
Payments		(25,403.45)
Cash book balance at 30/6/X3		9,277.41
Deposit for car paid by debit card, not recorded in cash book		(5,000.00)
Cash withdrawals, not recorded in cash book		(3,000.00)
Receipt from customer by BACS, not recorded in cash book		7,829.03
Amended cash book balance at 30/6/X3		9,106.44
Balance per bank statement at 30/6/X3		10,928.87
Add outstanding lodgement		648.93
Less unpresented cheques:		
8392	2,004.87	
8396	93.00	
8397	373.49	
		(2,471.36)
Amended cash book balance at 30/6/X3		9,106.44

Tasks 1, 6, 7 and 8

GENERAL LEDGER

ADMINISTRATION					
Date	**Details**	**Amount £**	**Date**	**Details**	**Amount £**
20X3			**20X3**		
1/6	Balance b/d	8,543.09			
30/6	Cash book	93.00			
30/6	Purchases day book	785.56			
30/6	Journal 7	189.62	30/6	Balance c/d	9,611.27
		9,611.27			9,611.27
30/6	Balance b/d	9,611.27			

ASSEMBLIES PURCHASES					
Date	**Details**	**Amount £**	**Date**	**Details**	**Amount £**
20X3			**20X3**		
1/6	Balance b/d	64,319.05			
30/6	Purchases day book	6,417.09	30/6	Purchases returns	
30/6	Journal 7	542.33		day book	207.50
			30/6	Balance c/d	71,070.97
		71,278.47			71,278.47
30/6	Balance b/d	71,070.97			

ASSEMBLIES STOCK					
Date	**Details**	**Amount £**	**Date**	**Details**	**Amount £**
20X3			**20X3**		
1/6	Balance	6,930.83			
			30/6	Balance c/d	6,930.83
		6,930.83			6,930.83
30/6	Balance b/d	6,930.83			

BPP PUBLISHING

Tasks 1, 6, 7 and 8, continued

GENERAL LEDGER

BANK					
Date	**Details**	**Amount £**	**Date**	**Details**	**Amount £**
20X3			**20X3**		
1/6	Balance	7,290.02	30/6	Cash book payments	33,403.45
30/6	Cash book receipts	35,219.87	30/6	Balance c/d	9,106.44
		42,509.89			42,509.89
30/6	Balance b/d	9,106.44			

CAPITAL					
Date	**Details**	**Amount £**	**Date**	**Details**	**Amount £**
20X3			**20X3**		
			1/6	Balance	70,000.00
30/6	Balance c/d	70,000.00			
		70,000.00			70,000.00
			30/6	Balance b/d	70,000.00

DEPRECIATION CHARGE					
Date	**Details**	**Amount £**	**Date**	**Details**	**Amount £**
20X3			**20X3**		
30/6	Journal 6 – factory	3,272.53			
30/6	Journal 6 – office	2,162.50			
30/6	Journal 6 – MV	13,350.00	30/6	Balance c/d	18,785.03
		18,785.03			18,785.03
30/6	Balance b/d	18,785.03			

Tasks 1, 6, 7 and 8, continued

GENERAL LEDGER

	DIRECT LABOUR				
Date	Details	Amount £	Date	Details	Amount £
20X3			**20X3**		
1/6	Balance	142,086.56			
30/6	Cash book	13,095.98	30/6	Balance c/d	155,182.54
		155,182.54			155,182.54
30/6	Balance b/d	155,182.54			

	DISPOSALS				
Date	Details	Amount £	Date	Details	Amount £
20X3			**20X3**		
30/6	Journal 5	2,500.00	30/6	Journal 5	693.75
			30/6	Journal 5	1,750.00
			30/6	Loss on disposal	56.25
		2,500.00			2,500.00

	DRAWINGS				
Date	Details	Amount £	Date	Details	Amount £
20X3			**20X3**		
30/6	Journal 1	36,000.00			
			30/6	Balance c/d	36,000.00
		36,000.00			36,000.00
30/6	Balance b/d	36,000.00			

Tasks 1, 6, 7 and 8, continued

GENERAL LEDGER

FACTORY EQUIPMENT: ACCUMULATED DEPRECIATION

Date	Details	Amount £	Date	Details	Amount £
20X3			20X3		
			1/6	Balance	7,126.87
30/6	Journal 5	693.75	30/6	Journal 6	3,272.53
30/6	Balance c/d	9,705.65			
		10,399.40			10,399.40
			30/6	Balance b/d	9,705.65

FACTORY EQUIPMENT: COST

Date	Details	Amount £	Date	Details	Amount £
20X3			20X3		
1/6	Balance	27,750.00			
30/6	Journal 2	3,000.00	30/6	Journal 5	2,500.00
			30/6	Balance c/d	28,250.00
		30,750.00			30,750.00
30/6	Balance b/d	28,250.00			

FACTORY OVERHEADS

Date	Details	Amount £	Date	Details	Amount £
20X3			20X3		
1/6	Balance	17,683.35			
30/6	Cash book	736.99			
30/6	Purchases day book	1,019.94			
30/6	Journal 7	105.00	30/6	Balance c/d	19,545.28
		19,545.28			19,545.28
30/6	Balance b/d	19,545.28			

Tasks 1, 6, 7 and 8, continued

GENERAL LEDGER

FINISHED GOODS STOCK					
Date	**Details**	**Amount £**	**Date**	**Details**	**Amount £**
20X3			**20X3**		
1/6	Balance	13,645.86			
			30/6	Balance c/d	13,645.86
		13,645.86			13,645.86
30/6	Balance b/d	13,645.86			

HIRE PURCHASE CREDITOR					
Date	**Details**	**Amount £**	**Date**	**Details**	**Amount £**
20X3			**20X3**		
30/6	Journal 4	5,000.00	30/6	Journal 3	29,305.00
30/6	Balance c/d	24,305.00			
		29,305.00			29,305.00
			30/6	Balance b/d	24,305.00

INTEREST EXPENSE					
Date	**Details**	**Amount £**	**Date**	**Details**	**Amount £**
20X3			**20X3**		
1/6	Balance	1,100.00			
30/6	Journal 3	125.00	30/6	Balance c/d	1,225.00
		1,225.00			1,225.00
30/6	Balance b/d	1,225.00			

MOTOR VEHICLES: ACCUMULATED DEPRECIATION					
Date	**Details**	**Amount £**	**Date**	**Details**	**Amount £**
20X3			**20X3**		
			1/6	Balance	12,150.00
30/6	Balance c/d	25,500.00	30/6	Journal 6	13,350.00
		25,500.00			25,500.00
			30/6	Balance b/d	25,500.00

Tasks 1, 6, 7 and 8, continued

GENERAL LEDGER

Date	Details	Amount £	Date	Details	Amount £
20X3			**20X3**		
1/6	Balance	36,750.00			
30/6	Journal 3	30,000.00	30/6	Balance c/d	66,750.00
		66,750.00			66,750.00
30/6	Balance b/d	66,750.00			

MOTOR VEHICLES: COST

Date	Details	Amount £	Date	Details	Amount £
20X3			**20X3**		
			1/6	Balance	2,912.50
30/6	Balance c/d	5,075.00	30/6	Journal 6	2,162.50
		5,075.00			5,075.00
			30/6	Balance b/d	5,075.00

OFFICE EQUIPMENT: ACCUMULATED DEPRECIATION

Date	Details	Amount £	Date	Details	Amount £
20X3			**20X3**		
1/6	Balance	8,650.00			
			30/6	Balance c/d	8,650.00
		8,650.00			8,650.00
30/6	Balance b/d	8,650.00			

OFFICE EQUIPMENT: COST

Tasks 1, 6, 7 and 8, continued

GENERAL LEDGER

PURCHASE LEDGER CONTROL					
Date	**Details**	**Amount £**	**Date**	**Details**	**Amount £**
20X3			**20X3**		
			1/6	Balance	21,548.55
30/6	Cash book	11,477.48	30/6	Purchases day book	20,529.70
30/6	Purchases returns day book	1,534.85			
30/6	Balance c/d	29,065.92			
		42,078.25			42,078.25
30/6	Balance c/d	31,469.26	30/6	Balance b/d	29,063.92
			30/6	Journal 7	2,403.34
		31,469.26			31,469.26
			30/6	Balance b/d	31,469.26

RAW MATERIALS PURCHASES					
Date	**Details**	**Amount £**	**Date**	**Details**	**Amount £**
20X3			**20X3**		
1/6	Balance	95,476.98			
30/6	Purchases day book	9,249.50	30/6	Purchases returns day book	1,098.76
30/6	Journal 7	1,208.45	30/6	Balance c/d	104,836.17
		105,934.93			105,934.93
30/6	Balance b/d	104,836.17			

RAW MATERIALS STOCK					
Date	**Details**	**Amount £**	**Date**	**Details**	**Amount £**
20X3			**20X3**		
1/6	Balance	15,019.86			
			30/6	Balance c/d	15,019.86
		15,019.86			15,019.86
30/6	Balance b/d	15,019.86			

Tasks 1, 6, 7 and 8, continued

GENERAL LEDGER

SALES					
Date	**Details**	**Amount £**	**Date**	**Details**	**Amount £**
20X3			20X3		
			1/6	Balance	408,243.67
30/6	Sales returns day book	6,015.42	30/6	Sales day book	28,120.93
30/6	Balance c/d	430,349.18			
		436,364.60			436,364.60
			30/6	Balance b/d	430,349.18

SALES LEDGER CONTROL					
Date	**Details**	**Amount £**	**Date**	**Details**	**Amount £**
20X3			20X3		
1/6	Balance b/d	52,754.01	30/6	Cash book	27,390.84
30/6	Sales day book	33,042.09	30/6	Journal 1	7,829.03
			30/6	Sales returns day book	7,068.11
			30/6	Balance c/d	43,508.12
		85,796.10			85,796.10
30/6	Balance b/d	43,508.12			

SUNDRY CREDITORS					
Date	**Details**	**Amount £**	**Date**	**Details**	**Amount £**
20X3			20X3		
			30/6	Journal 2	3,525.00
30/6	Balance c/d	4,345.00	30/6	Journal 3	820.00
		4,345.00			4,345.00
			30/6	Balance b/d	4,345.00

Tasks 1, 6, 7 and 8, continued

GENERAL LEDGER

SUSPENSE					
Date	**Details**	**Amount £**	**Date**	**Details**	**Amount £**
20X3			**20X3**		
1/6	Cash book	33,000.00	30/4	Cash book	1,750.00
30/6	Cash book	3,000.00	30/6	Cash book	7,829.03
30/6	Cash book	5,000.00	30/6	Journal 1	28,170.97
30/6	Journal 5	1,750.00	30/6	Journal 4	5,000.00
		42,750.00			42,750.00

VAT					
Date	**Details**	**Amount £**	**Date**	**Details**	**Amount £**
20X3			**20X3**		
			1/6	Balance	7,268.02
30/6	Journal 2	525.00	30/6	Sales day book	4,921.16
30/6	Sales returns day book	1,052.69	30/6	Purchases returns	
30/6	Purchases day book	3,057.61		day book	228.59
30/6	Journal 7	357.94			
30/6	Balance c/d	7,424.53			
		12,417.77			12,417.77
			30/6	Balance b/d	7,424.53

Task 2

Semiotix Associates

MEMO

Date: 20 July 20X3

To: Alex Beech

From: Ronnie Hall

Re: Suspense account

Thank you for your memo of yesterday. I can confirm that I am now able to clear some of the suspense account balance that has built up over the year as follows:

- A total of £36,000.00 needs to be credited to Suspense and debited to Drawings.

- £7,829.03 needs to be debited to Suspense and credited to Sales Ledger Control, as it is a reduction in the debt owed to us by Oonagh Shops Ltd. As the sales ledger is merely a subsidiary, memorandum ledger, the posting you made did not effect the full double entry.

There is still a balance outstanding on the suspense account to be cleared.

May I ask you in future to pass me the transaction slips after you have each made the withdrawals from ATM machines so I can account for drawings as they are made? In addition, I would appreciate it if you could pass me remittance advices from customers on a timely basis. Together these two actions will help me to monitor the cash situation for you much more effectively.

Ronnie

Tasks 2, 3, 4, 5 and 6

JOURNAL

Journal number	Date 20X3	Account names and narrative	Debit £	Credit £
1	30/6/X3	DEBIT Drawings	36,000.00	
		CREDIT Sales ledger control		7,829.03
		CREDIT Suspense		28,170.97
		Being reclassification of cash book entries posted to suspense		
2	30/6/X3	DEBIT Factory equipment: cost	3,000.00	
		DEBIT VAT	525.00	
		CREDIT Sundry creditors		3,525.00
		Being purchase of new Jig for factory		
3	30/6/X3	DEBIT Motor vehicles: cost	30,000.00	
		DEBIT Interest expense	125.00	
		CREDIT Sundry creditors (June payment)		820.00
		CREDIT Hire purchase creditor (30,000 – 695)		29,305.00
		Being acquisition of Mercedes 7 JH58 YTK on hire purchase		
4	30/6/X3	DEBIT Hire purchase creditor	5,000.00	
		CREDIT Suspense		5,000.00
		Being reclassification of deposit posted to suspense		
5	30/6/X3	DEBIT Factory equipment: accumulated depreciation	693.75	
		DEBIT Disposals	2,500.00	
		DEBIT Suspense	1,750.00	
		CREDIT Disposals		693.75
		CREDIT Factory equipment: cost		2,500.00
		CREDIT Disposals		1,750.00
		Being disposal of small frame machine during year		
6	30/6/X3	DEBIT Depreciation charge (factory equipment) (596.06 + 650.25 + 450.00 + 812.81 + 189.66 + 573.75)	3,272.53	
		DEBIT Depreciation charge (office equipment) (500.00 + 662.50 + 750.00 + 250.00)	2,162.50	
		DEBIT Depreciation charge (motor vehicles) (4,800.00 + 2,550.00 + 6,000.00)	13,350.00	
		CREDIT Factory equipment: accumulated depreciation		3,272.53
		CREDIT Office equipment: accumulated depreciation		2,162.50
		CREDIT Motor vehicles: accumulated depreciation		13,350.00
		Being depreciation for the year		

TASKS 3, 4 AND 5
FIXED ASSET REGISTER

Description/serial no	Date acquired	Original cost £	Depreciation £	NBV £	Funding method	Disposal proceeds £	Disposal date
Factory equipment							
Depreciation: 15% pa reducing balance							
High tensile cutter	1/7/X0	5,500.00			Cash		
Year ended 30/6/X1			825.00	4,675.00			
Year ended 30/6/X2			701.25	3,973.75			
Year ended 30/6/X3			596.06	3,377.69			
Small frame machine	1/7/X0	2,500.00			Cash	1,750.00	30/4/X3 Insurance
Year ended 30/6/X1			375.00	2,125.00			
Year ended 30/6/X2			318.75	1,806.25			
		2,500.00	693.75				
Large frame machine	31/12/X0	6,000.00			Cash		
Year ended 30/6/X1			900.00	5,100.00			
Year ended 30/6/X2			765.00	4,335.00			
Year ended 30/6/X3			650.25	3,684.75			
Jig	25/6/X3	3,000.00			Cash		
Year ended 30/6/X3			450.00	2,550.00			

TASKS 3, 4 AND 5, CONTINUED
FIXED ASSET REGISTER

Description/serial no	Date acquired	Original cost £	Depreciation £	NBV £	Funding method	Disposal proceeds £	Disposal date
Factory equipment							
Depreciation: 15% pa reducing balance							
Colour print machine	1/7/X0	7,500.00			Cash		
Year ended 30/6/X1			1,125.00	6,375.00			
Year ended 30/6/X2			956.25	5,418.75			
Year ended 30/6/X3			812.81	4,605.94			
Lifting machine	1/7/X0	1,750.00			Cash		
Year ended 30/6/X1			262.50	1,487.50			
Year ended 30/6/X2			223.12	1,264.38			
Year ended 30/6/X3			189.66	1,074.72			
Laminator	1/1/X2	4,500.00			Cash		
Year ended 30/6/X2			675.00	3,825.00			
Year ended 30/6/X3			573.75	3,251.25			

ANSWERS (TASKS 3, 4 AND 5, CONTINUED)
FIXED ASSET REGISTER

Description/serial no	Date acquired	Original cost £	Depreciation £	NBV £	Funding method	Disposal proceeds £	Disposal date
Office equipment							
Depreciation: 25% pa straight line							
Velox Pentium III PC	1/7/X1	2,000.00			Cash		
Year ended 30/6/X2			500.00	1,500.00			
Year ended 30/6/X3			500.00	1,000.00			
Velox Pentium III laptop	1/7/X1	2,650.00			Cash		
Year ended 30/6/X2			662.50	1,987.50			
Year ended 30/6/X3			662.50	1,325.00			
Photocopier	1/7/X0	3,000.00			Cash		
Year ended 30/6/X1			750.00	2,250.00			
Year ended 30/6/X2			750.00	1,500.00			
Year ended 30/6/X3			750.00	750.00			
Laser printer	1/7/X1	1,000.00			Cash		
Year ended 30/6/X2			250.00	750.00			
Year ended 30/6/X3			250.00	500.00			

TASKS 3, 4 AND 5, CONTINUED
FIXED ASSET REGISTER

Description/serial no	Date acquired	Original cost £	Depreciation £	NBV £	Funding method	Disposal proceeds £	Disposal date
Motor vehicles							
Depreciation: 20% pa straight line							
High sided delivery van JH54 HJK	1/7/X0	24,000.00			Hire purchase (30 months)		
Year ended 30/6/X1			4,800.00	19,200.00			
Year ended 30/6/X2			4,800.00	14,400.00			
Year ended 30/6/X3			4,800.00	9,600.00			
Delivery van JH56 ADF	1/5/X2	12,750.00			Cash		
Year ended 30/6/X2			2,550.00	10,200.00			
Year ended 30/6/X3			2,550.00	7,650.00			
Mercedes 7 JH58 YTK	12/6/X3	30,000.00			Hire purchase (36 months)		
Year ended 30/6/X3			6,000.00	24,000.00			

Task 4, continued

Semiotix Associates

MEMO

Date: 20 July 20X3

To: Alex Beech and Bridget Meadows

From: Ronnie Hall

Re: Authority for capital disposal and expenditure

I have been writing up the fixed asset register in preparation for the year end accounts. When I compared the register to the list of assets you had prepared I discovered a small frame machine in the factory had been destroyed by accident. I could then tie it in with the insurance monies received. However, in order to maintain proper control over fixed assets and their disposal, I would recommend that any disposal of fixed assets, for whatever reason, should be evidenced by you both in writing at the time of disposal.

I have also been accounting for the new Mercedes which has been acquired on hire purchase. While I now have evidence of your authority for the car's acquisition in the form of a sales invoice signed by you, this does not highlight the rather complicated hire purchase transaction that has been entered into to fund the purchase, nor the payment of the £5,000.00 by debit card as deposit which I picked up from the bank statement. As I did not know about this I am afraid that the June payment has already been missed. I would recommend that you pass me invoices for expenditure on fixed assets on a timely basis, and that you let me have any HP agreements signed by both of you promptly so we do not have this sort of problem again.

Ronnie

Task 7

Debtors' reconciliation

	£
Addlestone Town Council	7,930.84
Friary Shopping Mall	3,074.83
Granville Leisure Park	2,039.72
Highways Agency	2,928.03
Midlands Development Agency	15,920.39
Oonagh Shops Ltd	4,037.49
Pinewood plc	3,904.04
Warrington Town Council	3,672.78
Total = Balance per sales ledger control account	43,508.12

Creditors' reconciliation

	£
Adams Adhesives Ltd	4,920.37
Ericson plc	5,309.48
Jensen Plastics	253.39
Lentril Inks Ltd	1,028.39
MetalFramer Ltd	13,290.03
Orbitol Ltd	892.02
Plastika Inc	2,539.30
Tendrils plc	3,236.28
Total	31,469.26
Difference (page of purchases day book omitted from total for June)	(2,403.34)
Balance per purchase ledger control account	29,065.92

JOURNAL

Journal number	Date 20X3	Account names and narrative	Debit £	Credit £
7	30/6/X3	DEBIT Administration	189.62	
		DEBIT Assemblies purchases	542.33	
		DEBIT Factory overheads	105.00	
		DEBIT Raw materials purchases	1,208.45	
		DEBIT VAT	357.94	
		CREDIT Purchase Ledger Control		2,403.34
		Being posting of missing purchase day book page in June		

Tasks 8, 10 and 11
EXTENDED TRIAL BALANCE AT 30 JUNE 20X3

Ledger account name	Balance at 30/0/X3 £	£	Adjustments £	£	Profit and loss account £	£	Balance sheet £	£
Administration	9,611.27		1,000.00	630.00	9,981.27			
Assemblies purchases	71,070.97				71,070.97			
Assemblies opening stock	6,930.83				6,930.83			
Assemblies closing stock			6,900.00	6,900.00		6,900.00	6,900.00	
Bank	9,106.44						9,106.44	
Capital		70,000.00						70,000.00
Depreciation charge	18,785.03				18,785.03			
Direct labour	155,182.54				155,182.54			
Disposals	56.25				56.25			
Drawings	36,000.00						36,000.00	
Factory equipment: accumulated depreciation		9,705.65						9,705.65
Factory equipment: cost	28,250.00						28,250.00	
Factory overheads	19,545.28				19,545.28			
Finished goods opening stock	13,645.86				13,645.86			
Finished goods closing stock			15,132.34	15,132.34		15,132.34	15,132.34	
Hire purchase creditor		24,305.00						24,305.00
Interest expense	1,225.00				1,225.00			
Motor vehicles: accumulated depreciation		25,500.00						25,500.00
Motor vehicles: cost	66,750.00						66,750.00	
Office equipment: accumulated depreciation		5,075.00						5,075.00
Office equipment: cost	8,650.00						8,650.00	
Purchase ledger control		31,469.26						31,469.26
Raw materials purchasers	104,836.17				104,836.17			
Raw materials closing stock			13,997.92	13,997.92		13,997.92	13,997.92	
Raw materials opening stock	15,019.86				15,019.86			
Sales		430,349.18				430,349.18		
Sales ledger control	43,508.12						43,508.12	
Sundry creditors		4,345.00						4,345.00
VAT		7,424.53						7,424.53
Accruals/prepayments			630.00	1,000.00			630.00	1,000.00
Profit					50,100.38			50,100.38
Total	608,173.62	608,173.62	37,660.26	37,660.26	466,379.44	466,379.44	228,924.82	228,924.82

ANSWERS (Task 9)

STOCK VALUATION AT 30 June 20X3

	£
Raw materials	
Tungstra $(175 \times 32.00) + (200 \times 27.50)$	11,100.00
Miscellaneous items $(2,019.82 + 150.00 + 728.10)$	2,897.92
	13,997.92
Assemblies $(600.00 + 2,500.00 + 3,800.00)$	£6,900.00

Task 9, continued

Finished goods

MANUFACTURING ACCOUNT FOR THE YEAR ENDED 30 JUNE 20X3

	£	£
Raw material stock at 1 July 20X2		15,019.86
Assemblies stock at 1 July 20X2		6,930.83
Purchases: raw materials		104,836.17
assemblies		71,070.97
		197,857.83
Raw material stock at 30 June 20X3		
Tungstra	11,100.00	
Miscellaneous items	2,897.92	
		(13,997.92)
		183,859.91
Direct labour		155,182.54
Prime cost		339,042.45
Factory overheads	19,545.28	
Depreciation of factory equipment (Journal 6)	3,272.53	
		22,817.81
Factory cost of finished goods produced		361,860.26

Factory cost of signs made	Total costs £	Quantity made	Unit cost per sign £	Quantity in closing stock	Valuation £
Small signs (10%)	36,186.03	55	657.93	2	1,315.86
Large signs (50%)	180,930.13	110	1,644.82	4	6,579.28
Extra large signs (40%)	144,744.10	60	2,412.40	3	7,237.20
	361,860.26				15,132.34

ASSESSMENT CRITERIA

Task 1   The bank reconciliation should be presented neatly and accurately. Candidates should notice that the cash book balance must be adjusted for the receipt and payments. One error allowed in posting to the general ledger, and one in the reconciliation itself.

Task 2   Candidates should describe clearly the approach that should be taken to acting on the information obtained, and should point out tactfully the ways in which the partners can improve their record keeping, and why this would be a good idea. The journal should be clearly set out with narrative. One error allowed.

Task 3   Candidates must correctly distinguish between capital and revenue expenditure, and record both as appropriate. They should treat VAT correctly on each of the two fixed asset additions. The journals should be accurate and well presented, including dates and narratives. The candidate may choose whether to do one or two journals for the HP transaction. The double entry should be correct. One error allowed

Task 4   Candidates should notice the disposal and link it to the amount credited to the suspense account. Candidates should then record the disposal in the fixed asset register and draft a correct journal. The journals should be accurate and well presented, including dates and narratives. One error allowed. The memo should be tactful and constructive.

Task 5   Candidates must calculate individual amounts for recording in the register, and total amounts for recording in the ledger. One error of calculation or recording is allowed. The journals should be accurate and well presented, including dates and narratives.

Task 6   Candidates must post accurately to the correct ledger accounts. One error of posting is allowed.

Task 7   Candidates must prepare thorough reconciliations and should take the correct action to clear the reconciling item. One error allowed. The journal should be accurate and well presented, including dates and narrative.

Task 8   One error may be allowed in the calculation and listing of balances.

Task 9   Candidates should correctly apply the rule of 'lower of cost and NRV' when valuing miscellaneous raw material and assembly stocks. They should correctly apply the FIFO method when valuing the stock of tungstra. They should present a neat calculation of finished goods stock. Two errors of calculation one allowed.

Task 10   All adjustments should be correctly entered on the TB. In the presentation of adjustments some variety is evident in practice and candidates should not be penalised simply because their method of presentation differs slightly from that shown in the suggested solution. No errors allowed.

Task 11   One error may be allowed in extending or totalling the TB.

Answer to AAT sample simulation

ANSWER TO SAMPLE SIMULATION: BRANSON & CO

Tasks 1 and 2

EXTRACTS FROM FIXED ASSETS REGISTER

Description/ serial no	Location	Date acquired	Original cost £	Enhance- ments £	Total £	Dep'n £	NBV £	Funding method	Disposal proceeds £	Disposal date
Plant and equipment										
Milling machine										
45217809	Factory	20.6.X4	3,456.08		3,456.08			Cash		
Y/e 31.3.X5						864.02	2,592.06			
Y/e 31.3.X6						864.02	1,728.04			
Y/e 31.3.X7						864.02	864.02			
Y/e 31.3.X8						864.02	0.00			
Lathe 299088071	Factory	12.6.X5	4,008.24		4,008.24			Cash		
Y/e 31.3.X6						1,002.06	3,006.18			
Y/e 31.3.X7						1,002.06	2,004.12			
Y/e 31.3.X8						1,002.06	1,002.06			
Drill assembly										
51123412	Factory	12.2.X6	582.44		582.44			Cash		
Y/e 31.3.X6						145.61	436.83			
Y/e 31.3.X7						145.61	291.22			
Y/e 31.3.X8						145.61	145.61			
Punch drive										
91775321	Factory	12.2.X6	1,266.00		1,266.00			Cash plus		
Y/e 31.3.X6						316.50	949.50	trade-in		
Y/e 31.3.X7						316.50	633.00			
Y/e 31.3.X8						316.50	316.50			
Winding gear										
53098871	Factory	13.3.X6	1,082.68		1,082.68			Cash		
Y/e 31.3.X6						270.67	812.01			
Y/e 31.3.X7				341.79	1,153.80	384.60	769.20			
Y/e 31.3.X8						384.60	769.20			
Tender press										
44231809	Factory	8.8.X6	4,256.04		4,256.04			Cash		
Y/e 31.3.X7						1,064.01	3,192.03			
Y/e 31.3.X8						1,064.01	2,128.02			

Answer to AAT sample simulation

Description/ serial no	Location	Date acquired	Original cost £	Enhance- ments £	Total £	Dep'n £	NBV £	Funding method	Disposal proceeds £	Disposal date
Company cars										
M412 RTW	Yard	25.8.X4	8,923.71		8,923.71			Lease		
Y/e 31.3.X5						4,015.67	4,908.04			
Y/e 31.3.X6						2,208.62	2,699.42			
Y/e 31.3.X7						1,214.74	1,484.68			
Y/e 31.3.X8						668.11	816.57			
M104 PTY	Yard	15.3.X5	8,643.00		8,643.00			Cash		
Y/e 31.3.X5						3,889.35	4,753.65			
Y/e 31.3.X6						2,139.14	2,614.51			
Y/e 31.3.X7						1,176.53	1,437.98			
Y/e 31.3.X8									1,850.00	
N33 FGY	Yard	18.9.X5	10,065.34		10,065.34			Cash plus		
Y/e 31.3.X6						4,529.40	5,535.94	trade-in		
Y/e 31.3.X7						2,491.17	3,044.77			
Y/e 31.3.X8						1,370.15	1,674.62			
P321 HDR	Yard	13.12.X6	9,460.26		9,460.265			Cash		
Y/e 31.3.X7						4,257.12	5,203.14			
Y/e 31.3.X8						2,341.41	2,861.73			
R261 GHT	Yard	27.3.X8	12,807.50		12,807.50			Cash plus		
Y/e 31.3.X8						5,763.38	7,044.12	trade-in		

Tasks 1, 2, 4, 6, 7

NOMINAL (GENERAL) LEDGER

Account Debit	Administration overheads			Credit		
Date 20X8	Details	Amount £	Date 20X8	Details	Amount £
1 Mar	Balance b/f	15,071.23			
27 Mar	P/L control	140.00			
31 Mar	P/L control	991.24			
31 Mar	Bank	1,105.69	31 Mar	Balance c/d	17,308.16
		17,308.16			17,308.16
1 Apr	Balance b/d	17,308.16			

Account   Brandreth capital account

Debit			Credit		
Date 20X8	*Details*	*Amount* £	*Date* 20X8	*Details*	*Amount* £
			1 Mar	Balance b/f	17,063.24

Account   Brandreth current account

Debit			Credit		
Date 20X8	*Details*	*Amount* £	*Date* 20X8	*Details*	*Amount* £
1 Mar 31 Mar	Balance b/f Bank	11,056.73 500.00 11,556.73	31 Mar	Balance c/d	11,556.73 11,556.73
1 Apr	Balance b/d	11,556.73			

Answer to AAT sample simulation

Tasks 1, 2, 4, 6, 7 (continued)

Account Company cars: cost					
Debit			Credit		
Date 20X8	*Details*	*Amount* £	*Date* 20X8	*Details*	*Amount* £
1 Mar	Balance b/f	37,092.31	27 Mar	Disposal a/c	8,643.00
27 Mar	P/L control.	12,807.50	31 Mar	Balance c/d	41,256.81
		49,899.81			49,899.81
1 Apr	Balance b/d	41,256.81			

Account Company cars: depreciation charge					
Debit			Credit		
Date 20X8	*Details*	*Amount* £	*Date* 20X8	*Details*	*Amount* £
31 Mar	Accumulated depreciation	10,143.05			

Account Company cars: accumulated depreciation					
Debit			Credit		
Date 20X7	*Details*	*Amount* £	*Date* 20X7	*Details*	*Amount* £
			1 Apr	Balance b/f	25,921.74
20X8			20X8		
27 Mar	Disposal a/c	7,205.02	31 Mar	Charge for year	10,143.05
31 Mar	Balance c/d	28,859.77			
		36,064.79			36,064.79
			1 Apr	Balance b/d	28,859.77

Tasks 1, 2, 4, 6, 7 (continued)

Account Company cars: disposals					
Debit			Credit		
Date 20X8	*Details*	*Amount* £	*Date* 20X8	*Details*	*Amount* £
27 Mar	Cost	8,643.00	27 Mar	Accumulated depreciation	7,205.02
			27 Mar	Purchases ledger	
31 Mar	Balance c/d	412.02		control account	1,850.00
		9,055.02			9,055.02
			1 Apr	Balance b/d	412.02

Account Direct labour costs					
Debit			Credit		
Date 20X8	*Details*	*Amount* £	*Date* 20X8	*Details*	*Amount* £
1 Mar	Balance b/f	60,012.64			
31 Mar	Bank	6,014.73	31 Mar	Balance c/d	66,027.37
		66,027.37			66,027.37
1 Apr	Balance b/d	66,027.37			

Account Factory overheads					
Debit			Credit		
Date 20X8	*Details*	*Amount* £	*Date* 20X8	*Details*	*Amount* £
1 Mar	Balance b/f	27,109.67			
31 Mar	P/L control	1,451.09			
31 Mar	Bank	1,931.75	31 Mar	Balance c/d	30,492.51
		30,492.51			30,492.51
1 Apr	Balance b/d	30,492.51			

Tasks 1, 2, 4, 6, 7 (continued)

Account Other fixed assets: cost
Debit   Credit

Date 20X8	Details	Amount £	Date 20X8	Details	Amount £
1 Mar	Balance b/f	18,923.50			

Account Other fixed assets: depreciation charge
Debit   Credit

Date 20X8	Details	Amount £	Date 20X8	Details	Amount £
31 Mar	Accumulated depreciation	4,730.88			

Account Other fixed assets: accumulated depreciation
Debit   Credit

Date 20X7	Details	Amount £	Date 20X7	Details	Amount £
			1 Apr	Balance b/f	6,224.12
20X8			20X8 31 Mar	Charge for year	4,730.88
31 Mar	Balance c/d	10,955.00			————
		10,955.00			10,955.00
			1 Apr	Balance b/d	10,955.00

Tasks 1, 2, 4, 6, 7 (continued)

Account Debit	Other fixed assets: disposals		Credit		
Date 20X8	*Details*	*Amount* £	*Date* 20X8	*Details*	*Amount* £

Account Debit	Plant and equipment: cost		Credit		
Date 20X8	*Details*	*Amount* £	*Date* 20X8	*Details*	*Amount* £
1 Mar	Balance b/f	14,993.27			

Account Debit	Plant and equipment: depreciation charge		Credit		
Date 20X8	*Details*	*Amount* £	*Date* 20X8	*Details*	*Amount* £
31 Mar	Accumulated depreciation	3,776.80			

Tasks 1, 2, 4, 6, 7 (continued)

Account Debit	Plant and equipment: accumulated depreciation			Credit		
Date 20X7	*Details*	*Amount* £	*Date* 20X7	*Details*		*Amount* £
			1 Apr	Balance b/f		7,239.68
20X8 31 Mar	Balance c/d	11,016.48 11,016.48	20X8 31 Mar	Charge for year		3,776.80 11,016.48
			1 Apr	Balance b/d		11,016.48

Account Debit	Plant and equipment: disposals			Credit		
Date 20X8	*Details*	*Amount* £	*Date* 20X8	*Details*		*Amount* £

Account Debit	Purchases			Credit		
Date 20X8	*Details*	*Amount* £	*Date* 20X8	*Details*		*Amount* £
1 Mar 31 Mar	Balance b/f P/L control	54,231.89 4,871.22 59,103.11	31 Mar	Balance c/d		59,103.11 59,103.11
1 Apr	Balance b/d	59,103.11				

Tasks 1, 2, 4, 6, 7 (continued)

Account	Purchases ledger control				
Debit				Credit	
Date 20X8	*Details*	*Amount* £	*Date* 20X8	*Details*	*Amount* £
27 Mar	Car disposal a/c	1,850.00	1 Mar	Balance b/f	18,457.20
31 Mar	Bank	10,353.58	27 Mar	Purchase of new car	12,947.50
			31 Mar	Purchase invoices	
31 Mar	Balance c/d	28,334.30			9,133.18
		40,537.88			40,537.88
			1 Apr	Balance b/d	28,334.30

Account	Sales				
Debit				Credit	
Date 20X8	*Details*	*Amount* £	*Date* 20X8	*Details*	*Amount* £
			1 Mar	Balance b/f	225,091.42
31 Mar	Balance c/d	256,167.67	31 Mar	S/L control	31,076.25
		256,167.67			256,167.67
			1 Apr	Balance b/d	256,167.67

Account	Sales ledger control				
Debit				Credit	
Date 20X8	*Details*	*Amount* £	*Date* 20X8	*Details*	*Amount* £
1 Mar	Balance b/f	24,617.03	31 Mar	Bank	25,555.33
31 Mar	Sales invoices	36,514.59	31 Mar	Balance c/d	35,576.29
		61,131.62			61,131.62
1 Apr	Balance b/d	35,576.29			

Tasks 1, 2, 4, 6, 7 (continued)

Account   Selling and distribution overheads
Debit   Credit

Date 20X8	Details	Amount £	Date 20X8	Details	Amount £
1 Mar	Balance b/f	14,303.12			
31 Mar	P/L control	524.87			
31 Mar	Bank	1,427.88	31 Mar	Balance c/d	16,255.87
		16,255.87			16,255.87
1 Apr	Balance b/d	16,255.87			

Account   Sondin capital account
Debit   Credit

Date 20X8	Details	Amount £	Date 20X8	Details	Amount £
			1 Mar	Balance b/f	8,703.28

Account   Sondin current account
Debit   Credit

Date 20X8	Details	Amount £	Date 20X8	Details	Amount £
1 Mar	Balance b/f	12,912.29			
31 Mar	Bank	450.00	31 Mar	Balance c/d	13,362.29
		13,362.29			13,362.29
1 Apr	Balance b/d	13,362.29			

Tasks 1, 2, 4, 6, 7 (continued)

Account   Stock: raw materials

Date 20X7	Details	Amount £	Date 20X7	Details	Amount £
1 Apr	Balance b/f	6,294.33			

Account   Stock: finished goods

Date 20X7	Details	Amount £	Date 20X7	Details	Amount £
1 Apr	Balance b/f	12,513.77			

Account   Suspense

Date 20X8	Details	Amount £	Date 20X8	Details	Amount £
26 Jan	Bank	750.00	24 Feb	Bank	1,124.55
31 Mar	Balance c/d	374.55			
		1,124.55			1,124.55
			1 Apr	Balance b/d	374.55

Tasks 1, 2, 4, 6, 7 (continued)

Account	VAT				
Debit			Credit		
Date 20X8	Details	Amount £	Date 20X8	Details	Amount £
31 Mar	P/L control	1,294.76	1 Mar	Balance b/f	5,091.27
31 Mar	Balance c/d	9,234.85	31 Mar	S/L control	5,438.34
		10,529.61			10,529.61
			1 Apr	Balance b/d	9,234.85

Task 3

MEMORANDUM

To: Jenny Holden, Accountant

From: Val Denning, Accounts Assistant

Subject: Check on company cars at 31 March 20X8

Date: 20 April 20X8

I have compared the schedule of company cars actually on the premises at 31 March with the details in the fixed assets register. The only discrepancy is that the car M412 RTW was not on the premises, though listed in the register. I suggest that we check the physical existence of this car at another time.

Task 5

Bank reconciliation as at 31 March 20X8

	£	£
Balance per bank statement		(1,550.12) O/D
Outstanding lodgements		
27 March	6,071.88	
31 March	5,512.67	
		11,584.55
		10,034.43
Unpresented cheques		
19337	278.01	
19338	500.00	
19339	450.00	
		(1,228.01)
Balance per cash book		8,806.42

Tasks 7, 11, 12

Extended trial balance at 31 March 20X8

Account name	Balances per ledger £	£	Adjustments £	£	Profit and loss account £	£	Balance sheet £	£
Administration overheads	17,308.16		420.00	1,625.00	16,103.16			
Brandreth capital account		17,063.24						17,063.24
Brandreth current account	11,556.73		750.00				12,306.73	
Company cars: cost	41,256.81						41,256.81	
Company cars: depreciation charge	10,143.05				10,143.05			
Company cars: accum depreciation		28,859.77						28,859.77
Company cars: disposals		412.02				412.02		
Direct labour costs	66,027.37				66,027.37			
Factory overheads	30,492.51				30,492.51			
Other fixed assets: cost	18,923.50			2,317.69			16,605.81	
Other fixed assets: depreciation charge	4,730.88				4,730.88			
Other fixed assets: accum depreciation		10,955.00	946.23					10,008.77
Other fixed assets: profit/loss on disposal			246.91		246.91			
Plant and equipment: cost	14,993.27						14,993.27	
Plant and equipment: depreciation charge	3,776.80				3,776.80			
Plant and equipment: accum depreciation		11,016.48						11,016.48
Purchases	59,103.11				59,103.11			
Purchases ledger control		28,334.30						28,334.30
Sales		256,167.67				256,167.67		
Sales ledger control	35,576.29						35,576.29	
Selling & distribution overheads	16,255.87				16,255.87			
Sondin: capital account		8,703.28						8,703.28
Sondin: current account	13,362.29						13,362.29	
Stock: raw materials	6,294.33		8,136.55	8,136.55	6,294.33	8,136.55	8,136.55	
Stock: finished goods	12,513.77		18,714.47	18,714.47	12,513.77	18,714.47	18,714.47	
Suspense		374.55	1,124.55	750.00				
VAT		9,234.85						9,234.85
Bank balance	8,806.42						8,806.42	
Accruals and prepayments			1,625.00	420.00			1,625.00	420.00
Net profit for the year					57,742.95			57,742.95
Total	371,121.16	371,121.16	31,963.71	31,963.71	283,430.71	283,430.71	171,383.64	171,383.64

Task 8

This cheque probably represents payment of a personal expense incurred by one or other of the partners. If so it will need to be treated as drawings.

To establish that this is so I will first ask Jenny Holden, the Accountant, whether she knows about the payment. If she does not, it may then be necessary for either she or I to inquire tactfully of the partners themselves.

Tutorial note. This payment is in fact a payment for personal expenses incurred by Amy. Brandreth paid out of the business bank account.

Task 9

Journal

Date	Account names and narrative	Debit	Credit
20X8		£	£
31 March	Brandreth: current account	750.00	
	suspense		750.00
	Being cash paid for personal expenses, classified as drawings		
31 March	Other fixed assets: accumulated depreciation	946.23	
	Other fixed assets: loss on disposal	246.91	
	Suspense account	1,124.55	
	Other fixed assets: cost		2,317.69
		2,317.69	2,317.69
	Being disposal of fixed asset, removed from suspense account		

Task 10

Valuation of raw materials stock (lower of cost and net realisable value)

	£
Material X	3,417.22
Material Y	4,719.33
Total	8,136.55

Manufacturing account for the year ended 31 March 20X8

	£
Raw materials	
Opening stock	6,294.33
Purchases	59,103.11
	65,397.44
Closing stock	(8,136.55)
	57,260.89
Direct labour	66,027.37
Prime cost	123,288.26
Factory overheads	30,492.51
Factory cost of finished goods produced	153,780.77

The cost of 25,613 units is £153,780.77, a unit cost of production of £6.004.

The value of closing stock (3,117 units) is therefore £18,714.47.

Answers to practice central assessments

ANSWERS TO PRACTICE CENTRAL ASSESSMENT 1: INFORTEC

SECTION 1: PART A

Task 1

Trial Balance at 30th November 20X9

DESCRIPTION	Dr £	Cr £
Capital		134,230
Purchases	695,640	
Sales		836,320
Stock at 1 December 20X8	84,300	
Rent paid	36,000	
Salaries	37,860	
Motor vehicles (MV) at cost	32,400	
Provision for depreciation (MV)		8,730
Fixtures and fittings (F&F) at cost	50,610	
Provision for depreciation (F&F)		12,340
Purchase returns		10,780
Sales returns	5,270	
Drawings	55,910	
Insurance	4,760	
Debtors control account	73,450	
Creditors control account		56,590
Bad debts	3,670	
Provision for doubtful debts		3,060
Bank overdraft		10,800
Cash	1,980	
VAT (credit balance)		5,410
Discounts allowed	6,770	
Discounts received		4,380
Suspense account		5,980
Totals	1,088,620	1,088,620

Task 2

JOURNAL		
Details	DR £	CR £
a) Drawings account 　　Salaries	400	400
b) Suspense 　　Sales	100	100
c) Suspense 　　VAT	60	60
d) Creditor control account 　　Suspense	120	120
e) Suspense 　　Bank	6,000	6,000
f) Creditors control account 　　Suspense	10	10
g) Discounts received 　　Suspense	40	40
h) Insurance 　　Suspense	10	10

Task 3

	£
Total from list of balances	76,780
Adjustment for (a): add	400
Adjustment for (b): subtract	(100)
Adjustment for (c): subtract	(2,410)
Adjustment for (d): add	90
Adjustment for (e): subtract	(540)
Adjustment for (f): subtract	(770)
Revised total to agree with debtors control account	73,450

PART B

Task 4

	£
Depreciation for vehicle sold 1 March 20X9 ($^3/_{12} \times [18,000$ @20%])	900
Depreciation for vehicle purchased 1 June 20X9 ($^6/_{12} \times [10,000$ @20%])	1,000
Depreciation for vehicle purchased 1 September 20X9 ($^3/_{12} \times [12,000$ @20%])	600
Depreciation for other vehicles owned during the year ([28,400 – 18,000] @20%)	2,080
	4,580

Task 5

(a)   £247,000 – 231,000 = £16,000 profit

		£
(b)	Capital b/f	164,230
	Profit for the year	16,000
	Drawings	(46,000)
	Capital balance as at November 20X8	134,230

Task 6

		£
(a)	Leased	
	3 months @£500	£1,500
(b)	Purchased	£
	Loss in use (£8,000 – 7,000)	1,000
	Interest on the overdraft (8,000 × 12% × $^3/_{12}$)	240
		1,240

Task 7

(a) $\dfrac{£240,000}{£200} = 1200$ members

		£
(b)	Cash received	230,000
	Less prepayments	(10,000)
		220,000
	Subscriptions for the year	240,000
	Prepaid as at 31 December 20X8	20,000

$\dfrac{20,000}{200} = 100$ members prepaid during 20X8.

Task 8

MEMORANDUM

To:	Phil Townsend	Ref:	Valuation of stock
From:	Accounting Technician	Date:	29 November 20X9

The stock of ten Mica40z PCs is currently valued at £5,000 (10 × £500). This is valuation at cost.

Before we can sell, we would incur £100 of cost per machine and only be able to sell at £580. The net realisable value (NRV) is therefore £480 (£580 - £100).

Per SSAP 9, we must value stocks at the lower of cost and NRV.

This would be £4,800 (10 × £480).

If the Mica 40z PCs are to be scrapped or given away then we must write them off. We can only value them at cost if we will sell them for more than cost. If we cannot sell them at all then they have a NRV of zero.

SECTION 2

Task 1

	£
Money placed in new business bank account (50,000 – 40,000)	10,000
New machinery and equipment purchases	72,500
Capital invested by Phil Townsend on 1 January 20X0	82,500

Task 2

	£
Raw materials	180,000
Closing stock of raw materials	(15,600)
	164,400
Production wages	41,750
Prime cost	206,150

Task 3

	£
Prime cost (from **Task 2**)	206,150
Production supervisors' wages	22,000
Other production overheads	15,170
Depreciation of machinery and equipment (72,500 @10%)	7,250
	250,570
Less stock of work in progress	(10,170)
Total production cost of finished goods	240,400

Task 4

		£
Sales (220,000 @120%: see COS)		264,000
Cost of sales		
Opening stock	-	
Production cost of finished goods (from **Task 3**)	240,400	
Closing stock	(20,400)	
		(220,000)
Gross profit		44,000
Expenses		
Selling and distribution	38,800	
Loan interest (40,000 @8%)	3,200	
		(42,000)
Net profit		2,000

Task 5

	£	£
Opening balance (40,000 + 10,000)		50,000
Payments		
Raw materials	180,000	
Less creditors (180,000 × $^1/_{12}$)	(15,000)	
Production wages	41,750	
Production supervisor	22,000	
Production overheads	15,170	
Selling and distribution	38,800	
Interest on loan	3,200	
		(285,920)
Receipts		
Sales (from **Task 4**)	264,000	
Less debtors (264,000 × $^1/_{12}$)	(22,000)	
		242,000
Closing balance as at 31 December 20X0		6,080

ANSWERS TO PRACTICE CENTRAL ASSESSMENT 2: SIMPLE STATION

SECTION 1

Task 1.1

BANK ACCOUNT

	£		£
Balance b/d	811	General expenses	350
		General expenses	78
		Balance c/d	383
	811		811
Balance b/d	383		

Task 1.2

	£	
Amended cash book balance	383	
Add unpresented cheques	70	
Less outstanding lodgement	(690)	
Bank statement balance	(237)	Debit balance or overdraft

BPP
PUBLISHING

Task 1.3 and 1.4

	Ledger balances		Adjustments	
	DR	**CR**	**DR**	**CR**
	£	**£**	**£**	**£**
Capital		36,000		
Sales		313,740		
Sales returns	2,704			
Purchases	208,906			
Purchases returns		980		
Stock at 1 June 20X0	21,750			
Rent	22,000			
Wages	24,700			
General expenses (10,957 + 350 + 78)	11,385			
Motor expenses	4,134			200
Motor vehicles (MV) at cost	18,900			
Provision for depreciation(MV)		9,450		4,725
Office equipment (OE) at cost	27,410			
Provision for depreciation (OE)		8,152		2,741
Drawings	18,000			
Debtors control	30,450			
Creditors control		19,341		
Bank	383			
Cash	1,005			
VAT		3,664		
Suspense		400		
Depreciation (W1)			7,466	
Closing stock : P&L (W2)				25,760
Closing stock : balance sheet			25,760	
Prepayment (W3)			200	
Provision for doubtful debts P&L (W4)			609	
Provision for doubtful debts Balance sheet				609
	391,727	391,727	34,035	34,035

Workings

1   *Depreciation*

	£
Motor vehicles 25 × £18,900	4,725
Office equipment 10% × £27,410	2,741
Total charge	7,466

2   *Closing stock*

	£
Stock at cost	25,890
Less: damaged stock at cost	(200)
Add: damaged stock at NRV (110 – 40)	70
Closing stock at lower of cost and NRV	25,760

3   *Prepayment*

Motor insurance (£240 × 10/12) = £200

4   *Provision for doubtful debts*

Provision required (2% × £30,450) = £609

Task 1.5

DEBIT	Suspense account	£400	
CREDIT	Creditors control account (2 × 200)		£400
DEBIT	VAT account	£35	
CREDIT	Creditors control account		£35

Task 1.6

When the first instalment is paid.

Task 1.7

When fixed assets are purchased their cost is taken to the balance sheet as an asset rather than being charged to the profit and loss account as an expense. However the fixed asset is being used to earn the revenues and profits of the business, so some of its cost is charged as an expense to the profit and loss account each year to reflect this in the form of the depreciation charge.

Task 1.8

Capital is the amount that the business owes back to the owner of the business. It is made up of the amount that the owner originally paid into the business plus any profits that the business has made and less any losses made by the business, less any amounts previously taken out of the business by the owner as drawings.

SECTION 2

Task 2.1

DEBTORS ACCOUNT

Opening balance	580	Bank	12,010
Bar sales (bal fig)	12,330	Closing balance	900
	12,910		12,910

Task 2.2

CREDITORS ACCOUNT

	£		£
Bank	5,870	Opening balance	700
Closing balance	370	Bar purchases (bal fig)	5,540
	6,240		6,240

Task 2.3

	£	£
Bar sales		12,330
Less: cost of sales		
Opening stock	345	
Purchases	5,540	
	5,885	
Less closing stock	(680)	
		5,205
Gross profit		7,125
Less bar staff wages		3,600
Net profit		3,525

Task 2.4

Subscription income 80 members × £200 = £16,000

Task 2.5

SUBSCRIPTION ACCOUNT

	£		£
Opening subs in arrears	200	Bank	15,600
Subscription income	16,000	Closing subs in arrears	600
	16,200		16,200

Task 2.6

	£	£
Subscription income		16,000
Net profit from bar		3,525
Total income		19,525
Less: expenditure		
Maintenance	1,690	
General expenses		
(8,250 – 180 + 240)	8,310	
Club wages	9,750	
		(19,750)
Deficit		(225)

Task 2.7

(a) The accruals concept

(b) According to the accruals concept, the income to be included in an income and expenditure account is the amount of subscription income that is due for the period, whether or not it has been received in cash during the year. Similarly the expenditure to be included is the expenses incurred in the year, not necessarily those that have been paid for.

PUBLISHING

Task 2.8

MEMO

To: Edward Dyer   **Ref:** Expansion payments

From: **Date:** 19 June 20X1

When an organisation has expenditure it must be determined whether this is capital expenditure or revenue expenditure.

Capital expenditure is expenditure on the purchase or improvement of fixed assets. Fixed assets are assets that are for long term use of the business rather than assets that are due to be sold in the short term.

Revenue expenditure is all expenditure other than capital expenditure.

Revenue expenditure is charged to the income and expenditure account as an expense in the period in which it is incurred.

Capital expenditure is not immediately taken to the income and expenditure account. Instead it is taken to the balance sheet as a fixed asset. However the capital expenditure will eventually appear in the income and expenditure account as a charge for depreciation of the fixed assets should be made each year.

I hope that this addresses your concerns.

ANSWERS TO PRACTICE CENTRAL ASSESSMENT 3: FINE TIME

SECTION 1

Task 1.1

TRIAL BALANCE AS AT 31 OCTOBER 20X1

Description	Debit £	Credit £
Capital - Martin Fine		56,000
Capital - Helen Fine		42,000
Sales		296,857
Purchases	189,545	
Stock at 1 November 20X0	25,850	
Rent and rates	31,850	
General expenses	60,320	
Motor expenses	8,900	
Motor vehicles (MV) at cost	25,200	
Provision for depreciation (MV)		8,500
Office equipment (OE) at cost	42,800	
Provision for depreciation (OE)		12,760
Drawings - Martin Fine	12,000	
Drawings - Helen Fine	12,000	
Debtors control	55,890	
Provision for doubtful debts		1,560
Creditors control		42,230
Bank	2,450	
Cash	212	
VAT		8,370
Suspense	1,260	
	468,277	468,277

BPP PUBLISHING

Task 1.2

			Dr £	Cr £
(a)	DEBIT	Stock - balance sheet	19,750	
	CREDIT	Stock - profit and loss		19,750
(b)	DEBIT	Depreciation expense (5,040 + 4,506)	9,546	
	CREDIT	Provision for depreciation (MV) (25,200 × 20%)		5,040
	CREDIT	Provision for depreciation (OE) ((42,800 - 12,760) × 15%)		4,506
(c)	DEBIT	Bad debts expense	1,290	
	CREDIT	Debtors control		1,290
(d)	DEBIT	Bad debts expense (W1)	78	
	CREDIT	Provision for doubtful debts		78
(e)	DEBIT	Suspense account (2 × 270)	540	
	CREDIT	Bank (2 × 270)		540
(f)	DEBIT	Creditors control (4,212 – 2,412)	1,800	
	CREDIT	Suspense account		1,800
(g)	DEBIT	General expenses	5,100	
	DEBIT	VAT	3,654	
	CREDIT	Purchases		8,754

Working: Provision for doubtful debts

	£
Debtors control (per TB)	55,890
Less bad debt written off	(1,290)
Closing debtors control	54,600
Provision for doubtful debts required	
3% × 54,600	1,638
Less opening provision	1,560
Increase in provision	78

Task 1.3

(a)

	£
Sales:	
10 × £300	3,000
15 × £310	4,650
	7,650

(b)

	£
Closing stock:	
10 × £160	1,600
5 × £155	775
	2,375

Task 1.4

(a) Excludes VAT

(b) A business makes no profit out of VAT as it simply collects it on behalf of Customs and Excise by charging it to customers. The VAT is then paid over to Customs and Excise because it does not belong to the business. For this reason SSAP 5 states that VAT is excluded from sales in the profit and loss account.

Task 1.5

MEMO

To: **Martin and Helen Fine**   **Ref:**

From: **Accounting Technician**   **Date:**

If the receipt of a debt is uncertain then there are two options as to how to treat it:

(a)   to write it off as a bad debt
(b)   to make a provision against it as a doubtful debt

One of the fundamental accounting concepts from SSAP 2 (now replaced by FRS 18) is that of prudence. According to this concept financial statements should be prepared with a degree of caution. If it is felt that a loss or expense is likely then it must be accounted for immediately.

As the debtor has been declared bankrupt it would appear unlikely that you will receive the amount of the debt. Therefore under the concept of prudence it should be written off as a bad debt as has been done this year.

If it is realistic that the debt may be recovered then a provision against this amount may be more appropriate.

However in this case as the debtor has been declared bankrupt I feel that there is little chance that the debt will be recovered and therefore the accounting treatment of writing the debt off as a bad debt is the correct one.

If the debt is in fact recovered next year, the bad debt expense can be reversed in next year's profit and loss account.

BPP
PUBLISHING

SECTION 2

Task 2.1

CREDITORS ACCOUNT

	£		£
Bank	97,400	Opening balance	14,210
Closing balance	14,890	Purchases (bal fig)	98,080
	112,290		112,290

Task 2.2

	£	£
Raw materials used:		
Opening stock	9,800	
Purchases	98,080	
	107,880	
Less: closing stock	7,650	
		100,230
Production wages		24,000
Prime cost		124,230

Task 2.3

	£
Prime cost	124,230
Supervisory wages	28,000
Factory overheads	10,710
Depreciation of factory premises	
(100,000 × 2%)	2,000
Depreciation of factory equipment	
(48,000 × 10%)	4,800
Total production cost	169,740

Task 2.4

DEBTORS ACCOUNT

	£		£
Opening balance	18,700	Bank	201,010
Sales (bal fig)	203,620	Closing balance	21,310
	222,320		222,320

Task 2.5

	£	£
Sales		203,620
Cost of sales		
Opening stock of finished goods	12,540	
Production cost	169,740	
	182,280	
Less closing stock of finished goods	11,380	
		170,900
Gross profit		32,720

Task 2.6

	£	£
Gross profit		32,720
Less expenses		
Office wages	15,000	
Office overheads	7,780	
		22,780
Net profit		9,940

Task 2.7

MEMO

To: Scott George   **Ref:**

From: Accounting Technician   **Date: 20X0**

I refer to your concern about how expenditure on research should be treated in the accounts.

SSAP 13 covers the subject of research and development expenditure. SSAP 13 recognises two categories of research known as pure and applied research. Both types of research should be written off in the profit and loss account as an expense in the year that it is incurred.

However development expenditure is of a different nature. Development expenditure is expenditure that is due to provide the business with future benefits in the form of a new product or new production processes. As such this development expenditure can be initially treated as a fixed asset on the balance sheet and then written off (amortised) to the profit and loss account when the new product is sold or the new process comes into operation.

However as one of the fundamental accounting concepts is that of prudence, in order to treat the development expenditure as a fixed asset SSAP 13 states five criteria that must be met. These are:

(a)   There is a clearly defined project.
(b)   Adequate resources exist to complete the project.
(c)   The development expenditure is separately identifiable.
(d)   It is expected that the revenue from the project will exceed the costs.
(e)   The project is both technically feasible and commercially viable.

I hope that this information is useful.

Task 2.8

(a) Yes

(b) As the capital expenditure is of such a small amount then the concept of materiality would allow it to be written off to the profit and loss account as an expense instead of being shown as a fixed asset in the balance sheet and depreciated.

ANSWER TO PRACTICE CENTRAL ASSESSMENT 4: SLEEPEASY

SECTION 1

Task 1.1

SLEEP EASY
EXTENDED TRIAL BALANCE AS AT 31 MAY 20X1

DESCRIPTION	LEDGER BALANCE		ADJUSTMENTS	
	Debit £	*Credit* £	*Debit* £	*Credit* £
Capital		150,750		
Sales		757,210		
Sales returns	2,850			
Purchases	439,400			
Purchases returns		5,090		
Stock at 1 June 20X0	112,410			
Rent	71,500		6,500	
Wages	185,400			
Insurance	6,900			
Motor expenses	10,790			
Motor vehicles (MV) at cost	101,850			
Provision for depreciation (MV)		38,150		9,555
Fixtures and fittings (F&F) at cost	31,300			
Provision for depreciation (F&F)		6,330		6,260
Drawings	31,000			
Bad debts	2,500			
Provision for doubtful debts		6,050	2,111	
Debtors control account	78,780			
Creditors control account		38,220		
Bank	5,680			
VAT		8,800		
Bank loan		60,000		
Bank interest	3,750		750	
Suspense		13,510		
Depreciation			15,815	
Closing stock: P&L				98,400
Closing stock: balance sheet			98,400	
Provision for doubtful debts: adjustment				2,111
Loan interest owing				750
Other accruals				6,500
TOTALS	**1,084,110**	**1,084,110**	**123,576**	**123,576**

Answers to practice central assessments

Workings

1   *Depreciation*

	£
Motor vehicle (£101,850 – 38,150) × 15%)	9,555
Fixtures and fittings (£31,300 × 20%)	6,260
	15,815

2   *Loan*

	£
£60,000 × 7.5%	4,500
As per TB	3,750
Accrual	750

3   *Rent*

	£
£6,500 × 12 months	78,000
As per TB	71,500
Accrual	6,500

4   *Provision for doubtful debts*

	£
£78,780 × 5%	3,939
As per TB	6,050
Reduction in provision	2,111

Task 1.2

JOURNAL			Debit £	Credit £
(a)	DEBIT	Motor expenses	150	
	CREDIT	Motor vehicle at cost		150
(b)	DEBIT	Suspense	400	
	CREDIT	VAT account		400
(c)	DEBIT	Disposal account	11,000	
	CREDIT	Fixtures and fittings at cost		11,000
	DEBIT	Provision for depreciation (F&F)		
		(£11,000 × 20% × 2)	4,400	
	CREDIT	Disposal account		4,400
	DEBIT	Suspense	7,000	
	CREDIT	Disposal account		7,000
	DEBIT	Disposal account	400	
	CREDIT	Profit and loss account		400
OR	DEBIT	Provision for depreciation (F&F)	4,400	
	CREDIT	Fixtures and fittings at cost		11,000
	DEBIT	Suspense	7,000	
	CREDIT	Disposal account		400
	DEBIT	Disposal account	400	
	CREDIT	Profit and loss account		400
(d)	DEBIT	Suspense	3,600	
	CREDIT	Sales (£9,500 – £5,900)		3,600
(e)	DEBIT	Suspense	2,510	
	CREDIT	Bank		2,510

Task 1.3

SUSPENSE ACCOUNT

	£		£
		Balance b/d	13,510
Journal (b)	400		
Journal (c)	7,000		
Journal (d)	3,600		
Journal (e)	2,510		
	13,510		13,510

Task 1.4

(a) Decrease

(b) Consistency

Task 1.5

(a)

	£
Direct materials	35,760
Closing stock of raw materials	(3,060)
Production wages	22,410
Prime cost	55,110

(b)

	£
Prime cost	55,110
Supervisory wages	15,000
Factory overheads	18,080
Total production cost	88,190

SECTION 2

Task 2.1

DEBTORS ACCOUNT

	£		£
Opening balance	52,300	Bank	722,800
Credit sales	729,520	Closing balance	59,020
	781,820		781,820

Note. Alternative formats are acceptable.

Task 2.2

CASH ACCOUNT

	£		£
Opening cash float	1,000	Closing cash float	800
Cash sales	291,980	Cash banked	292,180
	292,980		292,980

	£
Cash sales	291,980
Credit sales (Task 1.1)	729,520
Total sales	1,021,500

Task 2.3

CREDITORS

	£		£
Bank	789,950	Opening balance	46,750
Closing balance	64,100	Credit purchases	807,300
	854,050		854,050

Note. Alternative formats are acceptable, eg a column.

Task 2.4

	£	£
Sales (from Task 2.2)		1,021,500
Opening stock	43,160	
Purchases (from Task 2.3)	807,300	
Closing stock (bal. fig.)	(33,260)	
Cost of sales		817,200
Gross profit (£1,021,500 × 20%)		204,300

Task 2.5

	£	£
Gross profit (from Task 2.4)		204,300
General expenses (£8,110 + £700 + £210)	9,020	
Salaries	92,420	
Depreciation		
Premises (£104,000 × 2%)	2,080	
Fixtures (£22,750 × 10%)	2,275	
		105,795
Net profit		98,505

Task 2.6

	£	£
Fixed assets		
Freehold premises at cost	104,000	
Depreciation to date (20,800 + 2,080)	22,880	
		81,120
Fixtures and fittings at cost	22,750	
Depreciation to date (13,650 + 2,275)	15,925	
		6,825
Total		87,945

Task 2.7

(a) Any two of:

    (i)   Accruals
    (ii)   Prepayments
    (iii) Debtors
    (iv) Creditors
    (v)   Depreciation
    (vi) Provision for doubtful debts

(b) Any one of:

    (i)   Purchase of fixed asset
    (ii)   Disposal of fixed asset (if no profit or loss is made)
    (iii) Taking out or increasing loans or other long-term debt
    (iv) Drawings or injections of capital

Task 2.8

MEMO

To: **Sarah Glass**   **Date: 18 June 20X1**

From: **Accounting Technician**

Subject: **Partnership accounts**

Thank you for your recent query regarding partnership accounts. I understand that you are concerned about keeping track of each partner's money. In fact, partnership accounts are designed to do just that.

Each partner in the business – two in the case of your proposed partnership – has a capital account and a current account.

- Capital accounts only show important capital transactions, for example, a partner leaving or joining a partnership and introducing capital. In your proposed business you and your brother will each have a capital account.

- Current accounts are used much more regularly to show salaries, drawings, interest on capital and share of profit.

I hope this answers your queries. Please feel free to contact me if you need any further assistance.

Signed

AAT Student

Answer to trial run central assessment

ANSWER TO TRIAL RUN CENTRAL ASSESSMENT (December 2001)

SECTION 1

Task 1.1

KW ENTERPRISE
TRIAL BALANCE AS AT 31 OCTOBER 20X1

DESCRIPTION	LEDGER BALANCE		ADJUSTMENTS	
	Debit £	Credit £	Debit £	Credit £
Capital		61,280		
Sales		487,360		
Sales returns	8,900			
Purchases (W3)	286,330		2,000	
Purchases returns		650		
Stock at 1 November 20X0	25,870			
Rent (W2)	33,000		3,000	
General expenses	87,700			
Motor expenses	28,540			
Bad debts	1,220		300	
Provision for doubtful debts (W5)		3,200	950	
Motor vehicles (MV) at cost	36,000			
Provision for depreciation (MV) (W1)		19,560		4,110
Fixtures and fittings (F&F) at cost	57,020			
Provision for depreciation (F&F) (W1)		34,580		8,553
Drawings	30,000			
Debtors control account	56,550			300
Creditors control account (W3)		31,500		2,350
Bank		2,700		
VAT (W3)		10,070	350	
Suspense		230		
Depreciation (W1)			12,663	
Provision for doubtful debts: adjustment (W5)				950
Closing stock: P&L (W4)				29,665
Closing stock: balance sheet (W4)			29,665	
Accruals (W2)				3,000
TOTALS	**651,130**	**651,130**	**48,928**	**48,928**

Workings

1   *Depreciation*

		£
Motor vehicles: $36,000 - 19,560 \times 25\%$		4,110
Fixtures and fittings: $57,020 \times 15\%$		8,553
Total depreciation		12,663

2   *Rent*

		£
£3,000 × 12		36,000
Per trial balance		33,000
Accrual		3,000

3   *Purchases*

		£
Total invoice		2,350
VAT element @ 17.5%		350
Net invoice		2,000

4   *Stock*

	£	£
Per task		30,040
Lower of		
Cost	625	
NRV (300–50)	250	
Therefore reduce by		375
Revised stock valuation		29,665

5   *Provision for doubtful debts*

		£
Debtors per trial balance		56,550
Less bad debt		300
Net outstanding debtors		56,250
Provision for doubtful debts @ 4%		2,250
Provision as per trial balance		3,200
Reduction in provision for doubtful debts		950

Task 1.2

JOURNAL			Debit £	Credit £
(a)	DEBIT	Suspense	380	
	CREDIT	VAT		380
(b)	DEBIT	Sales	870	
	CREDIT	Suspense		870
(c)	DEBIT	Suspense	720	
	CREDIT	Debtors control		720

Task 1.3

		£
Total from purchase ledger		33,770
Adjustment for (a)	Add creditor balance	290
Adjustment for (b)	Add credit purchase	960
Adjustment for (c)	Subtract	80
Adjustment for (d)	Subtract	1,000
Adjustment for (e)	Subtract	90
Revised total to agree with creditors control account		**33,850**

Task 1.4

(a) £8,400 − (£8,400 × 15% × 19/12) = £6,405

(b) £6,405 − £6,000 = £405 loss

Task 1.5

(a) Customs and Excise

(b) This balance shows the excess of the VAT payable on sales over the VAT recoverable on purchases and other inputs.

Task 1.6

MEMO

To:	Kelly Wainwright	**Ref:**	Reconciliations
From:	Accounting Technician	**Date:**	3 December 20X1

Thank you for your enquiry regarding the purpose of the reconciliation between the purchases ledger and the creditors control account.

The purchase ledger is used to record the transactions in the personal accounts of the individual creditors. It is a memorandum account only, and is not part of the double entry accounting system.

A creditors control account is also used to record all of the transactions of individual creditors. However, this is done on a summary or total basis. A creditors control account **is** part of the double entry system.

The creditors control account and the total of the individual accounts in the purchase ledger should agree. However, often they do not, because one or both is incorrect. For example, the entries made in the personal accounts may be inaccurate, as may the amounts transferred from the purchases day book or cash payments book to the creditors control account.

Performing a reconciliation will identify that such discrepancies exist so that they can be investigated and eliminated.

I hope that answers your query.

A Technician

SECTION 2

Task 2.1

CREDITORS

	£		£
Bank	6,400	Balance b/d	1,000
Balance c/d	540	Purchases (bal. fig.)	5,940
	6,940		6,940

Task 2.2

	£	£
Bar sales from bank		8,700
Opening stock	680	
Purchases (from Task 2.1)	5,940	
Closing stock	(890)	
		(5,730)
Gross profit		2,970
Wages: 25,500 × 20%	5,100	
General expenses: (4,850 + 250 – 150) × 30%	1,485	
		(6,585)
Net loss		(3,615)

Task 2.3

SUBSCRIPTIONS

	£		£
Balance b/d	1,000	Bank	33,000
Subscriptions due (bal. fig.)	36,000	Balance c/d	4,000
	37,000		37,000

$\therefore$ Number of members who should have paid is $\dfrac{36,000}{100} = 360$

Task 2.4

	£	£
Subscriptions receivable (from Task 2.3)		36,000
Wages: 25,500 × 80%	20,400	
General expenses: (4,850 + 250 – 150) × 70%	3,465	
Loss on bar (from Task 2.2)	3,615	
Loan interest: 5,400 × 8% × 11/12	396	
		27,876
Surplus		8,124

2.5

Assets

	£
Land	12,000
Stock	890
Subscriptions	4,000
	16,890

Liabilities

	£
Bank	800
Creditors	540
Accrual	250
Loan	5,400
Interest	396
	7,386

Task 2.6

Land is classified as a non-wasting fixed asset. This means that as the value of the land does not diminish over time, it should not be depreciated.

Task 2.7

MEMO

To: Chairperson

From: Accounting Technician

Subject: Loan

Date: 3 December 20X1

Thank you for your enquiries about the treatment of the bank loan in the accounts of the tennis club. I will answer each of your points in turn.

Loan interest

The loan interest is an **expense** of the club, to be set off against any **income** that the club generates. The correct place for it is therefore the **income and expenditure account**.

Loan as income

The bank loan is not income generated by the club, it is a liability owed by the club to the bank. It would therefore be inappropriate to show it in the income and expenditure account. This would imply that the club had made the money instead of borrowing it from the bank.

Where to show the loan

As well as an income and expenditure account, the club has a balance sheet. This is a list of what it owns (assets) and what it owes (liabilities) at a given point in time. The loan would be classified as a liability.

I hope this clarifies the matter for you.

A Technician

Lecturers' resource pack activities

CHAPTER 1: DOUBLE ENTRY ACCOUNTING

1   BRITNEY

On 1 January 20X4 Britney's business has assets of £10,000 and liabilities of £4,000. What is the value of her investment?

2   BALANCE SHEET

Explain a balance sheet to a layman.

3   PROFIT

On 1 January 20X2, a business had assets of £15,000 and liabilities of £14,000. By 31 December 20X2 it had assets of £20,000, liabilities of £18,000. The owner had contributed capital of £2,000. How much profit had the business made over the year?

4   SOURCE

(a) Which of the following business documents is the source of information for purchases made on credit?

    A   Invoice
    B   Copy of the invoice
    C   Credit note
    D   Bank statement

(b) A document from a seller notifying the purchaser that an overcharge has been made is called:

    A   An advice note
    B   A credit note
    C   A consignment note
    D   A debit note

5   TIFFANY

During May 20X2, the following transactions took place involving Tiffany's cash account and the bank account.

May 1   Received a loan of £2,000 from Dave and paid it into the bank
        2   Paid rent of £100 by cheque
        3   Transferred £320 to the cash till
        4   Paid office cleaner £60 in cash
        5   Purchased goods amounting to £1,540 by cheque
        6   Cash sales £288
        8   Paid cash for stationery: £56
      10   Cash sales £464
      11   Paid cash for goods for resale £400
      12   Banked £516 of cash takings from the till
      13   Tiffany drew a cheque for £60 for her own use

Task

Draw up the cash account and bank account as two separate ledger accounts. Enter the above transactions into the accounts. Balance both accounts at the end of May 20X2 and carry down the balances.

CHAPTER 2: FROM LEDGER ACCOUNTS TO TRIAL BALANCE

6 CUSTOMS & EXCISE

In the second quarter of 20X2, a business had taxable outputs, net of VAT of £85,560, and taxable inputs, net of VAT of £60,720. All are subject to VAT at standard rate. At the end of the quarter, how much is payable to or recoverable from HM Customs & Excise?

7 DEBTORS

A debtors control account contains the following entries.

	£
Balance brought forward at 1 January	42,800
Bank	204,000
Discounts allowed	16,250
Credit sales	240,200

There are no other entries in the account. What is the closing balance carried forward at 31 December?

8 CREDITORS

A creditors control account contains the following entries.

	£
Bank	159,000
Credit purchases	166,400
Discounts received	7,500
Contra with debtors control account	8,000
Balance c/f at 31 December 20X7	25,840

There are no other entries in the account. What was the opening balance brought forward at 1 January 20X7?

9 BIGEND

Bigend Ltd has an accounting year ended 31 December 20X1. At that date, the balance on the sales ledger control account was £130,000, but the total of the individual accounts in the sales ledger came to £127,240. Upon investigation the following facts were discovered.

(a) The sales day book total for week 22 had been overcast by £600.

(b) A credit balance of £420 on Camshaft's account in the sales ledger had been incorrectly treated as a debit entry, when balancing off his account.

(c) A purchase ledger contra of £3,000 had been entered in Gasket's account in the sales ledger but no other entry had been made.

What are the adjusted totals of the sales ledger control account and the sales ledger balances?

10 APPALING

You have been given the following list of balances from the accounts of Appaling Ltd as at 31 December 20X6.

	£
Stock as at 1 January 20X6	44,000
Purchases	446,000
Sales	681,400
Discounts allowed	9,200
Discounts received	11,000
Returns in	13,400
Returns out	11,200
Wages and salaries	69,000
Bad debts	6,200
Carriage in	2,800
Carriage out	4,400
Other operating expenses	49,000
Trade debtors	68,000
Trade creditors	43,200
Provision for bad debts	900
Cash on hand	1,600
Bank overdraft	46,800
Profit and loss account at 1 January 20X6	17,100
Share capital	60,000
Property	100,000
Equipment	128,000
Provisions for depreciation at 1 January 20X6	
Property	20,000
Equipment	50,000

Task

Lay out the trial balance and add up the debit and credit columns.

11 HIBBERT

On 30.11.20X8, which is one month before the end of his financial year, the ledger accounts of Hibbert were as follows.

CASH

	£		£
Capital	19,000	Rent	5,500
Bank loan	6,000	Creditors	1,400
Sales	22,400	Interest	700
Debtors	800	Electricity	800
		Telephone	360
		Drawings	2,600

CAPITAL

	£		£
		Cash	19,000

BANK LOAN

	£		£
		Cash	6,000

SALES

	£		£
		Cash	22,400
		Debtors	9,200

BPP PUBLISHING

DEBTORS

	£		£
Sales	9,200	Cash	800

RENT

	£		£
Cash	5,500		

PURCHASES

	£		£
Creditors	4,200		

CREDITORS

	£		£
Cash	1,400	Purchases	4,200

INTEREST

	£		£
Cash	700		

ELECTRICITY

	£		£
Cash	800		

TELEPHONE

	£		£
Cash	360		

DRAWINGS

	£		£
Cash	2,600		

During the last month of his financial year, Hibbert recorded the following transactions.

(a) He bought goods for £4,000, half for credit and half for cash.

(b) He paid the following:

  (i) interest £40;
  (ii) electricity £50;
  (iii) telephone £24.

(c) He made sales of £7,000 of which £1,000 were for cash.

(d) He received £440 from debtors.

Tasks

(a) Post the transactions for December 20X8 into the ledger accounts.

(b) Balance off the ledger accounts and draw up a trial balance.

(c) Prepare a balance sheet as at 31.12.20X8 and a trading, profit and loss account for the year ended 31.12.20X8.

CHAPTER 3: CONTENT OF FINAL ACCOUNTS

12 REASONS

What are the main reasons for and purposes behind preparing accounts?

13 VAT

The following transactions were recorded in a company's books during one week of its trading year.

	£
Trade purchases (at list price)	9,000
Sales on credit (at list price)	12,000
Purchase of a van	20,920
Entertaining	720
Purchase of a car for a sales representative	17,200

A settlement discount of £600 is available on the sales. All figures are given exclusive of VAT at 17.5%. If the balance on the VAT account was £4,330 at the beginning of the week, what is the balance at the end of the week?

14 ASSETS

Note down which of the following would be an asset on the balance sheet, which would be an expense in a period end profit and loss account and which would be neither (in which case, have a stab at saying what it is).

(a) Freehold property

(b) Payment of wages for a director with a two year service contract

(c) Payments into a pension fund

(d) A debtor who will pay in 18 months time

(e) A bad debt written off

(f) A patent

(g) A company car

(h) Interest on a bank overdraft

(i) A bank loan repayable in five years

(j) Petty cash of £25

(k) The portion of uniform business rate paid covering the period after the balance sheet date

15 LEASES

How is an asset obtained under a finance lease shown in the financial statements and how does this differ to an asset obtained under an operating lease?

CHAPTER 4: ACCOUNTING CONCEPTS AND STANDARDS

16   HISTORICAL COST ACCOUNTING

What is historical cost accounting?

17   MUD

You make Mud for a living. Mud has two components: an Ice and a Coal. Each Ice costs £1 and each Coal costs 50 pence. Mud sells for £5.00 per unit.

In January 20X2 you sell 30 units of mud, although the money for ten will not be received until February. You have acquired 40 Coals which you paid for at the beginning of the month, and 50 Icess which do not have to be paid for until March.

What is the surplus for January on the basis of:

(a)   Cash accounting?
(b)   Accruals accounting?

18   SSAPS AND FRSS

What are SSAPs and FRSs used for?

19   INTANGIBLE FIXED ASSET

Which one of the following assets may be classified as an intangible fixed asset in the accounts of a business?

A   Trade investment
B   Goodwill
C   Preliminary expenses of incorporation
D   Leasehold premises

CHAPTER 5: CAPITAL ACQUISITION AND DISPOSAL

20 FIXED ASSET REGISTER

What events give rise to entries in a fixed assets register?

21 DISPOSALS

What details would you expect to find on an asset disposal authorisation form?

22 RECONCILE

Give reasons why the fixed assets register might not reconcile with the fixed assets actually present.

23 DON

At 30 June 20X2 the following balances were extracted from the ledger accounts of Don in respect of motor vehicles.

	Debit £	Credit £
Motor vehicles: cost	127,000	
Accumulated depreciation at 1 July 20X1		76,000
Motor vehicles: disposals		1,600

During the year to 30 June 20X2, the following took place.

(a) A delivery van which was fully depreciated and had cost £2,000 was scrapped. No proceeds were received.

(b) A car which had cost £5,000 and which had an accumulated depreciation balance of £3,000 was traded in for a new model priced at £8,000. A trade in allowance of £1,500 was received. Only the net cost of £6,500 has been entered into the books.

(c) A car which cost £4,000 and had a written down value of £1,250 was sold for £1,600 (credited to the disposals account).

(d) A delivery van was sold for £2,500. It had cost £10,000 and a loss of £750 was made on its sales. The proceeds have been credited to the fixed asset account.

(e) The depreciation charge for the year is £25,000.

Tasks

(a) Prepare the motor vehicles (cost) account, the motor vehicles accumulated depreciation account and the motor vehicles disposals account, taking into consideration the information above.

(b) Show the amounts which would appear in the company's balance sheet as at 30 June 20X2 in respect of motor vehicles.

CHAPTER 6: FINAL ACCOUNTS AND THE ACCOUNTING SYSTEM

24 A TRADER

A trader, registered for VAT, undertook the following transactions during the year ended 31 May 20X8.

	£
Sales taxable at standard rate	1,000,000
Sales taxable at zero rate	50,000
Exempt sales	150,000
Expenses subject to input tax	600,000

Included in expenses is the purchase of a motor car for £16,000 and a delivery van for £20,000. All figures are given exclusive of VAT. No particular purchase is attributable to any particular sale.

How much input tax can be reclaimed by the trader?

25 ROCKFORD

Rockford Ltd has incurred research and development costs of £234,000 during 20X8, which have been analysed as follows.

	£
Pure research	70,000
Development work for contract with James Ltd	30,000
Applied research	44,000
Project development costs (including market research £6,000)	90,000
	234,000

Task

State how the figures for R & D would be shown in the balance sheet and profit and loss account of Rockford Ltd, according to the rules in SSAP 13.

26 GEEZER

Geezer plc wishes to capitalise the development expenditure incurred on its new product, the Topbloke, an improved version of its successful existing product, the Drinkingbuddy. Which of the following would make this impossible under SSAP 13?

A   Legislation on product safety is currently going through Parliament which would make it difficult to produce the Topbloke at a profit

B   No market research has been carried out to verify the sales director's estimated sales figures

C   The Topbloke's development has been funded in part by a government grant

D   The development work will not be complete for another year

CHAPTER 7: CONTROL ACCOUNTS AND THE CORRECTION OF ERRORS

27 BANK STATEMENT

A company's bank statement shows £1,430 direct debits and £706 investment income not recorded in the cash book. The bank statement does not show a customer's cheque for £1,750 entered in the cash book on the last day of the accounting period. If the cash book shows a credit balance of £1,220 what balance appears on the bank statement?

A   £1,254 overdrawn
B   £2,246 overdrawn
C   £3,694 overdrawn
D   £194 overdrawn

28 CLOSING BALANCE

A debtors control account contains the following entries:

	£
Balance b/f 1 January	85,600
Bank	408,000
Discounts allowed	32,500
Credit sales	480,400

Assuming there are no other entries into the account, what is the closing balance at 31 December?

29 DEBTORS CONTROL ACCOUNT

The balances in a company's sales ledger at 31 December 20X3 were totalled and their sum was found to be £502,770. At the same date, the debit balance on the company's debtor control account was found to be £495,066. Upon investigation the following facts were discovered.

(a)   One customer, whose balance was £2,520 credit, had been omitted from the list of sales ledger balances.

(b)   A bad debt of £3,000 had not been entered in the control account.

(c)   Cash received of £1,680 had been debited to the customer's individual account.

(d)   A customer's cheque for £4,824 had been dishonoured by the bank, but no adjustment had been made in the control account.

Task

Reconcile the debtors control account with the list of balances as at 31 December 20X3.

CHAPTER 8: ACCRUALS, PREPAYMENTS AND BAD/DOUBTFUL DEBTS

30 BOTCHER

Botcher is a business dealing in building work. Its owner, Troy Bent, employs a team of eight who were paid £24,000 per annum each in the year to 31 December 20X4. In the following year 20X5 he raised salaries by 10% to £26,400 per annum each. On 1 July 20X5, he hired a trainee at a salary of £16,800 per annum. He pays his work force on the first working day of every month, one month in arrears, so that his employees receive their salary for January on the first working day in February, and so on.

Tasks

(a) Calculate the cost of salaries which would be charged in the profit and loss account of Botcher for the year ended 31 December 20X5.

(b) Calculate the amount actually paid in salaries during the year (the amount of cash received by the workforce).

(c) State the amount of accrued charges for salaries which would appear in the balance sheet of Botcher as at 31 December 20X5.

31 SHANTA

The following balances were extracted from the ledger accounts of Shanta as at 31 March 20X4.

	Debit £	Credit £
Insurance	564	
Commission		300
Telephones	1,172	
Carriage	308	

The following adjustments are required in respect of these items:

Insurance is prepaid by £156
The business is owed £100 commission
There is a telephone bill outstanding of £304
Carriage costs of £60 are owing

Task

Show the ledger account for each item above after the adjustment has been made and the transfer to the profit and loss account.

32 WAGES

On 1 January 20X4 the wages account had a credit balance brought forward of £350.20. During the year, £36,696.80 was paid in cash for wages. On 31 December 20X3 £443.04 was owed for wages.

Task

Show the wages account after adjustment.

CHAPTER 9: COST OF GOODS SOLD AND THE TREATMENT OF STOCKS

33 EH? LTD

Eh? Ltd is a manufacturer of card. During the stocktake it is discovered that a quantity of the large standard size card has been damaged. Only the edges of the sheets are affected, so it would be possible to cut the card down to the smaller standard size.

The production cost of this quantity of large card was £51,000 and it would normally sell for £84,000. The same number of sheets of the smaller card would normally cost £36,000 to produce and they would sell for £54,000.

The company's selling and distribution costs are calculated as 5% of selling price. The estimated cost of reducing the damaged card to the smaller size is £1,500.

Task

Calculate the balance sheet value of this stock item.

34 CHRISTINE

Christine started a business on 1 May 20X4. During the month the following transactions took place.

May	1	Started business with £19,200 cash
	2	Put £18,000 of the cash into a bank account
	3	Purchased shop fittings by cheque for £3,000
	5	Bought goods by cheque for £2,600
	8	Cash sales of £368
	9	Paid £80 rent in cash
	11	Sold £580 of goods on credit to Emily
	13	Cash sales of £520. £400 cash banked
	15	Bought a secondhand delivery van, paying £6,600 by cheque
	16	Christine withdrew £180 in cash for her own use. Paid motor expenses by cheque: £528
	17	Emily paid her account by cheque (£560) taking advantage of a £20 discount
	19	Sold more goods on credit to Emily for £152
	20	Purchased more goods by cheque for £1,160
	21	Paid advertising bill of £60 in cash
	22	Christine withdrew £220 from the business bank account
	29	Cash sales of £376
	31	Banked all cash in hand

Task

(a) Draw up any ledger accounts required to record the above transactions. Enter the transactions in the accounts. Balance off the accounts.

(b) Extract a trial balance at the end of the month.

Note. Ignore VAT.

CHAPTER 10: INCOMPLETE RECORDS

35 OOMPALUMPA

Oompalumpa Ltd is a retail company and sales are all on cash terms. During 20X5 their bank account shows cash banked of £285,900 which included £1,320 in respect of the repayment of a director's loan. About £900 was taken from the till every month for wages and £120 was taken weekly for sundry expenses. The cash in the till amounted to £1,860 on 1 January 20X5 and £1,560 on 31 December 20X5.

Task

Calculate the sales figure for Oompalumpa Ltd for 20X5.

36 REX-UM

The following trading account was produced by Rex-um Ltd for the year ended 31 March 20X7.

	£	£
Sales		1,290,000
Opening stock	150,000	
Purchases	937,500	
	1,087,500	
Closing stock	114,000	
Cost of sales		973,500
Gross profit		316,500

The following figures have been extracted from Rex-um Ltd's balance sheet as at 31 March 20X7.

	£
Trade debtors	180,000
Prepayments	12,000
Cash in hand	18,000
Bank overdraft	24,000
Trade creditors	120,000
Accruals	9,000
Proposed dividend	15,000

Tasks

Calculate:

(a) The stock turnover period in days
(b) The debtors' collection period in days
(c) The creditors' payment period in days
(d) The current ratio at 31 March 20X7
(e) The quick ratio (or acid test ratio) at 31 March 20X7.

37 HELEN

Helen Blinking, a sole trader, makes all her business payments by cheque and pays all her takings into the bank account. She does not keep a full set of accounting records, but you have managed to obtain the following information relating to balances as at 31 March 20X3 and as at 31 March 20X4, the current year.

	31 March *20X4* £	*31 March* *20X3* £
Trade debtors	9,376	7,600
Trade creditors	7,720	6,520
Stock	7,392	8,160
Fixtures and fittings		
(at net book value)	1,440	1,600
Bank	3,264	1,920

The following is a summary of the business's bank statements for the year.

	£
Receipts	
Cash received from debtors	126,240
Payments	
Trade creditors	99,200
General expenses	10,096
Rent	1,200
Drawings	14,400
	124,896

Tasks

(a) Calculate the balance of Helen Blinking's capital as at 31 March 20X3.

(b) Prepare the trading, profit and loss account for the year ended 31 March 20X4 and a balance sheet at that date.

CHAPTER 11: CLUB ACCOUNTS, MANUFACTURING ACCOUNTS AND PARTNERSHIPS

38 ROTUND PIE-EATING CLUB

The following balances were taken from the books of the Rotund Pie-Eating Club as at 1 January 20X6.

	£	£
Pie-making facility at cost		140,000
Clubhouse at cost		30,000
Building fund – represented by investments:		
£40,000 4% consolidated stock	14,800	
Deposit with building society	20,000	
		34,800
Subscriptions in advance (20X6)		800
Creditors for bar supplies		700
Life membership fund		8,000
Subscriptions in arrears		1,200
Bar stock		9,600
Clubhouse equipment at cost		6,400
Cash in hand	200	
Cash at bank	1,700	
		1,900

An analysis of the bank account operated by the club showed the following summary of receipts and payments during the year ended 31 December 20X6.

Receipts	£
Subscriptions	50,000
Life members	4,000
Sale of recipe books	1,400
Pie-facility fees	600
Sale of old carpet from clubhouse	44
Bar takings	57,000
Consolidated stock interest	1,600

Payments	£
Upkeep of facility	32,300
General clubhouse expenses (including bar wages of £8,400)	24,300
Petty cash (expenses paid to treasurer)	3,100
Bar supplies	46,300
Purchase of instruction manuals	500
Piano	1,000
Deposited with building society	1,600
Replacement carpet for clubhouse	2,520

The following information is significant for the preparation of the club's accounts.

(a) The club maintains a building fund separate from the capital fund and life membership fund. The building fund is invested in consolidated stock and a building society, whilst the capital fund and life membership fund are represented by the general assets of the club.

(b) The building society has been instructed to credit the interest on the club's account direct to the account at each half year. The society computes interest half yearly on 30 June and 31 December. This year the interest amounted to £1,480. Interest paid on the consolidated stock is also added to the building fund by paying it into the building society account.

(c) There were four life members at the beginning of the year, one of whom has since died due to obesity. Two other life members have, however, joined the club.

(d) Renewals of clubhouse furnishings are to be treated as revenue expenditure.

(e) Outstanding at 31 December 20X6 were:

	£
Creditors for bar supplies	3,200
Subscriptions in advance (20X7)	1,800
Subscriptions in arrear (20X6)	600
Bar chits not yet settled	70

(f) Bar stocks at 31 December 20X6 were valued at £8,600.

(g) It is a rule of the club that a cash float of £200 shall be maintained in the treasurer's hands. To this end an imprest petty cash account is operated.

(h) An insurance premium of £960 has been paid by cheque during 20X6 for the year to 31 March 20X7.

Tasks

(a) Prepare an income and expenditure account for the year ended 31 December 20X6.

(b) Prepare a balance sheet as at that date.

39 BOLLAK

From the information given below your task is to prepare the manufacturing, trading and profit and loss account of Bollak Ltd for the year ended 31 December 20X6.

Balances at 31 December 20X5

	£
Authorised and issued share capital	
Ordinary shares of £1 each fully paid	200,000
Reserves	2,000
Creditors	114,800
Fixed assets (cost £120,000)	78,000
Stocks	
Raw materials	50,000
Work in progress, valued at prime cost	11,600
Finished goods	102,000
Debtors	70,000
Cash at bank	4,000
Administration expenses prepaid	1,200

The following transactions occurred during 20X6.

Invoiced sales, less returns	486,000
Cash received from debtors	469,400
Discounts allowed	10,800
Bad debts written off	2,200
Invoiced purchases of raw materials, less returns	160,000
Payments to creditors	165,000
Discounts received	3,400
Factory wages paid	66,600
Manufacturing expenses paid	123,800
Administration expenses paid	32,400
Selling and distribution expenses paid	33,600
Payment for purchase of fixed assets	60,000

Balances at 31 December 20X6

	£
Fixed assets (cost £180,000)	120,000
Stocks	
Raw materials	48,000
Work in progress	10,000
Finished goods	104,000
Administration expenses accrued	2,200
Factory wages accrued	1,400
Selling and distribution expenses prepaid	2,400

The following information is given.

(a) Depreciation of fixed assets is to be apportioned between manufacturing, administration and selling in the proportions of 7: 2: 1.

(b) Discounts allowed and bad debts written off are to be regarded as selling and distribution expenses.

(c) Discounts received are to be credited to administration expenses.

(d) Taxation is to be ignored.

Tutorial notes

1   A manufacturing account is a detailed breakdown of what would be the 'Purchases' line in cost of sales in a non-manufacturing organisation. Your aim is to set out how raw materials, work in progress, direct wages and indirect factory expenses are gathered together to arrive at the 'Factory cost of finished goods produced'.

2   Most of the figures can be taken straight from the figures given, but don't forget accruals and depreciation.

3   Once you have the figure for finished goods produced you can prepare the trading and profit and loss account in the normal way.

4   Beware! You do not need all of the figures you are given in this question.

40   PRIME COST

Which one of the following costs would be included in the calculation of prime cost in a manufacturing account?

   A   Wages of factory workers engaged in machine maintenance
   B   Depreciation of lorries used for deliveries to customers
   C   Cost of indirect production materials
   D   Cost of transporting raw materials from suppliers' premises

41   FINISHED GOODS

The factory cost of finished goods produced by a manufacturing company in 20X6 was £1,276,800. Opening and closing stocks of finished goods were £89,600 and £100,800 respectively, each valuation including a factory profit of 12% on production cost. Goods are sold to customers at a mark-up of 25% on production cost.

What is the sales figure for 20X6?

CHAPTER 12: EXTENDED TRIAL BALANCE

42 EXTENDED TRIAL BALANCE

Why do we prepare an extended trial balance?

43 JOURNALS

Why would journals be used on an extended trial balance?

44 DOUBLE ENTRY

Does the extended trial balance ensure that double entry rules are complied with?

BPP PUBLISHING

Lecturers' practice devolved assessment: Mogginosh

Performance criteria

The following performance criteria are covered in this Devolved Assessment.

Element 5.2: Record income and expenditure

1   All income and expenditure is correctly identified and recorded in the appropriate records

2   Relevant accrued and prepaid income and expenditure is correctly identified and adjustments are made

3   The organisation's policies, regulations, procedures and timescales in relation to recording income and expenditure are observed

4   Incomplete data is identified and either resolved or referred to the appropriate person

Element 5.3: Collect and collate information for the preparation of final accounts

1   Relevant accounts and reconciliations are correctly prepared to allow the preparation of final accounts

2   All relevant information is correctly identified and recorded

4   The organisation's policies, regulations, procedures and timescales relating to preparing final accounts are observed

5   Discrepancies and unusual features are identified and either resolved or referred to the appropriate person

6   The trial balance is accurately prepared and, where necessary, a suspense account is opened and reconciled

Element 5.4: Prepare the extended trial balance

1   The trial balance is accurately extended and totalled

2   Totals from the general ledger or other records are correctly entered on the extended trial balance

3   Any errors disclosed by the trial balance are traced and corrected

4   Any adjustments not dealt with in the ledger accounts are correctly entered on the extended trial balance

5   An agreed valuation of closing stock is correctly entered on the extended trial balance

6   The organisation's policies, regulations, procedures and timescales are observed

7   Discrepancies, unusual features or queries are identified and either resolved or referred to the appropriate person

Notes on completing the Assessment

This Assessment is designed to test your ability to prepare journals to clear a suspense account and to prepare the extended trial balance.

You are provided below with data which you must use to complete the tasks.

You are allowed 3 hours to complete your work.

A high level of accuracy is required. Check your work carefully.

Correcting fluid should not be used. Errors should be crossed out neatly and clearly. You should write in ink and not in pencil.

A full suggested solution to this Assessment is provided in the Lecturers' Resource Pack.

Do not turn to the suggested solution until you have completed all parts of the Assessment.

Data

Mogginosh has been in business for around ten years, manufacturing and selling tinned catfood for wholesale customers. The business operates from leasehold premises in Catford, South London.

The Managing Director is Tom Price, the Chief Accountant is Felix Thompson. You are Tabitha Mouser, an Accounting Technician. You have joined the firm in January 20X2, only to be thrown in at the deep end. Felix has gone skiing, leaving you with a trial balance which needs adjusting in the light of various pieces of information contained in a memo.

In order to complete the tasks listed at the end of this assignment, you should find attached the following items.

(a) Memorandum from Felix Thompson
(b) Trial balance as at 31 December 20X1
(c) Proforma suspense account
(d) Pages of the journal
(e) Extended trial balance proformas.

Tasks

(a) Write up the suspense account eliminating the balance.

(b) Show the journal entries required in order to clear the suspense account in (a).

(c) Calculate the adjustments required in respect of items (d), (m) and (n) in the memorandum.

(d) Show the journal entries required in respect of any other adjustments you need to make, excluding accruals and prepayments.

(e) Enter the opening trial balance on the attached proforma after making the adjustments required in (c) (items (d), (m) and (n) in the memorandum).

(f) Make any other adjustments arising from journal entries, accruals or prepayments on the ETB.

(g) Extend the trial balance, calculate the profit and balance the ETB.

MEMORANDUM

To: Tabitha Mouser
From: Felix Thompson
Date: 2 January 20X2

Please find attached the trial balance as at 31 December 20X1. As you can see, I've had to open up a suspense account because the trial balance didn't balance.

Before the final accounts can be prepared, some adjustments will need to be made. Some of these will affect the suspense account, others will not. I'll leave you to work this out for yourself! I have attached proforma journals, ETBs and a suspense account.

(a) The stock count has been done and the stock has been valued at £19,768. However, one particular line, 'Paw Relation' is not selling too well. There are cans of them in stock which cost £500 to make, but which we can now only sell for £400.

(b) Rent and rates include £320 which relates to this year.

(c) A balance of £174 on a debtors account has been omitted from the schedule of debtors, the total of which was entered as debtors in the trial balance.

(d) A small piece of machinery purchased for £2,400 has been recorded as an expense under repairs in error, rather than as a fixed asset.

(e) The receipts side of the cash book has been undercast by £1,440.

(f) The provision for doubtful debts is to be 5% of debtors at the year end.

(g) Insurance includes £164 for motor insurance which is to be transferred to motor expenses.

(h) Mr Price has taken goods, costing £370 from the business for his own private use.

(i) The total of one page of the sales day book has been carried forward as £16,038, whereas the correct amount was £16,308.

(j) A credit note for £358 received from a supplier has been posted to the wrong side of his account.

(k) An electricity bill in the sum of £304, not yet accrued for, has been discovered in a filing tray in my office.

(l) Mr Ferral, whose past debts to the business had been the subject of a provision, at last paid £1,462 to clear his account. The personal account has been credited but the cheque has not yet been entered in the cash book.

(m) Depreciation is to be charged on both plant and machinery and motor vehicles at 20% of cost. As you know, we charge a full year's depreciation in the year of purchase and none in the year of sale.

(n) During the year we sold a van for £500 which had been purchased in 20W8 at a cost of £2,000. The only entry which has been made in respect of the disposal is to credit the £500 to a disposals account and record the cash received.

BPP PUBLISHING

MOGGINOSH
TRIAL BALANCE AS AT 31 DECEMBER 20X1

Folio		Debit £	Credit £
F100	Freehold property	20,000	
P110	Plant and machinery: cost	18,500	
P120	Plant and machinery: provision for depreciation		7,400
M110	Motor vehicles: cost	12,000	
M120	Motor vehicles: provision for depreciation		6,000
C100	Capital		56,147
D120	Drawings	4,314	
D100	Debtors	15,360	
C200	Creditors		10,924
S100	Sales		163,484
P100	Purchases	124,202	
R100	Rent and rates	1,760	
L100	Lighting and heating	2,358	
W100	Wages and salaries	16,536	
B100	Bad debt expense	494	
B120	Bad debt provision		652
R120	Repairs	3,842	
S200	Stock at 1.1.X1	18,548	
S100	Insurances	344	
K100	Cash at bank	3,164	
K200	Cash in hand	821	
D300	Discounts received		1,600
M130	Motor vehicles disposals		500
M140	Motor expenses	942	
S300	Suspense account	3,522	
		246,707	246,707

SUSPENSE ACCOUNT

	£		
Balance b/f	3,522		

JOURNAL

Date	Details	Folio Ref	£	£

BPP PUBLISHING

Lecturers' practice devolved assessment

FOLIO	DESCRIPTION	REF.	TRIAL BALANCE		ADJUSTMENTS	
					DEBIT	CREDIT

PROFIT AND LOSS ACCOUNT		BALANCE SHEET	
DEBIT	CREDIT	DEBIT	CREDIT

BPP PUBLISHING

Lecturers' practice central assessment: Mr Singh

Notes on completing the Assessment

This Assessment is designed to test your ability to maintain financial records and prepare accounts. It purpose is to give you an idea of what an AAT Central Assessment looks like. It is not intended as a definitive guide to the tasks you may be required to perform.

The suggested time allowance for this Assessment is three hours. It is in three sections. You are advised to spend approximately 100 minutes on Section 1 and 80 minutes on Section 2.

You are reminded that competence must be achieved in each section. You should therefore attempt and aim to complete every task in each section. All essential workings should be included within your answer where appropriate.

A high level of accuracy is required. Check your work carefully. Errors should be crossed out neatly and clearly.

Calculators may be used but no reference material is permitted.

Do not turn to the suggested solution until you have completed all parts of the Assessment.

A full suggested solution to this Assessment is provided in the Lecturers' Resource Pack.

SECTION 1

The suggested time allocation for this extended trial balance exercise is 80 minutes.

Mr Singh owns a small manufacturing business which makes and sells toys in the Bradford area. You are Jenny Russ, responsible for the payroll and producing the trial balance.

At 31 May 20X6 the following balances were extracted from the nominal ledger.

BPP PUBLISHING

	£
Property, at cost	90,000
Equipment, at cost	57,500
Provisions for depreciation (as at 1 June 20X5)	
Property	12,500
Equipment	32,500
Stock, as at 1 June 20X5	27,400
Purchases	259,600
Sales	405,000
Discounts allowed	3,370
Discounts received	4,420
Wages and salaries	52,360
Bad debts	1,720
Loan interest	1,560
Carriage out	5,310
Other operating expenses	38,800
Trade debtors	46,200
Trade creditors	33,600
Provision for bad debts	280
Cash in hand	151
Bank overdraft	14,500
Drawings	28,930
13% loan	12,000
Capital	98,101

On investigation you discover the following.

(a)   Stock as at the close of business was valued at £25,900.

(b)   Depreciation for the year ended 31 May 20X6 has yet to be provided as follows.

Property: 1% using the straight line method.
Equipment: 15% using the straight line method.

(c)   Wages and salaries are accrued by £140.

(d)   'Other operating expenses' include certain expenses prepaid by £500. Other expenses included under this heading are accrued by £200.

(e)   The provision for bad debts is to be adjusted so that it is 0.5% of trade debtors as at 31 May 20X6.

(f)   'Purchases' include goods valued at £1,040 which were withdrawn by Mr Singh for his own personal use.

Task 1

Using the journal extract below, show the journal entry, if any, required to correct the error in part (f) above.

JOURNAL   Page 1

Details   £   £

Task 2

Calculate the adjustments required in respect of:

(a) Depreciation
(b) Bad debts

Task 3

Assuming that the error, if any, in part (f) has been corrected, complete the first two columns of the extended trial balance on the next page.

Task 4

Complete the adjustments, accruals and prepayment columns.

Task 5

Extend the trial balance into the columns for profit and loss account and balance sheet. Total and complete all columns.

Account	Trial balance		Adjustments		Accrued	Prepaid	Profit and loss a/c		Balance sheet	
	Debit	Credit	Debit	Credit			Debit	Credit	Debit	Credit
	£	£	£	£	£	£	£	£	£	£
Property: cost										
Equipment: cost										
Property: depreciation provision										
Equipment: depreciation provision										
Stock as at 1 June 20X5										
Purchases										
Sales										
Discounts allowed										
Discounts received										
Wages and salaries										
Bad debts										
Loan interest										
Carriage out										
Other operating expenses										
Trade debtors										
Trade creditors										
Provision for bad debts										
Cash in hand										
Bank overdraft										
Drawings										
13% loan										
Capital										
SUB-TOTAL										
Profit for the year										
TOTAL										

BPP PUBLISHING

SECTION 2

The following short answer questions are mainly based on the scenario outlined in Section 1. You may have to refer back to the information in that exercise in order to answer the questions.

Your answers should be complete but as concise as possible.

The suggested time allocation for this set of short answer questions is 40 minutes.

Task 6

(a) The property, recorded at £90,000 in the accounts, is now worth £120,000. Should it still be depreciated?

(b) A customer whose debt had been provided for has gone bankrupt. What is the correct double entry to record this?

Task 7

The following information is available in respect of two product lines.

	Direct costs of material and labour £	Production overheads Incurred £	Expected selling price £
Product 1	2,470	2,100	5,800
Product 2	9,360	2,730	12,040

(a) At what amount should Product 1 be stated in the company's balance sheet?

(b) At what amount should Product 2 be stated?

(c) One debtor has a credit balance on his account. How might this have arisen?

Task 8

(a) There is a figure in Mr Singh's profit and loss account for discounts received. Do you think that these will be trade discounts, settlement discounts or a mixture of both?

(b) What is the correct accounting treatment for:

(i) Trade discounts?
(ii) Settlement discounts?

SECTION 3

Mary Grimes, retail fruit and vegetable merchant, does not keep a full set of accounting records. However, the following information has been produced from the business's records.

1 Summary of the bank account for the year ended 31 August 20X8

	£		£
1 Sept 20X7 balance brought forward	1,970	Payment to suppliers	72,000
Receipts from trade debtors	96,000	Purchase of motor van (E471 KBR)	13,000
Sale of private yacht	20,000	Rent and rates	2,600
Sale of motor van (A123 BWA)	2,100	Wages	15,100
		Motor vehicle expenses	3,350
		Postages and stationery	1,360
		Drawings	9,200
		Repairs and renewals	650
		Insurances	800
		31 August 20X8 balance carried forward	2,010
	120,070		120,070
1 Sept 20X8 balance brought forward	2,010		

2 Assets and liabilities, other than balance at bank

At	1 Sept 20X7	31 Aug 20X8
	£	£
Trade creditors	4,700	2,590
Trade debtors	7,320	9,500
Rent and rates accruals	200	260
Motor vans:		
A123 BWA - At cost	10,000	-
Provision for depreciation	8,000	-
E471 KBR - At cost	-	13,000
Provision for depreciation	-	To be determined
Stock in trade	4,900	5,900
Insurance prepaid	160	200

3 All receipts are banked and all payments are made from the business bank account.

4 A trade debt of £300 owing by John Blunt and included in the trade debtor at 31 August 20X8 (see 2 above), is to be written off as a bad debt.

5 It is Mary Grimes' policy to provide depreciation at the rate of 20% on the cost of motor vans held at the end of each financial year; no depreciation is provided in the year of sale or disposal of a motor van.

6 Discounts received during the year ended 31 August 20X8 from trade creditors amounted to £1,100.

Task 1

Prepare Mary Grimes' trading and profit and loss account for the year ended 31 August 20X8.

Task 2

Prepare Mary Grimes' balance sheet as at 31 August 20X7.

Task 3

Prepare Mary Grimes' balance sheet as at 31 August 20X8.

BPP
PUBLISHING

See overleaf for information on other
BPP products and how to order

AAT Order

To BPP Publishing Ltd, Aldine Place, London W12 8AW

Tel: 020 8740 2211. Fax: 020 8740 1184

E-mail: Publishing@bpp.com Web:www.bpp.com

Mr/Mrs/Ms (Full name) _____

Daytime delivery address _____

Postcode _____

Daytime Tel _____

E-mail _____

	5/02 Texts	5/02 Kits	Special offer	8/02 Passcards	Tapes
FOUNDATION (£14.95 except as indicated)					
Units 1 & 2 Receipts and Payments	☐	☐	Foundation	£6.95 ☐	£10.00 ☐
Unit 3 Ledger Balances and Initial Trial Balance	☐	☐			
Unit 4 Supplying Information for Mgmt Control	☐	☐			
Unit 20 Working with Information Technology (£9.95) (6/02)	☐	☐			
Unit 22/23 Healthy Workplace/Personal Effectiveness (£9.95)	☐				
INTERMEDIATE (£9.95)					
Unit 5 Financial Records and Accounts	☐	☐	All	£5.95 ☐	£10.00 ☐
Unit 6 Cost Information	☐	☐	Inter'te Texts	£5.95 ☐	£10.00 ☐
Unit 7 Reports and Returns	☐	☐	and Kits (£65) ☐	£5.95 ☐	
Unit 21 Using Information Technology	☐	☐		£5.95 ☐	
TECHNICIAN (£9.95)					
Unit 8/9 Core Managing Costs and Allocating Resources	☐	☐	Set of 12	£5.95 ☐	£10.00 ☐
Unit 10 Core Managing Accounting Systems	☐	☐	Technician		
Unit 11 Option Financial Statements (A/c Practice)	☐	☐	Texts/Kits	£5.95 ☐	£10.00 ☐
Unit 12 Option Financial Statements (Central Govnmt)	☐	☐	(Please		
Unit 15 Option Cash Management and Credit Control	☐	☐	specify titles	£5.95 ☐	
Unit 16 Option Evaluating Activities	☐	☐	required)	£5.95 ☐	
Unit 17 Option Implementing Auditing Procedures	☐	☐	(£100) ☐	£5.95 ☐	
Unit 18 Option Business Tax (FA02)(8/02 Text & Kit)	☐	☐		£5.95 ☐	
Unit 19 Option Personal Tax (FA 02)(8/02 Text & Kit)	☐	☐			
TECHNICIAN 2001 (£9.95)					
Unit 18 Option Business Tax FA01 (8/01 Text & Kit)	☐	☐			
Unit 19 Option Personal Tax FA01 (8/01 Text & Kit)	☐	☐			
SUBTOTAL	£ [____]	£ [____]	£ [____]	£ [____]	£ [____]

TOTAL FOR PRODUCTS £ [____]

POSTAGE & PACKING

Texts/Kits

	First	Each extra	
UK	£2.00	£2.00	£
Europe*	£4.00	£2.00	£
Rest of world	£20.00	£10.00	£

Passcards

UK	£2.00	£1.00	£
Europe*	£2.50	£1.00	£
Rest of world	£15.00	£8.00	£

Tapes

UK	£1.00	£1.00	£
Europe*	£1.00	£1.00	£
Rest of world	£4.00	£4.00	£

TOTAL FOR POSTAGE & PACKING £ [____]

(Max £10 Texts/Kits/Passcards)

Grand Total (Cheques to *BPP Publishing*) I enclose

a cheque for (incl. Postage) £ [____]

Or charge to Access/Visa/Switch

Card Number [_____]

Expiry date _____ Start Date _____

Issue Number (Switch Only) [_____]

Signature _____

We aim to deliver to all UK addresses inside 5 working days; a signature will be required. Orders to all UK addresses should be delivered within 6 working days. All other orders to overseas addresses should be delivered within 8 working days. * Europe includes the Republic of Ireland and the Channel Islands.

REVIEW FORM & FREE PRIZE DRAW

All original review forms from the entire BPP range, completed with genuine comments, will be entered into one of two draws on 31 January 2003 and 31 July 2003. The names on the first four forms picked out on each occasion will be sent a cheque for £50.

Name: _____   Address: _____

_____

_____

How have you used this Assessment Kit?
(Tick one box only)

☐ Home study (book only)

☐ On a course: college _____

☐ With 'correspondence' package

☐ Other _____

Why did you decide to purchase this Assessment Kit? *(Tick one box only)*

☐ Have used BPP Texts in the past

☐ Recommendation by friend/colleague

☐ Recommendation by a lecturer at college

☐ Saw advertising

☐ Other _____

During the past six months do you recall seeing/receiving any of the following?
(Tick as many boxes as are relevant)

☐ Our advertisement in *Accounting Technician* magazine

☐ Our advertisement in *Pass*

☐ Our brochure with a letter through the post

Which (if any) aspects of our advertising do you find useful?
(Tick as many boxes as are relevant)

☐ Prices and publication dates of new editions

☐ Information on Interactive Text content

☐ Facility to order books off-the-page

☐ None of the above

Have you used the companion Interactive Text for this subject?   ☐ Yes   ☐ No

Your ratings, comments and suggestions would be appreciated on the following areas

	Very useful	Useful	Not useful
Introductory section (How to use this Assessment Kit etc)	☐	☐	☐
Practice activities	☐	☐	☐
Practice devolved assessments	☐	☐	☐
Trial run devolved assessments	☐	☐	☐
AAT Sample Simulation	☐	☐	☐
Practice central assessments	☐	☐	☐
Trial run central assessment	☐	☐	☐
Lecturers' Resource Pack activities	☐	☐	☐
Content of answers	☐	☐	☐
Layout of pages	☐	☐	☐
Structure of book and ease of use	☐	☐	☐

	Excellent	Good	Adequate	Poor
Overall opinion of this Kit	☐	☐	☐	☐

Do you intend to continue using BPP Assessment Kits/Interactive Texts? ☐ Yes ☐ No

Please note any further comments and suggestions/errors on the reverse of this page.

The BPP author of this edition can be e-mailed at: katyhibbert@bpp.com

Please return to: Nick Weller, BPP Publishing Ltd, FREEPOST, London, W12 8BR

REVIEW FORM & FREE PRIZE DRAW (continued)

Please note any further comments and suggestions/errors below

FREE PRIZE DRAW RULES

1 Closing date for 31 January 2003 draw is 31 December 2002. Closing date for 31 July 2003 draw is 30 June 2003.

2 Restricted to entries with UK and Eire addresses only. BPP employees, their families and business associates are excluded.

3 No purchase necessary. Entry forms are available upon request from BPP Publishing. No more than one entry per title, per person. Draw restricted to persons aged 16 and over.

4 Winners will be notified by post and receive their cheques not later than 6 weeks after the relevant draw date.

5 The decision of the promoter in all matters is final and binding. No correspondence will be entered into.